D1557557

AFTER THE WHALE

AFTER THE WHALE

Melville in the Wake of *Moby-Dick*

Clark Davis

The University of Alabama Press

Tuscaloosa and London

Copyright © 1995
The University of Alabama Press
Tuscaloosa, Alabama 35487–0380
All rights reserved
Manufactured in the United States of America

Library of Congress Cataloging-in-Publication Data

Davis, Clark.
    After the whale : Melville in the wake of Moby-Dick / Clark Davis.
      p. cm.
    Includes bibliographical references and index.
    ISBN 0-8173-0774-5
    1. Melville, Herman, 1819–1891—Criticism and interpretation.
  2. Melville, Herman, 1819–1891. Moby-Dick. I. Title.
  PS2387.D39   1995
  813′.3—dc20   94-43179

British Library Cataloguing-in-Publication Data available

The illustration on the cover jacket is an engraving entitled *Cutting Away the Masts* by J. T. Willmore after C. Stanfield. (Courtesy of Berkshire Athenaeum, Herman Melville Memorial Room, Pittsfield, Massachusetts.)

The illustration on the title page is an engraving entitled *Figures on a Shore in a Storm,* after Claude Joseph Vernet. (Courtesy of Berkshire Athenaeum, Herman Melville Memorial Room, Pittsfield, Massachusetts.)

For my parents
and for Hillary

CONTENTS

PREFACE

Truth uncompromisingly told will always have its ragged edges.
—*Billy Budd*

AMONG THOSE nineteenth-century American writers who maintain canonical status, Melville continues to attract, almost simultaneously, both an extreme attention and a benign neglect. As with most authors whose reputations have grown from the single seed of one great book, the light shed on the "supporting" works, those leading to and away from the *chef d'oeuvre*, is not only less strong but tends, more often than not, to catch only the burnished surfaces of arguably weaker texts in whose pages readers often find the shrunken, sometimes warped image of the principal work. Such a method is both understandable and practical; nevertheless, in certain cases, it seems to promote a continuous inattention to those individual productions that stand furthest from the masterwork in accomplishment as well as to the process by which the author discovers new forms and expression.

In this respect, a large portion of Melville's career—the period extending from *Pierre* to *Billy Budd*—has itself suffered not so much from a lack of interest as from a willful dissociation, a frequent refusal to envision this long period of generic uncertainty as a whole, to see Melville not simply as the author of a few famous prose fictions but as a writer whose lifelong engagement with language pushed him through generic boundaries in search of new ways of shaping and questioning his world. This study attempts just such a vision of the middle and later Melville in the hope that by linking prose to poetry, short tale to novel, epic to sketch, we can begin to examine Melville's later work consecutively and completely and understand the development of his attitude toward reality and language as it unfolds from work to work.

As every Melvillean seemingly does, I too have begun with *Moby-Dick,* because it remains the center, the vortex toward which the early fictions swirl and out of which pour the troubled waters of the still mysterious later career. I have argued that this vast dispersal and dissemination of energies flows principally from the dualistic conflict, both linguistic and philosophical, that Ishmael and Ahab embody, that it is their voices, elements of Melville's own, strained and altered by time and temper, that fill the volumes that follow their advent. Thus part 1 attempts to provide a basic understanding of Ahabian/Ishmaelean dualism through a reading of *Moby-Dick*'s topographical division of the body into head and heart and further follows the resultant dialectic into the opposing visions of language it creates and employs. Similar studies of *Pierre*, "Bartleby," and *Israel Potter* continue to uncover the development of this dualism in the incipient fragmentation and bodily deferral of the works immediately following *Moby-Dick*. Part 2 traces the dominance of the Ahabian-ascetic vision of world and language in a series of works that emphasize both fragmentation and the deceptiveness of reality and language. Part 3 considers the nature of Melville's shift to poetry in the politically and psychologically dualistic *Battle Pieces* and *Clarel*. It also attempts to follow the evolution of Ishmaelean and Ahabian strains in the late poetry—from the consideration of memory and distance in *John Marr and Other Sailors* through the dualism of *Timoleon* to the celebration of sensuality in *Weeds and Wildings*. Finally, part 4 acts as a conclusion by offering a reading of *Billy Budd* that considers its position both as potential answer to the long-stated questions of Ahabian desire and as the ultimate, but potentially ironic, development of the now largely Christianized Ishmaelean vision.

In service of these ends, I have attempted to follow the oeuvre as chronologically and with as few omissions as possible. In the case of the *Piazza Tales*, for instance, I have chosen to consider the stories separately, according to their thematic links to other works, rather than as a book both because their dating remains uncertain and because they individually reflect important changes in the development of Melville's thought. Furthermore, in the interests of space I have chosen to omit extended discussion of a few of the shorter pieces ("The Piazza," "The Lightning-Rod Man," "The Bell-Tower," "The Two Temples," "The 'Gees," and "The Apple-Tree Table") in favor of those more pertinent to the study. Other than these tales and some uncollected lyrics, however, I have not consciously ignored any of Melville's standard works and have tried, to the extent that it is possible, to follow the trail he himself created in writing them.

To begin with *Moby-Dick*, of course, is to ignore five early novels, but the genesis of the masterwork remains a tale frequently retold in Melville criticism, and the thematic links of the white whale to its younger siblings have been clearly and solidly defined. On the other hand, the dissolution, the aftermath of the *Pequod*'s disaster seems more troubling as a subject for criticism, a sometimes mournful narrative notable for its stops, starts, and odd shifts of scene and method. Perhaps because it ends in a less spectacular triumph, or because most of us would rather look beyond these dark, awkward years of broken prose and irregular verse, we have generally ignored the full development of Melville's later career. This study hopes to bring it closer to the light.

ACKNOWLEDGMENTS

I OWE ENDLESS thanks to a number of people for their guidance, patience, and support. At the State University of New York at Buffalo, to Martin Pops, whose direction made this study possible and whose kindness and wit made writing it a pleasure rather than a burden. To Leslie Fiedler and Kenneth Dauber, who provided fruitful suggestions, sound judgments, and memorable conversations. At Northeast Louisiana University, to my colleagues and students who have helped create a productive atmosphere and given me the opportunity to solidify many of the ideas in this study. At the University of Alabama Press to editors and readers for valuable suggestions. To members of my family, Mr. and Mrs. Henry E. Cole and Mr. and Mrs. Elvis C. Davis, Jr., who helped reduce many of the anxieties inevitable over three years of writing. And, most of all, to my wife, Hillary, who gives ceaselessly her patience, endurance, and love.

Portions of chapter one were originally published in *American Transcendental Quarterly* 5, no. 1 (March 1991). They are reprinted by permission of the University of Rhode Island. A section of chapter two appeared in *ESQ: A Journal of the American Renaissance*, copyright 1992 by the Board of Regents of Washington State University. A previous version of chapter three appeared in *Studies in American Fiction*, copyright 1991 by Northeastern University. My thanks to the editors of these journals for permission to reprint this material.

I

Moby-Dick and After

1

MOBY-DICK AND THE DIVIDED BODY

A MONG MELVILLE'S EARLY influences, both comic and serious, Rabelais plays a major role. Along with Shakespeare, Browne, Burton, and Sterne, Rabelais fired Melville's linguistic imagination during the period of reading that preceded and profoundly affected *Mardi* and continued as a favorite, if not always an influence, beyond the composition of *Moby-Dick*.[1] Though many critics have consistently acknowledged the Rabelaisian presence in Melville's language, however, few have significantly investigated the roots of the Rabelaisian sensibility in an attempt to discover not only what attracted Melville to Rabelais but also what this attraction may reveal about the deeper composition of Melville's worldview and of his vision of language. In this respect, in order to gain a clearer understanding of Melville's attitudes toward his and his characters' languages, we should look beneath the surface textures of variously resembling styles to the vision of reality that shapes language into a revelation of the speaker.

In reference to Rabelais, we can locate one such analysis in Mikhail Bakhtin's *Rabelais and His World,* in which Bakhtin outlines the foundation of the early Renaissance's "topographical" division of both world and body, as well as Rabelais's grounding in the process of "degradation" that his "grotesque realism" enacts:

> Degradation and debasement of the higher do not have a formal and relative character in grotesque realism. "Upward" and "downward" have here an absolute and strictly topographical meaning. "Downward" is earth, "upward" is heaven. Earth is an element that devours, swallows up (the grave, the womb) and at the same time an element of birth, of renascence (the maternal breasts). Such is the meaning of "upward" and "downward" in their cosmic aspect, while in their purely bodily aspect, which is not clearly distinct from the cosmic, the upper part is the face or the head and the lower part is the genital organs, the belly, and the buttocks.[2]

The themes of duality, resurrection, sexuality, and sexual comedy that this description invokes help us to understand Rabelais's depiction of the world in *Gargantua and Pantagruel* as well as his creation of characters and the modes of perception and communication through which those characters engage reality. To realize that these themes also comprise a major portion of the inner structure of *Moby-Dick,* one only has to glance at the book itself or its ample criticism. With this comparison in mind it is easy to see that the relation between Melville and Rabelais extends beneath the superficial evidence of stylistics and into the realm of deep interpretation of the human body and its world. It is to this Rabelaisian ordering and description of experience that we must turn in order to understand more completely Melville's link in *Moby-Dick* to the renaissance sensibility that in part helps establish the identities and languages of the novel and its major characters.[3]

Bakhtin's analysis describes the "topographical meaning" of reality, a dualism of high and low, head and body, a division readily available in *Moby-Dick.* For instance, the *Pequod* encounters its first whale in the chapter entitled "The First Lowering," a linguistic play that echoes Ahab's "the little lower layer" and "I lack the low, enjoying power."[4] One "lowers" for whales, in other words, in a motion that is more than physical, that is, in fact, a metaphysical (or as Bakhtin might say, "cosmic") descent into the "lower stratum," the level of sexuality, animality, the level of body, death, and rebirth. One descends to the sea, the locus of the "very pelvis of the world" (118) where sperm whales "mostly swim in *veins*" (199), the sea that is "gored" (234) by the *Pequod.* Or one ascends to the masthead, the "thought-engendering altitude" (158), the ship-world's farthest point from the "catacombs" (476) of the hold that are "disembowelled" (477) to fix a leaking cask. Above waits the "sweet childhood of air and sky!" (543), "immortal infancy, and innocency of the azure!" (543); below, the cannibalism and "sharkishness" of the sea.

For Rabelais, such a topographical dualism relies chiefly upon the regenerative power of the lower stratum, located in both the body and the land. As Bakhtin notes, "degradation . . . means coming down to earth, the contact with earth as an element that swallows up and gives birth at the same time" (21). In *Moby-Dick,* however, the imagination of a locus of death and rebirth shifts from the now sterile land, the frozen, hostile topography of New Bedford and Nantucket—the land that brings "hypos" to Ishmael and seems "scorching" to the feet of Bulkington (106)— to a sea that Ishmael attempts to reinvigorate with a primordial power, the mythological sea of Osiris and Vishnu, the "cosmic" ocean and locus of miracle: "Wherein differ the sea and the land, that a miracle upon one is not a miracle upon the other? Preternatural terrors rested upon the Hebrews, when under the feet of Korah and his company the live ground opened and swallowed them up for ever; yet not a modern sun ever sets, but in precisely the same manner the live sea swallows up ships and crews" (273–74). Having noted that "man has lost that sense of the full awfulness of the sea which aboriginally belongs to it" (273), Ishmael considers the "subtleness of the sea," its mystery, and "universal cannibalism" (274), redescribing a place of power, the seat of both the "appalling" and death-dealing energies of the world, as well as the "creamy" pool of rebirth. The ocean contains within its "tornadoed Atlantic" (389) the sacred, maternal circles of "The Grand Armada." Ishmael's sea is both the place of a truth-seeking "negative capability" (Bulkington's "landlessness") and the vision of "God's foot upon the treadle of the loom" (Pip's madness) (414). It is allied to the cosmic body in its fleshly reality and its deepening mysteries, and, as a result, participates in the Rabelaisian vision of a "reproductive lower stratum" of reality.

It therefore comes as no surprise not only that land and sea metaphors mix but also that metaphors describing the sea often speak directly of the grave and resurrection. In "The Pacific," for instance, Ishmael describes the "sweet mystery about this sea, whose gently awful stirrings seem to speak of some hidden soul beneath; like those fabled undulations of the Ephesian sod over the buried Evangelist St. John" (482). He calls the extending waves "Potters' Fields of all four continents" (482), just as the captain of the *Delight* answers Ahab by crying that "the rest were buried before they died; you sail upon their tomb" (541). Likewise, in a reversal of this alignment, the blacksmith's wife "dived down into the long church-yard grass," causing Perth to "put up [his] gravestone, too, within the churchyard" and go to the death-dealing cries of sirenic mermaids (485–86); and Ahab, bitterly transferring this metaphor to the ship in chapter 29, descends the "narrow scuttle, to go to [his] grave-dug berth" (127).

With the Rabelaisian, "primordial" vision of the sea comes the corresponding vision of the body, the "cosmic" body that "represents the entire material bodily world in all its elements. It is an incarnation of this world at its absolute lower stratum, as the swallowing up and generating principle . . . " (Bakhtin 27). For Melville this "incarnation" takes place, at least partially, in the creatures that inhabit the ocean. These include the sharks, "with their jewel-hilted mouths" (293), images of the "universal cannibalism" of which all nature, including and especially man, is capable, yet representative as well of simple animality, the flesh that "swarming round the dead leviathan, smackingly feasted on its fatness" (293). More dramatically, however, the feeding sharks also represent the swirling grotesque of the "unfinished and open body" (Bakhtin 27) as they "viciously snapped, not only at each other's disembowelments, but like flexible bows, bent round, and bit their own; till those entrails seemed swallowed over and over again by the same mouth, to be oppositely voided by the gaping wound" (302). As Bakhtin notes, "the unfinished and open body (dying, bringing forth and being born) is not separated from the world by clearly defined boundaries; it is blended with the world, with animals, with objects" (27). A certain formlessness indicates not only an identification with the basic material of bodily existence, a faceless, boneless corporeality, but also a participation in the power of the lower stratum, the seat of death-birth energy.

In *Moby-Dick*, at least part of this conception finds expression in the "great live squid" (276): "A vast pulpy mass, furlongs in length and breadth, of a glancing cream-color, lay floating on the water, innumerable longs arms radiating from its centre, and curling and twisting like a nest of anacondas, as if blindly to clutch at any hapless object within reach. No perceptible face or front did it have; no conceivable token of either sensation or instinct; but undulated there on the billows, an unearthly, formless, chance-like apparition of life" (276). The faceless lack of form and serpentine twisting clearly echo the sharks' swirling cannibalism, but at the same time Ishmael adds the language of supernatural interpretation, noting that the formlessness lends the "pulpy mass" a ghostly quality, an apparitional, "unearthly" appearance that suggests the absence of a body.[5] What this language reveals is that an encounter with the "cosmic body," which the squid certainly represents, often promotes a denial of its power and an attempt to explain it in terms other than physical. As Bakhtin suggests, "[i]t is this concept [the grotesque body] that also forms the body images in the immense mass of legends . . . connected with . . . Western miracles of the Celtic sea. It also forms the body images of ghostly vision and of the legends of giants" (27). In other words, the history of man's encounter with the grotesque body records the tendency to fabulize and spiritualize the physical and so create the legends of Saint George and Perseus, for instance, that Ishmael himself records in chapter 82. But as we will later see, the novel makes clear that such interpretations, including the "superstitious" accounts of the whale, result from an inability to embrace the lower stratum and that at the point of the ship's encounter with the squid, Ishmael remains under the influence of Ahab, the book's most significant representative of that failure.

If the squid represents the formless, most primal manifestation of the cosmic body, then the variously encountered whales (excluding, for the moment, Moby-Dick) represent an at once more formal and sentient—and therefore less primal but more dangerous—form of the lower stratum. Leviathan possesses "the strength of a thousand thighs in his tail"

(356) and is associated at times with bodily ailments (352–53), fleshly fatness (293), and gallons "of clotted red gore" (286). He possesses the "jet-
black" "grandissimus" (419) and a head often figured sexually: "Why, diving after the slowly descending head, Queequeg with his keen sword had
made side lunges near its bottom, so as to scuttle a large hole there; then
dropping his sword, had thrust his long arm far inwards and upwards,
and so hauled out our poor Tash by the head" (343). Furthermore, the
whale body appears in land and grave metaphors as well and is described
as "fat English loam" full of "old Roman tiles and pottery" (407). On
the other hand, unlike the squid, the whale possesses a certain organizable
power and knows an "infantileness of ease" (376) and a strength that "has
much to do with the magic" of beauty (376). In short, the whale represents the lower stratum and cosmic body in its most dangerous form, a
seemingly purposeful, powerful, "infantile" body, pitted against the controlling forces of the upper, mentalizing world.

Moby-Dick, on the other hand, clearly inhabits and embodies the active forces of the lower stratum in a way that the other whales in the book
do not; for, to a large degree, the various sea creatures encountered participate in the "lower" reality of the sea less as individuals than as a whole
that reveals the reality, omnipresence, and omnivorousness of the grotesque body. Moby-Dick clearly forms a distinct entity, significant unto
himself as the lower stratum incarnate, equal if not superior in weight to
all the sea creatures that inhabit the book.

As in the episode of the squid, the descriptions and, to a small extent,
the actual encounters with Moby-Dick reveal that it is not his "whaleness"
that excites and appalls but the unusual qualities of his appearance. As in
the case of the "Albino man," it is "this mere aspect of all-pervading
whiteness [that] makes him more strangely hideous than the ugliest abor-
tion" (191). His hump, his deformed lower jaw, his hieroglyphic forehead
present not the face of evil but the uncontextual disproportion of the
grotesque—the unexpected, troubling crux or illogical generic violation
that irritates the viewer into the act of reading. As a result, one gets to
know two Moby-Dicks: the "White Whale" of the sailors' superstitions,
Ahab's monomaniacal, neurotic readings, and the "Whiteness" chapter
of Ishmael; and the other whale, the narratively encountered Moby-Dick,
seemingly malicious, seemingly gentle and pacifistic, the whale as grotesque body that incites the mind's desire for control.[6] It is this latter
Moby-Dick that originates the former, for in a sense the whale-as-gro-
tesque body accounts both for itself *and* for all the interpretations the
various characters give it. Its identity is, in effect, inscribed upon itself,
embodied by its own body. In this sense the "actual" whale, the encoun-

tered white sperm whale of the narrative, physically *is* a disproportionate grotesque. What results from the perception of this fact constitutes Ahab's whale, Ishmael's whale, and the "gliding great demon of the seas of life" (187) that the sailors have created.[7]

That Ahab, consciously or unconsciously, understands the true nature of the whale is clear from Ishmael's description of his captain and the obvious rhyming of his and Moby-Dick's bodies. For instance, Ahab's scar threads "its way out from among his gray hairs, and continuing right down one side of his tawny scorched face and neck, till it disappeared in his clothing, you saw a slender rod-like mark, lividly whitish" (123). He stands upon a "barbaric white leg" "fashioned from the polished bone of the sperm whale's jaw" (124) and wears "unsmoothable" wrinkles in his brow (488). Likewise, Moby-Dick possesses "a peculiar snow-white wrinkled forehead," a "streaked, and spotted, and marbled" body, and a "deformed lower jaw" (183). The question of whether Ahab acquired his scar or was born with it forms one of the book's mysteries, but by the time of his entrance into the narrative, we can see that by means of his primary "dismasting" encounter with Moby-Dick, Ahab has gradually grown into a reflection of the White Whale.[8] His body, in response to his deep recognition of the "cosmic" corporeality of Moby-Dick, has followed the process of the mind and identified "with him [Moby-Dick], not only all his bodily woes, but all his intellectual and spiritual exaspirations" (184). Subsequently, it has, to some extent, deformed itself. Ahab struck at the whale, it is said, with a "passionate, corporal animosity" (184) that originated his madness. The physical precedes, generates the spiritual ailment, at the same time that the recognition of the cosmic body, if repressed, reshapes the warped perceiver.[9]

Above all, it is Ahab's failure to accept the corporeality of Moby-Dick, first physically, then mentally, that drives him mad. Ahab "pitted himself, all mutilated, against it" (184). He desires to "dismember [his] dismemberer" (168), not only to take apart Moby-Dick but to deprive him of "membership," of connection to the world, and to sexuality, as the whale has done to Ahab. In short, Ahab, topographically divided into head and body, has rejected the corporeal (he orders from the carpenter a man with "no heart at all, brass forehead, and about a quarter of an acre of fine brains" [470]), has lost the "low, enjoying power" (167), and, sexually wounded by his whale-bone leg (463), has refused to give in to the melding of head and heart. As a result, Ahab is neurotic and represents one of the most basic neuroses of western man: he has recognized his own connection with the lower stratum and denied it, asceticizing his vision of human reality.[10] Therefore, despite H. Bruce Franklin's identification of the captain with Osiris,[11] Ahab never achieves rebirth, never actually descends into the true "grave-dug berth" (127). Sterile Ahab, "split" by his scar, torn apart by the unembraced cosmic body, knows "the general rage and hate felt by his whole race from Adam down" (184). He feels "deadly faint, bowed, and humped, as though [he] were Adam, staggering beneath the piled centuries since Paradise" (544). In other words, at least on one level, Ahab represents the first man, driven from the garden, incapable of rebirth. Though "[h]e sleeps with clenched hands; and wakes with his own bloody nails in his palms" (201), he is no Christ and can have no resurrection.

Thus Ahab's much-examined fascination with the penetration of the mask, his desire to know spiritual truth, is not so much the cause of his monomaniacal quest for the whale as it is the effect of his neurotic duality: "Would now the wind but had a body; but all the things that most exasperate and outrage mortal man, all these things are bodiless, but only bodiless as objects, not as agents. There's a most special, a most cunning, oh, a most malicious difference!" (564). This voice comes not from a god-angry, Miltonic Satan, but a man whose inability to accept the body as body, the world's body and his own part in it, has led him to see his own conception of himself behind it—a maliciously intent brain, "a most cunning" captain. Were Ahab to "strike through the mask," the "inscrutable thing" he would find (164), that upon which he "wreak[s] [his] hate" (164), would be nothing more than himself.

If Ahab gives us an image of self-destructive sterility, however, Ishmael brings us closer to the vision of plenty, an infantile, intellectually and spiritually fertile self, a figure of flux to Ahab's stasis, love to Ahab's hate, and, eventually, body to Ahab's scarred, raging head.[12] As a figure of change and motion, Ishmael, like Moby-Dick, to some extent always defies identification. Likewise, as a dialectical, endlessly growing self, he participates in a repeatedly circular pattern of death and rebirth, the images of which constitute one of the major structural components of the book. In fact, it seems clear that Ishmael undergoes at least three major rebirths in the course of the narrative: first, in the "pagan" arms of "bridegroom" Queequeg; second, in the equally comic but warmly embracing chapter 94, "A Squeeze of the Hand"; and third, in the circular, coffin-bearing vortex of the epilogue.[13] And yet, between these resurrections, Ishmael slips into, or is drawn toward, a vision of reality that springs directly or indirectly from Ahab. There operates, in short, a dialectic in the novel between the many and the one, fertility and sterility, an opposition that extends to Ishmael's changing vision of the whale as well as, ultimately, to the language with which he constructs his book.

At book's beginning Ishmael is, as is often noted, depressed. Though some commentators have labeled his misanthropy a ruse or at least comically, and therefore less sincerely, drawn, we cannot deny that he seems genuinely concerned with the "drizzly November in [his] soul" (3) and, if not exactly suicidal, is, in fact, serious enough to embark on a whaling voyage for the first time, an act that cannot be denied its dangers.[14] Thus by the time he encounters Queequeg, Ishmael has demonstrated his mind's bent, has, while searching the barren New Bedford night, encountered "a negro church" that he mentally alters to "the great Black Parliament sitting in Tophet" (9). He has considered the "ominous" associations of "Coffin" and "Spouter" (10), puzzled himself over a "squitchy picture" that he eventually interprets as a cetological suicide (12–13), and provided a generous target for the knowing barbs of Peter Coffin, who cannot resist pricking the fears of this overly suspicious, self-importantly depressed young man. Thus by the time tropical Queequeg embraces this rather combatively "self-reliant" Ishmael, we can see a dualism emerge: a young sailor, caught in depression, misanthropic, culturally paranoid, individually cold and suggestive of sterility; and a tropical pagan, warmly physical, whose tattoos call attention to his body as body, a shrinker of heads, an image of death, the worshiper of a phallic idol—in short, head against head-hunter, neurotic mind versus unconscious, grotesque body.[15]

If, therefore, Queequeg equally embodies the lower stratum's fertility-death power complex, then the "marriage" of Ishmael to Queequeg constitutes a genuine instance of death and rebirth—an embrace of grave and body and an emergence from that embrace as from Ishmael's boyhood dream, in a "resurrection" (26) both from his hypos and from the original darkness imposed by the "step-mother" world that would not allow him to remain an infant, "to crawl up the chimney" (25) and thus cease to grow. The result of this resurrection, however, becomes a kind of infantility, a re-acknowledgment of the physical and a renewed love of others. Ishmael becomes a figure of infantile play, a polymorphous, body-centered self, content to seek the sensuous for its own sake. This conversion is eventually revealed in his subsequent willingness to give himself to the tactile pleasures of squeezing sperm and indicates a descent of the head into the loins, an acknowledgement of, and surrender to, the cosmic body: "Would that I could keep squeezing that sperm for ever! For now, since by many prolonged, repeated experiences, I have perceived that in all cases man must eventually lower, or at least shift, his conceit of attainable felicity; not placing it anywhere in the intellect or the fancy; but in the wife, the heart, the bed, the table, the saddle, the fire-side, the country; now that I have perceived all this, I am ready to squeeze case eternally. In visions of the night, I saw long rows of angels in paradise, each with his hands in a jar of spermaceti" (416). Norman O. Brown states that "the human body would become after resurrection polymorphously perverse, delighting in that full life of the body which it now fears. The consciousness strong enough to endure full life would be no longer Apollonian but Dionysian—consciousness which does not observe the limit, but overflows; consciousness which *does not negate any more*."[16] In this respect, Ishmael's statement constitutes a clear perception of the "low, enjoying power." He denies "intellect," cites the loci of sexuality, animality, and regenerative production, and, in a final, suitably playful vision, brings the bodiless angels, images of spirituality itself, down to earth to baptize their hands in "sperm."

It becomes clear that after both of his early, direct encounters with the lower stratum, Ishmael becomes such a figure of positivity. After the comically frightening night with Queequeg, for instance, he likes "nothing better than to have Queequeg smoking by me, even in bed, because he seemed to be full of such serene household joy then" (54). He comes alive to the "condensed confidential comfortableness of sharing a pipe and a blanket" (54) and, as Rosenberry points out, quickly transforms into a knowing joker, the antithesis of the greenhorn he arrived as.[17] In fact, both Ishmael's attitude toward the world and his resultant language fluctuate throughout the book between the renewed depression of the early chapters—the first encounter and subsequent identification with Ahab and his quest—and those periods of renewal after each rebirth.[18]

The Division of Language

The fluctuations of Ishmael's dialectical self also make evident the undeniable and significant differences between his linguistic roots and those of Ahab, differences of time and space that parallel the book's dualism and dialectic of head and heart. Ahab is past, Elizabethan, his language the cadence of Shakespeare, his vision that of the late Renaissance mind, Doctor Faustus, a seeker of absolute knowledge and amateur of black magic. Ishmael is present, nineteenth-century American, a dialectically progressing self, full of the play of his polymorphousness, a product of revolutions, both political and psychological. As he narrates, Ishmael recalls the fluctuations of self passed through, and we can discern at times both old and new, the language of the reborn and the portrait of the Ahab-shadowed sailor; for it is between the need to define and control and the desire to delight in the concretized textures of speech that the book's linguistic tensions, in reflection of its psychological and narrative ones, take place.

To begin to understand Ahab's language, it must be taken in soliloquy. It is his defining genre:

> I own thy speechless, placeless power; said I not so? Nor was it wrung from me; nor do I now drop these links. Thou canst blind; but I can then grope. Thou canst consume; but I can then be ashes. Take the homage of these poor eyes, and shutter-hands. I would not take it. The lightning flashes through my skull; mine eye-balls ache and ache; my whole beaten brain seems as beheaded, and rolling on some stunning ground. Oh, oh! Yet blindfold, yet will I talk to thee. Light though thou be, thou leapest out of darkness; but I am darkness leaping out of light, leaping out of thee! (507)

As both Matthiessen and Olson have told us, Ahab's speeches act and sound Shakespearean.[19] But beyond their blank verse rhythms and jagged bursts of energy, they further echo Ahab's duality of vision and so provide a key into the structure of his thought. The rhetorical patterns, forged within the great dualism of his quest, emerge in conflicting pairs, each utterance fractured into equal and opposing halves. The natural force registered elicits the defiant, humanistic response. Human force, force of will and determination, stands forehead to forehead, rhythmically jammed against its natural opposite by the syntax of the speech. The nature of the address, the abstraction of its intended audience, mirrors the defiant intention not only to kill the whale but also to harpoon the unbodied, "inscrutable thing" that moves "behind the unreasoning mask" (164). For Ahab, language is as much agent as is Moby-Dick or the "foundling fire"; it is a human instrument to be employed against the instruments of the unknowable, the tool by which he attempts to consummate his relation to reality. It is a substitute for his lost body.[20]

The internal structure of this soliloquy, the organizing tension between duality and singular definition, can be located in most of Ahab's speeches. In fact, we may benefit from dividing all of Ahab's language into two different but related categories: (1) utterances that attempt to wrest a single, hidden and unknowable truth from a complex of oppositions, to, as though it were a body, "consummate" a desire for truth; and (2) utterances that, because frustrated, descend to dark humor, prophecy, or magic. The two may at first seem contradictory, but, like his renaissance prototypes, Ahab has turned to magic in an attempt to subvert the failures of normal human reasoning. Thus the futility and self-punishment of his search for the unknowable, the results of a commitment to the first type of language, have led him to the Faustian pact, and in consequence, the man who has "been in colleges" (79) has also become a believer of spells.

The questing man's turn to magic and prophecy has frequently formed the subject of tragedy because in essence it helps clarify one of language's inherent traps. Whether Macbeth's, Doctor Faustus's, or Ahab's, the passionately curious and ambitious mind that rejects its own intellectual and linguistic powers because of natural limitations inevitably falls prey to the very spirit of language itself by stumbling into a trap of words: though Ahab is at times acutely sensitive to both the denotative and symbolic properties of speech, in the company of the Parsee he fails to consider the possibilities of multiple meaning. His determination to force language into singular reference, coupled with a distrust of his own ability to define the subject of his search, verbally blinds him. Ahab places both too great a faith in language and too little. His conclusions resurrect the model of seventeenth-century tragedy: a technocratic mind, muddled by an ambition of intellect that supersedes the wisdom of the body, frustrated by its own failures, fails itself by creating a false logic of success. As the book begins its end and Ahab seizes its focus, his frustrated mind cannot live up to the proliferation of utterance; it cannot grasp the ancient fact that all prophecy, while baited with the promise of escape, actually only describes, in symbolic language, the teeth of the trap itself.

As a result, during those periods between the denial of his own linguistic powers and the acceptance of the prophecy's pledge, Ahab appears in scenes of self-lacerating humor. Frustration, the inability to act or determine the target of the action, as in the late Elizabethan mind, as in *Hamlet,* often leads to a humor of negation and darkness that ironically consists of the sort of word play that, were it not the result of the very blindness that destroys him, might save Ahab from the Parsee's riddles:

> What art thou thrusting that thief-catcher into my face for, man? Thrusted light is worse than presented pistols.
> I thought, sir, that you spoke to carpenter.
> Carpenter? why that's—but no;—a very tidy, and, I may say, an extremely gentlemanlike sort of business thou art in here, carpenter;—or would'st thou rather work in clay?
> Sir?—Clay? clay, sir? That's mud; we leave clay to ditchers, sir.
> The fellow's impious! What art thou sneezing about?
> Bone is rather dusty, sir.
> Take the hint, then; and when thou art dead, never bury thyself under living people's noses. (470–71)

While the dualism of other speeches here remains in the concern with light and dark, this passage serves best to demonstrate Ahab's sensitivity to the meanings of acts and words and, at the same time, his failure to allow that sensitivity to work in his favor. Throughout this episode he demonstrates an undeniable playfulness and sensitivity to language, and yet this humor, the negative of Ishmael's polymorphous creativity, remains inherently destructive and self-punishing. Without rebirth and without the acceptance of death and its mysteries that the lower stratum provides, Ahab can use language only to frustrate, entrap, or punish himself.

It may be said that, like Pierre, Ahab possesses a pair of opposing angels, each of whom either provokes or tempts him toward his seemingly predestined end. Fedallah—whose language functions in an almost completely symbolic manner and is allied to magic—assumes the traditional role of the "evil" angel whose intent is to tempt and mislead his charge.[21] Worrying in Ahab's other ear, however, is Starbuck, the "earnest," almost ascetic chief mate, whose flesh is "hard as twice-baked biscuit" (115) and whose "conscientiousness" and "deep natural reverence" (116) establish him as the voice of expediency and restraint. In this respect he undoubtedly functions as a rather careful though impotent "good" angel, willing to challenge his captain if necessary but nevertheless cowed by the "more spiritual terrors" (117) Ahab is able to evoke in him.

More important than any alteration he may attempt in Ahab, however, is his role as catalyst for his captain's fierier speeches. In these moments Starbuck becomes the representative of the world's compromising voice and perhaps, despite Ahab's denials, a figure of conscience as well, as though in being who and what he is, Starbuck inevitably scrapes Ahab's unhealed wounds and so reminds him of what he himself has lost and become. In addition, Starbuck's "careful bravery"—"a daring so strangely respectful and cautious that it almost seemed not only every way seeking to avoid the slightest outward manifestation of itself, but within also seemed more than half distrustful of itself" (474)—frequently allows him the ability to accurately analyze his captain's words and actions: "Thou hast outraged, not insulted me, sir; but for that I ask thee not to beware Starbuck; thou wouldst but laugh; but let Ahab beware of Ahab; beware of thyself, old man" (474–75). Thus, though Starbuck is a part of the opposing force that, by its very existence, insults and provokes Ahab into speech, he is also the missing voice of Ahab's sanity. Ahab can and does recognize the truth of Starbuck's criticisms ("What's that he said—Ahab beware of Ahab—there's something there!" [475]) but the monomania of his quest and the domination of his overdeveloped head refuse to allow its influence.

More interesting, however, is the relationship between Ahab's and

Starbuck's languages. For while the rigidly dualistic captain pushes his aggressive speech into the ungiving walls of reality, Starbuck, in a similar though less powerful fashion, linguistically pushes against Ahab, the authority of the captain's position, and the moral and ethical bounds of society that prevent the chief mate from becoming the man of more than physical action he needs to be: "What! hope to wrest this old man's living power from his own living hands? Only a fool would try it. Say he were pinioned even; knotted all over with ropes and hawsers; chained down to ring-bolts on this cabin floor; he would be more hideous than a caged tiger, then. I could not endure the sight; could not possibly fly his howlings; all comfort, sleep itself, inestimable reason would leave me on the long intolerable voyage" (515). What Ahab possesses in relation to Moby-Dick, Starbuck lacks in relation to Ahab: the spiritual fearlessness to strike, to ignore the world's objections and at least attempt to destroy that which opposes him. As a result, the language of this passage is aggressive in an Ahabian sense yet weak and "pinioned" itself in its attacks. It questions and seeks but does not have the force of will to vault into the extra-logical realms of magic or self-destructive frustration to which Ahab's unstoppable intention resorts. In short, Starbuck's is the speech of self-compromise and control, the linguistic equivalent of the lowered gaze and tone of voice he usually employs in Ahab's presence. In the end his speeches, though seeming to wrestle with insoluble dilemmas, inevitably apologize for and negativize his inner desires and, as a result, typically conclude with the simple or silent admission that he cannot or will not do what he knows he must.

Perhaps more dangerous to Ahab's intention is Pip, the "gloomy-jolly," "over tender-hearted" (411) witness of "God's foot upon the treadle of the loom" (414). At once a less reasoning, more rounded soul than Starbuck, he acts as a figure for orphaned consciousness, full of the wisdom of loss, reborn but nevertheless one of the dead. In this sense Pip exists somewhere beyond Ahab because, lacking the "globular brain" and "ponderous heart" (73), he also lacks the ability either to oppose the depths of what he experiences in the vastness of the open sea or to accept the immensity he finds within himself. As a result, his heart and mind have equally burst and, in ultimately tragic fashion, become one. Thus his language is both deeply sad and unconsciously playful, remarkably wise and full of nonsense: "Ha, ha! old Ahab! the White Whale; he'll nail ye! This is a pine tree. My father, in old Tolland county, cut down a pine tree once, and found a silver ring grown over in it; some old darkey's wedding ring. How did it get there? And so they'll say in the resurrection, when they come to fish up this old mast, and find a doubloon lodged in it, with bedded oysters for the shaggy bark. Oh, the gold! the precious, precious gold!—the green miser'll hoard ye soon! Hish, hish! God goes 'mong the worlds blackberrying" (435).

What gives this speech its position in the book's linguistic spectrum is its combination of extreme consciousness and near unconsciousness. It is fair to say, for instance, that Pip has undergone a remarkably Ahabian experience, has in fact reached a level of self-consciousness so great it has driven him into a madness one step beyond Ahab's. At the same time, however, we can also claim that the result of that self-consciousness is a regression to the unconscious realm of pre-reason and nonsense talk.[22] Thus the undeniable playfulness of the onomatopoeic animal cries, for instance, is undercut by the emptiness beneath that play, while in a similar fashion, the deeply perceptive wisdom and prophetic utterances are compromised by their often playful constructions. As a result, the "crazy wittiness" that Melville gleaned from Shakespeare's fools participates in both spheres of the book's dualism at the same time that it lacks the constructive results of Ishmael's repeated rebirths.

It is precisely this conscious unconsciousness, much more than the simple pull of pity, that Ahab finds threatening in Pip, for in his identification with "the little negro" (411), Ahab sees not only what he believes himself to be at this moment but also what he may become. Pip offers a model of both a more intense madness and a type of sanity that, in its sobering clarity, may be the most horrific condition of all. As a result, in order to escape the vision of himself, Ahab rejects Pip's offers, represses the insight he invokes, and recommits himself to his quest, refusing, as he has throughout the book, to acknowledge both past and future, family and fate.

In a letter to Evert A. Duyckinck, Melville provides what is perhaps a key to the essence of Ahab's limitations: "—I would to God Shakspeare had lived later, & promenaded in Broadway. Not that I might have had the pleasure of leaving my card for him at the Astor, or made merry with him over a bowl of the fine Duyckinck punch; but that the muzzle which all men wore on their souls in the Elizabethan day, might not have intercepted Shakspers full articulations."[23] As Olson tells us, this important passage underscores Melville's aversion to those moments in Shakespeare when "truth-speakers" are forbidden a voice because of a self-censorship that, in Melville's view, became unnecessary after the Declaration of Independence.[24] The distinction made here, however, is more than political. It speaks a difference not only of time but of place, each of which radically alters the sensibility and "soul" of its inhabitants. The freewheeling pride with which Melville mentions Broadway, the Astor, and the prospect of entertaining Shakespeare in a distinctly American fashion alerts us to the likelihood that for all his admiration of the playwright, Melville saw him as less than perfect precisely because he wasn't American, because he hadn't been a product of revolution. Furthermore, those characters in Melville's own fiction drawn from Shakespearean influence may in fact be subject to a similar limitation, not because they are not born American but because they do not act and think along American lines.

If Shakespearian Ahab represents seventeenth-century man, however, then Ishmael—the prideful Yankee, who would indeed enjoy "a bowl of the fine Duyckinck punch" just as he enjoys fowls "broiled, judiciously buttered, and judgmatically salted and peppered" (5)—represents Broadway, the Astor, and the revolutionized, continually reborn sensibility of Melville's nineteenth-century American. As Ahab is attuned to the ambitions of the humanistic mind, Ishmael, when not under Ahab's spell, is aware of the pleasures of both mind and body, of the joys of companionship and conversation, the Whitmanian love of self and other.[25] Consequently, his language expands and explains, converses and creates; it enjoys not only its ability to signify the knowledge it seeks and sometimes finds but also its very activity as language, its existence as word of mouth or pen: "It was while gliding through these latter waters that one serene and moonlight night, when all the waves rolled by like scrolls of silver; and, by their soft, suffusing seethings, made what seemed a silvery silence, not a solitude; on such a silent night a silvery jet was seen far in advance of the white bubbles at the bow" (232).

What immediately strikes the reader accustomed to Ahab's tense rhythms and frustrated logic is the ease and acceptance of this sentence. It takes what comes to it rather than searching for an unknown. It describes and dilates, allows for variation of rhythm and subject, and, above all, enjoys itself, plays, within the contours of its own utterance. This is prose both self-effacing and unafraid of the mythological magic of the world it describes. It is the product of psychological and political revolutions, the melding of head and heart in the voice of Melville's modern American.

As Ahab's language attacks in order to define, Ishmael's digresses in order to explain:

> The casket of the skull is broken into with an axe, and the two plump, whitish lobes being withdrawn (precisely resembling two large puddings), they are then mixed with flour, and cooked into a most delectable mess, in flavor somewhat resembling calves' head, which is quite a dish among some epicures; and every one knows that some young bucks among the epicures, by continually dining upon calves' brains, by and by get to have a little brains of their own, so as to be able to tell a calf's head from their own heads; which, indeed, requires uncommon discrimination. (299)

This passage typifies Ishmael's primary linguistic mode. It begins in a straightforward style of explanation, veers quickly into detailed, and often fanciful, description, which in turn leads a meandering syntax and thought process into a more general level of comment that, more often than not, concludes comedically. It is a trajectory that mirrors the playful man's thinking, a productive searching out of both small truths and delicate mirths, and a vision of the sentence that is wholly inclusive, an instrument with which to embrace information, explanation, and, in the end, comedy. It forms an excellent synecdoche for the pattern of those chapters that Ishmael dominates and initiates us further into the sensitivity and versatility of the continually reborn mind. After all, it is digression, the desire and ability to delay the consummation of both syntax and thought, to delight in the fore-pleasure of information and description, that is most characteristic of Ishmaelean language and that forms the heart of his sense of play. The very aesthetic of delay, from sentence to paragraph to plot, informs and animates Ishmael's mind and *Moby-Dick* and provides us with the very "body" of the book itself—the cetology chapters, the explanations of whaling, and the many subgenres and added tales that fatten the text itself.

Perhaps a better example of the purely comic aspect of Ishmael's dilatory speech occurs just after the first of his rebirths, in chapter 17, "The Ramadan." His bedside lecture to Queequeg on the "nonsense" of "prolonged" religious "ham-squattings" (85) serves to demonstrate his unique ability to be both earnest and comic without compromising either the seriousness of what he says or the delight with which he says it—to construct, via the accumulation of puns and unexpected usages, a delicate blend of disarming charm and intent hortatory.[26] Such a passage reveals the uniqueness of Melville's creation, for one of the qualities that makes *Moby-Dick* unforgettably different from other nineteenth-century novels is the idiosyncratic construction of such Ishmaelean language, the use of culturally mixed phrases such as "sensible and sagacious savage" or "ridiculous Ramadan," as well as the subtle punning on "fast" and "half-starved" (85). As we later learn, "fast" is a term that denotes control, definition, the pinning down of truth and life that Ahab fiercely desires. Thus body-centered Ishmael argues that one should not deny the flesh lest the thoughts that result from that denial, like those born of a desire to "make fast to" the whale, be undernourished, "starved" both physically and spiritually. It is this ability to tap into the book's thematic structure via the complexities of a seriocomic, dilating language that makes Ishmael unique. Only he, Melville's representative democrat and body-wise American, could create the phrase "dyspeptic religionists" (85) and trans-

mit with it all the common man's distrust of religious denial and ideological manipulation, while delighting in the humor with which he de-
bunks the seriousness of the temporarily ascetic Queequeg. For it is the
body and its relation to language, the "cosmic" body of the sea's creatures and the flesh of the book itself, that energize and inform Ishmael's
text. In the book's higher moments of psychological rebirth, he reaches
a playfulness not only of word but of self, a baptismal breaching that
pours into his language and recreates, both in thought and word, the
polymorphous perversity of childhood:

> As I sat there at my ease, cross-legged on the deck; after the bitter exertion
> at the windlass; under a blue tranquil sky; the ship under indolent sail, and
> gliding so serenely along; as I bathed my hands among those soft, gentle
> globules of infiltrated tissues, woven almost within the hour; as they richly
> broke to my fingers, and discharged all their opulence, like fully ripe grapes
> their wine; as I snuffed up that uncontaminated aroma,—literally and truly,
> like the smell of spring violets; I declare to you, that for the time I lived as
> in a musky meadow; I forgot all about our horrible oath; in that inexpressible
> sperm, I washed my hands and my heart of it; I almost began to credit the
> old Paracelsan superstition that sperm is of rare virtue in allaying the heat
> of anger; while bathing in that bath, I felt divinely free from all ill-will, or
> petulance, or malice, of any sort whatsoever. (415–16)

There is an Eastern tranquillity about this passage. Once again, in a single
sentence, the verbal action is delayed in a fore-pleasure of description.
The rhythms are predominately slow and anapestic, a rocking, maternal
motion. The details are fully enjoyed, word-sounds fondled in imitation
of the squeezing process itself. The language enacts a world without an-
ger, a place of unconsummated pleasure, and represents the height of
Ishmaelean play, the deep pleasure of infantility, and the alternative to
the Ahabian frustration of unconsummated desire.

Of the book's other important characters, Stubb clearly comes closest
to Ishmael's playfulness, though without the depth of character and fullness of experience Ishmael draws upon. Though it is clear that Stubb
maintains a comic vision of existence, has "converted the jaws of death
into an easy chair," for instance (118), the "happy-go-lucky," "neither cra-
ven nor valiant" (118) second mate has not, as far as we can tell, undergone
the self-shaping process of rebirth, nor does his genial philosophy rest
upon the intricate superstructure of a probing mind: "What he thought
of death itself, there is no telling. Whether he ever thought of it at all,
might be a question; but, if he ever did chance to cast his mind that way
after a comfortable dinner, no doubt, like a good sailor, he took it to be
a sort of call of the watch to tumble aloft, and bestir themselves there,

about something which he would find out when he obeyed the order, and not sooner" (118). This is praise and criticism combined, for though Ishmael may admire Stubb's ability to ignore the serious, he nevertheless questions the depth of being that permits such ignorance. Likewise, in his encounter with Ahab in chapter 29 as well as in "The Doubloon" chapter, Stubb does indeed seem a rather shallow character after all; unable to think his way past Ahab or understand the dream he invokes, too weak to listen to Pip's mad truth telling, he slinks away, overwhelmed. As Rosenberry has noted, during these episodes Stubb is indeed a "spiritual scarecrow."[27]

Nevertheless, in times of less vital challenge, Stubb's ability to transcend physical danger or enliven a quiet scene helps balance the presentation of his character. Appropriately enough, though, it is not by virtue of action or thought but by means of his buoyantly comic speech, his language, that Stubb reveals his greatest value and most nearly approaches the Ishmaelean sensibility: "Give way there, give way! The devil fetch ye, ye ragamuffin rapscallions; ye are all asleep. Stop snoring, ye sleepers, and pull. Pull, will ye? pull, can't ye? pull, won't ye? Why in the name of gudgeons and ginger-cakes don't ye pull?—pull and break something! pull, and start your eyes out!" (218–19). The combination of earnestness, excitement, and comedy, as well as the obvious delight in blusteringly comic phrases and unique sonic combinations, identifies Stubb's as an uplifting, comically transcendent voice, one that not only sees the lighter side of reality but also radiates delight in its own activity. This is the same voice, for instance, that exhorts Fleece to berate the sharks in mockingly sermonized form and, while it feasts on the "fatness" of its own words, enjoys the taste of whale flesh (293).[28] Nevertheless, this identical episode also demonstrates Stubb's harder qualities, perhaps even his bigotry, as with much the same callousness that he left Pip to float in the sea, he forces the notably unwilling Fleece to play preacher.

An at once more rounded and less blithe character close to Ishmael is the deeply experienced Father Mapple. Like the Ishmael of the epilogue, Father Mapple, "a sailor and harpooneer in his youth" (38), has also experienced resurrection: "At the time I now write of, Father Mapple was in the hardy winter of a healthy old age; that sort of old age which seems merging into a second flowering youth, for among all the fissures of his wrinkles, there shone certain mild gleams of a newly developing bloom—the spring verdure peeping forth even beneath February's snow" (38). This vegetable metaphor for rebirth—one Melville uses concerning himself in a letter to Hawthorne—is a sure sign of the self-maturation of the minister.[29] From the text of his sermon and the vividness of his descriptions of Jonah's experience, it is also safe to assume that he himself has experienced, if not a similar trial, then at least enough of life's depths to render his concern with this topic more than merely dutiful. In short, like Ishmael, Father Mapple, having "survived the wreck," has "escaped alone to tell thee" (573). It is precisely his isolation that asserts itself and claims importance—isolation not only as one who has lived through the disaster and reformed himself, but as truth teller, alone, "impregnable in his little Quebec" (39), roaring, as Melville himself so often does, of the need "to preach the Truth to the face of Falsehood!": "Woe to him who seeks to pour oil upon the waters when God has brewed them into a gale! Woe to him who seeks to please rather than to appal!" (48). That this prophetic warning is a version of the Melvillean manifesto of "chronometrical" or uncorrupted truth telling is difficult to doubt. That it is similar to Ishmael's own project in telling his story is likewise clear, as is its likeness to those moments in Ishmael's own speech when, employing the wisdom his cyclical experience of death and rebirth has afforded him, he quickly converts comedy into appalling truth.

It is equally clear that Father Mapple's resurrection is at once riper and less playful in some sense than Ishmael's. Nevertheless, he too demonstrates a taste for language that rings more of rhetoric than aggression, more of explanation and exegesis than definition and delimitation. Though not tactilely playful in an Ishmaelean sense, his speech generally participates in an imaginative wholeness that results from the transcendent experience of its speaker. It reveals an attempt to dramatize the psychomachian text, to give body and form to scripture in order to express the truth of its narration—the dangers and possible values of psychological trauma. It is, in other words, a preaching of acceptance, both of destiny and of the world's engulfing and empowering body, the doctrine of the embrace that becomes but a hoarier version of Ishmael's sperm squeezing: "And eternal delight and deliciousness will be his, who coming to lay him down, can say with his final breath—O Father!—chiefly known to me by thy rod—mortal or immortal, here I die. I have striven to be Thine, more than to be this world's, or mine own. Yet this is nothing; I leave eternity to Thee; for what is man that he should live out the lifetime of his God?" (48). Though orthodoxly religious in a way Ishmael himself often avoids, this relinquishment of self is nevertheless a vital part of his vision. Ishmael does indeed approach an "eternal delight and deliciousness" that is, among other things, a realization and acceptance of the facts of existence.

"Like One of Those Seeds"

Despite the structural patterns Rabelais and Bakhtin's analysis of Rabelais provides in leading to a clearer understanding of the languages of the novel, and despite recent attempts to prove some unity of structure and intention, *Moby-Dick* remains an awkward, sometimes sloppy book. In part because of his pursuit of organic form and seemingly personal differences with the novel as a genre, Melville ultimately constructed a book that may fall short of perfection but nevertheless wears its imperfections proudly and is indeed at times as "ungainly as the gambols of the whales themselves."[30] Moreover, any attempt to ascribe to him or the book a sense of triumph or generically comic satisfaction, despite its ending, is too easily undercut by the later domination, for instance, of Ahab as a character and of Ahab's story in general. In short, what is perhaps most Melvillean about *Moby-Dick* is that, in the end, we cannot pin it down, cannot say with certainty that its final form or statement is one of victory or defeat. Though Ishmael does survive, the epilogue is nevertheless heavily laden with the Jobian allusion of worldly cruelty and is equally expressive of the orphanage of the surviving self. At the same time, however, taken as a whole it seems to strike a rough balance between formal playfulness and linguistic versatility on the one hand and earnest intent and the "appetite for God" on the other.

Melville has nevertheless left another shaft of light to train upon the problem: the letters written during the book's composition. Here, not only do we see a degree of playfulness not unlike Ishmael's but also the maturity and preoccupation with resurrection that both Ishmael and Father Mapple often demonstrate: "I am like one of those seeds taken out of the Egyptian Pyramids, which, after being three thousand years a seed and nothing but a seed, being planted in English soil, it developed itself, grew to greenness, and then fell to mould."[31] Many of the major preoccupations of theme and style in *Moby-Dick* can be found in such a passage without the confusing intervention of character. The impulse toward expansion and identification, the concern with vegetable metaphors of rebirth—with their particularly Rabelaisian conception of reality—as well as the mixture of hopeful and sorrowful visions of experience this quotation reveals can but remind us of Ishmael and those characters closest to him. Even so, it is difficult to suggest that Melville's own voice was completely Ishmaelean or that it can be represented solely by a single quotation. In the same letter, as a matter of fact, there are moments of deep despair that, if not exactly Ahabian, hint at the frustrated emotion with which Melville is able to endow Ahab's speeches. Admittedly, it is the final compromise in attempting to understand a complex mind to say that it contains all, accounts for everything, and yet to a certain extent in Melville's case this is true. The one thing that is clear in relation to his language is that the amounts of one voice in relation to another are variable, that they change, attenuate, swell, and blend, and that even over the subsequent years of his life and writing, these two primary strands continue to develop, ultimately producing a body of work of even greater complexity and diversity than *Moby-Dick* itself.

2

LANGUAGE AND THE ASCETIC BODY IN *PIERRE* AND "BARTLEBY"

Asceticism and the Fictive

THE INTERVAL BETWEEN *Moby-Dick* and *Pierre* has puzzled commentators not so much because Melville, despite feeling "grated to pieces,"[1] continued his shattering pace of work but because, with the small time intervening, the two books at first glance seem very different. Nevertheless, in spite of some initial disconcertion, those in search of deeper connections have certainly found them, especially and most significantly between the two questing protagonists, Pierre and Ahab.[2] Despite the undeniable importance of this clear link between the two novels, however, there nevertheless remains an equally significant, and often undervalued, difference of context and world composition that must be taken into account if we are to understand either Pierre himself as a less forceful version of the Ahabian sensibility or Pierre's language (and the language of the novel) as the result of an essentially Ahabian attitude towards reality. For instance, the most obvious and often-noted difference between the two books is the change from sea to land. *Pierre,* with the exception of the embryonic "Fragments From a Writing Desk," holds the qualified distinction of being Melville's first predominately land-locked work, but this change of milieu signifies more than a mere turn to greener pastures; it alerts us to the loss of the most potent force Melville's fiction had yet to reveal—the primal, mythopoeic ocean. After all, the energy that animates *Moby-Dick,* that is responsible for the very foundation of that book's world, springs in large part from the existence of a protean stratum of sexuality, death, and rebirth that Melville locates in the textures and depths of the sea. What is immediately clear at the beginning of *Pierre,* with its evocation of "the green and golden world" of Saddle Meadows,[3] is that in addition to presenting a self-conscious pastoral idyll—a fiction, it seems, that often senses its own fictionality—Melville avoids the potency of the sea and gives us instead a world whose body and consciousness of that body is, at least for a time, deeply repressed. In short, we are

introduced for the first time to a Melvillean world without flesh, a noticeably fictive landscape asceticized by worldly propriety, familial religion, and genealogical authority and therefore unable to imagine or allow
the existence of a warm, aboriginal sea and its potent, thousand-thighed
monsters.[4]

Though the land in *Moby-Dick* seems "scorching" or induces "hypos,"
though it is, as we first encounter it, sterile and frozen, the land of *Pierre*
is different only in the guise of its sterility, its deceptive makeup. As there
exists no "substitute for pistol and ball"[5] in the world of *Pierre,* no "live
sea" that "swallows up ships and crews,"[6] it becomes clear from the opening pages that the balancing impulses of vitality, sexuality, and indeter-
minacy that Ishmael locates in the sea have instead been overlooked by a
vision that cannot, or will not, account for them. This failure to allow the
lower stratum its existence results in artificiality, a nature gilded with the
denied but nevertheless hoarded golds of the ascetic sensibility: "There
are some strange summer mornings in the country, when he who is but
a sojourner from the city shall early walk forth into the fields, and be won-
der-smitten with the trance-like aspect of the green and golden world.
Not a flower stirs; the trees forget to wave; the grass itself seems to have
ceased to grow; and all Nature, as if suddenly become conscious of her
own profound mystery, and feeling no refuge from it but silence, sinks
into this wonderful and indescribable repose" (3). The almost pictorial
emphasis on stasis here, on a stillness of "all Nature" contemplating its
own previously unconscious mysteries, alerts us to the forced rigidity of
this landscape at the same time that it reveals as background a world in
which an excess of interiority has led to a kind of external coma. It is thus
no surprise that in the book's early sections, the characters, themselves
partial beings, move stiffly and the land, far from the mythological "live
ground" that "swallowed up" "Korah and his company,"[7] is covered with
an evergreen grass that serves only to hide lifeless stone.

In fact, Saddle Meadows presents the very image of repression, the
world as mask that betrays its hidden nature through exaggerated gestures, and it is equally clear that this repression results partially from the
combined domination of history and religion. Not only does Pierre, "the
only surnamed male Glendinning extant" (7), seem shadowed by an idealized, masculine past, but also that past, with all its heroism and bellicose
grandeur, is deeply and, as Pierre will discover, paradoxically linked to
Christianity. As a result, "the illuminated scroll of his life" (7)—an image
that combines monkish asceticism, gilded materialism, and the distance
of textuality—is filled to some extent with a concern for his sexuality
in the absence of a male model as well as with the weight of that now-

idealized past in which the "horological" and "chronometrical" seem wedded:

> The grandfather of Pierre measured six feet four inches in height; during a
> fire in the old manorial mansion, with one dash of his foot, he had smitten
> down an oaken door, to admit the buckets of his negro slaves; Pierre had
> often tried on his military vest, which still remained an heirloom at Saddle
> Meadows, and found the pockets below his knees, and plenty of additional
> room for a fair-sized quarter-cask within its buttoned girth; in a night-scuffle
> in the wilderness before the Revolutionary War, he had annihilated two In-
> dian savages by making reciprocal bludgeons of their heads. And all this was
> done by . . . the kindest of masters to his slaves; . . . a sweet-hearted, chari-
> table Christian; in fine, a pure, cheerful, childlike, blue-eyed, divine old man;
> in whose meek, majestic soul, the lion and the lamb embraced—fit image of
> his God. (29–30)

It is fitting and emblematic of Pierre's condition that his grandfather's clothes seem to swallow him; he can live up neither to the image in his mind nor to its physical traces. Furthermore, the figure of the "Christian-militant" Indian killer (an early version of Colonel Moredock perhaps) is here heavily ironized due both to the contradiction between his actions and his "beliefs" and to the young Pierre's failure to see what Melville clearly understood at this time—the undeniable split between the teachings of Christ and the mechanisms of the world. Indeed, the overall effect on Pierre of such an illustrious and burdening ancestral figure appears to be a mixture of phallic anxiety and ambition, the desire to "have a monopoly of glory in capping the fame-column, whose tall shaft had been erected by his noble sires" (8).

As though to add to rather than diminish this pressure, the death of Pierre's father when Pierre was twelve seems to have cemented in his mind the childhood conception of an unblemished, deific figure, an idealization that experience and consciousness have had little opportunity to qualify. In other words, in addition to possessing a grandfather who is made largely of tall tales rather than flesh and blood, Pierre also retains a father, his physical progenitor, who has become to him a bodiless image of ideal good. The "unclouded, snow-white" (68) figure in Pierre's shrine consti-tutes a fleshless vision, an allegorization of the father as "fatherhood" rather than an actual being who possesses, among other things, a physical body. The combination in Pierre's world of an idealizing religion and such mental images of his male progenitors helps form part of a complexly repressive atmosphere that takes form in the exterior landscape of Saddle Meadows and in the artificiality of its construction. Thus at least one function of the stilted presentation of Pierre's early world is to cast the shadow of Pierre's mind and immaturity, to reveal the remarkably unreal, aphysical manner in which he sees and constructs his reality.

Pierre's male ancestors, however, form only part of the solution to understanding his early condition. After all, his present world is populated primarily by women. Of these, Pierre's "haughty" mother dominates, both as the sole possessor of parental authority and, more subtly, as artificial "sister" to Pierre. First of all, as mother, Mrs. Glendinning, while retaining her beauty, nevertheless manages to exude distance, an aura of unattainability that is similar to what Pierre feels when remembering his father, so much so, in fact, that Pierre refuses to consider a paternal replacement by childishly imagining the magical disappearance of any "man—gray-beard, or beardless—who should dare to propose marriage to his mother . . . " (5). In other words, not only is Pierre's vision of his father so sacred and unreal that he would imaginatively deny any physical surrogate, but his image of his mother, as real as she is, is at this early stage similarly unable to account for her sexuality. Such innocence would be understandable, of course, had not both Pierre and Mrs. Glendinning placed the youth in the position that might have been filled by one of the "train of infatuated suitors" (5). But in an incestuous as well as narcissistic play, both mother and son distort their natural relationship and further ignore Pierre's developing sexuality by "innocently" playing at love despite their inability to proceed with "the final banns and the rite" (16) to which their sexless play naturally leads.[8] As a result, all aspects of pure physicality, anything that speaks of the flesh in its unidealized state, qualifies and sullies the "pure" nature of their constructed world and, because in Pierre such signs indicate growth, strikes a subtle blow at the "practical sorcery" Mrs. Glendinning maintains over him.

On the other hand, as Pierre's "sister," Mrs. Glendinning cuts off, by artificially fulfilling, what may have been a different escape for Pierre. For the presence of an equally developing yet sexually opposite sibling might have allowed him to depend less upon his mother simply because his relationship with her, in the presence of an equally worthy counterpart, may well have been less intimate. Pierre himself seems to sense this unfulfilled need: "So perfect to Pierre had long seemed the illuminated scroll of his life thus far, that only one hiatus was discoverable by him in that sweetly-writ manuscript. A sister had been omitted from the text. He mourned that so delicious a feeling as fraternal love had been denied him. Nor could the fictitious title, which he so often lavished upon his mother, at all supply the absent reality" (7). Mrs. Glendinning's willingness to play the sister not only fails to satisfy Pierre's need for a more balanced family structure but also functions for her as another way to keep in check and redirect whatever sexual impulses he may have otherwise allowed to de-velop.[9] By constructing such a "fictitious" relationship, she is furthering the falsity—the sense of textuality and allegorization that the narrator's metaphor contains—of Pierre's early life and assuring that when his consciousness of physical sexuality arrives, it will shatter both his world and all of its relationships, past and future.

Furthermore, her need to dominate Pierre arises in part from the lack of a counterbalancing force, either husband or daughter, to oppose her. In fact, at times she seems to have consumed rather than lost Pierre's father and now attains a near mythic power of maternal masculinity that contradictorily wishes both to engender and to bear, to cut the cord while keeping Pierre tied to her:

> So saying she crossed the room, and—resting in a corner—her glad proud eye met the old General's baton. . . . She lifted it, and musingly swayed it to and fro; then paused, and staff-wise rested with it in her hand. . . .
>
> "This is his inheritance—this symbol of command! and I swell out to think of it. Yet but just now I fondled the conceit that Pierre was so sweetly docile! Here sure is a most strange inconsistency! For is sweet docility a general's badge? and is this baton but a distaff then?—Here's something widely wrong." (20)

The obviously masculine sexual gestures and language of this passage seem to produce the momentary vision that allows her to see partially through the fiction, the dream-within-dreams and its contradictory demands, that she has helped to create for Pierre. So great a repression of natural development wedded to so fierce a demand for developed achievement can lead only to disaster in her relations with Pierre. She demands that he grow, become, conquer (i.e., possess a body), and at the same time remain within her realm—unconscious, bodiless, the secret prisoner of her fleshless womb.

The "other" woman of Pierre's early life, Lucy Tartan, plays no less a role in his loss of a bodily self. Whether because of his tendency to over-idealize or some inherent characteristic in Lucy's behavior and background, it is clear from our first glimpse of them together that theirs is a relationship in which sexuality will appear only indirectly; only figuratively in this textual world can Pierre "dislodge the flower" that rests on her "snow-white glossy pillow" (3–4).[10] Thus the language employed in the initial description of Lucy reflects her remarkable unreality in Pierre's eyes. She cannot be described except through textual reference, the distance of mythological trope. In fact, she often seems as unreal herself as the conceits of which Pierre makes her, "arrayed in colors harmonious with the heavens"; "light blue" is her "perpetual color" (33). When Pierre enters her "chamber . . . with feelings of a wonderful reverentialness," "the carpet seem[s] holy ground" (39):

> Now, crossing the magic silence of the empty chamber, he caught the snow-white bed reflected in the toilet-glass. This rooted him. For one swift instant, he seemed to see in that one glance the two separate beds—the real one and the reflected one—and an unbidden, most miserable presentiment thereupon stole into him. . . . Then again his glance fixed itself upon the slender, snow-white, ruffled roll; and he stood as one enchanted. Never precious parchment of the Greek was half so precious in his eyes. Never trembling scholar longed more to unroll the mystic vellum, than Pierre longed to unroll the sacred secrets of that snow-white, ruffled thing. (39)

The uncomfortable fragility of Pierre's idealizations becomes clear in this passage's tremulous restraint and textual metaphorizing, for despite his pilgrim's reverence for the white space he calls Lucy's chamber, he cannot avoid an intensity of curious desire when he contemplates his own symbolization of her temple. Thus the sight of the two beds, one a mirror image of the other, not only suggests that Pierre is beginning to see the potential for representation and fictionality in all nature but also that he glimpses here the falsity of his own imaginative transformation of Lucy, her room and bed, and, more generally, the fictionality of his entire youthful world.

The third figure in Pierre's female-dominated circle, Isabel, both joins and disrupts his fictive life. Of the blows she deals, however, there is no question that the most serious emanates from the content of her cloudy story and ultimately strikes at the central beam of Pierre's flimsily constructed world, his conception of his father. Because Pierre has idealistically enshrined his father and imagines "the perfect mold in which his virtuous heart had been cast" (69), he proves unable to accept or understand, except as evil, not only his father's alleged illegitimate production of the dark Isabel but, more specifically, the very notion that his father is capable of any sexuality at all, that the idealized form in his memory is made not of marble but of flesh and blood: " . . . up to this period, in his breast, all remained as it had been; and to Pierre, his father's shrine seemed spotless, and still new as the marble of the tomb of him of Arimathea" (69). "In one breath, Memory and Prophecy, and Intuition tell him—'Pierre, have no reserves; no minutest possible doubt;—this being is thy sister; thou gazest on thy father's flesh' " (112). The hypocritical brand of Christianity that dominates Pierre's world, that knows little of forgiveness and denies the reality of the body, helps equate in Pierre's mind the memory of his father and the image of the fallen Christ at the same time that it provides him, despite his subsequent moral idealism, with a structure for condemning his father and his father's sexuality as evil. His discovery is all the more stunning because in realizing the presence of physical desire in his father, he simultaneously becomes conscious of his own desires, long re-channeled by the maneuvers of his mother and the deceptiveness of Saddle Meadows. In short, in seeing and condemning his own father's sexuality, he has seen and condemned his father's body, and simultaneously discovered and become horrified at his own.

As Pierre discovers his father's sexuality, he also encounters Isabel and a new strain of femininity that is itself more openly sexual than anything he has experienced before. The Poe-esque figure of Isabel not only participates in gothic patterns of the sexually powerful, dark woman, but also more directly acts as the embodiment of Pierre's own recently experienced encounter with lower reality. Her frequently mentioned "long and unimprisoned hair" and magical evocation of the "speaking" guitar connect her both to a mysterious sexuality in general and to the youthful sexuality of his father. That she is, and will become even more so, a substitute for Mrs. Glendinning has been often suggested, as well as the notion that Pierre, in finding such a replacement, is only furthering the unproductive, fictitious relationship he maintained with his mother. It is to the purposes of Melville's tragic mode that the body found after so long an absence should lead not to health but to an intensification, in different form, of the kind of avoidance that caused so violent a discovery in the first place. Both Isabel and the physically and emotionally wronged Delly Ulver—a possible figure for Pierre's own "ruin" by sexuality—suggest by their histories the negative vision of the body Pierre is likely to have formed after so sudden, and so long delayed, an introduction to it.

The result of Pierre's sudden body-consciousness, as in Ahab's case, is not a commitment to this newly found realm of experience but a denial of it, a pronounced asceticism and an emphasis on the development of the head in the absence of an acceptable lower body. Convinced now of both his father's sin and his mother's unwillingness to acknowledge or accept it, he equates sexuality and physicality with evil and begins to see the body as a deception, a beautiful mask that can no longer be trusted because it conceals the truth about itself: "Oh, small thanks I owe thee, Favorable Goddess, that didst clothe this form with all the beauty of a man, that so thou mightest hide from me all the truth of a man. Now I see that in his beauty a man is snared, and made stone-blind, as the worm within its silk" (90). Pierre thus denies not only his own flesh but also his own procreators by burning his father's portrait and assigning his

mother to the "heartless, proud, ice-gilded world" of Pride (90). Having
figuratively abolished his own physical origin, he then declares his Christly
mission, an ascetic devotion not to Ishmael's "heart"—a figure for both
compassion and Eros—but to the head's idealization of ascetic good:

> And dimmed be all beauty that must own the clay; and dimmed be all
> wealth, and all delight, and all the annual prosperities of earth, that but gild
> the links, and stud with diamonds the base rivets and the chains of Lies. Oh,
> now methinks I a little see why of old the men of Truth went barefoot,
> girded with a rope, and ever moving under mournfulness as underneath a
> canopy. . . . Oh, men are jailers all; jailers of themselves; and in Opinion's
> world ignorantly hold their noblest part a captive to their vilest; as disguised
> royal Charles when caught by peasants. The heart! the heart! 'tis God's
> anointed; let me pursue the heart! (90)

The figures of "the men of Truth," ascetically "barefoot, girded with a
rope," become Pierre's representatives of the life he wishes now to lead.
He condemns worldly reality and appearances, including his own body,
as deceptive and false and portrays "the heart"—here a figure for bodiless
idealism or simply the exalted mind—as captive in the body.

In fact, we can take it as yet another warning of Pierre's final downfall
that he falsely applies the Melvillean distinction between head and heart,
between that which is rigidly idealistic without regard to physical consequences and that which acknowledges the needs, benefits, and pains of
the body as well as the strong, and often illogical, pull of the feelings. In
the Melvillean oeuvre, those characters who commit themselves to an un-
swerving ideal, whether that ideal is revenge, desire, or even the need to
act "chronometrically"—that is, without reference or attention to public
opinion—have devoted themselves first and foremost to a bodiless principle and by so doing have blinded themselves to the reality of the physical
world, the result of which, no matter what the intention, is unfailingly
tragic.[11] Such an alliance to pure principle too often leads these characters
to a declaration of bodiless deification; for as Pierre transforms himself
into his own fleshless Christ, has a sacramental supper with Isabel (162),
and, in the case of Delly Ulver, denies "official" religion as too worldly
to live up to his projected idealism, his mind also learns to deny what does
not fulfill its preconceived notion of the Christly as well as what fails
to match its division of the world into worthy ideality and unworthy reality.[12]

It is finally Pierre's life in the Dantean city that confirms his new convictions and engraves his now openly ascetic vision into a life of deprivation accompanied by mental and sexual frustration. Having seen the final

fragments of his Saddle Meadows illusion destroyed in the episode with Glendinning Stanly, Pierre sets up the sexually tense but unfulfilling household of himself, Isabel, and Delly in the stony chambers of the Apostles and, attempting to "gospelize the world anew" by writing (297), assumes his own monkish lifestyle. Like the other "Apostles," the narrator subsequently tells us, Pierre has been "deluded . . . into the Flesh-Brush Philosophy" (300), an ascetic idealism that elicits what may be Melville's most conclusive sermon on the proper, but separate, nourishments of body and soul: "The gods love the soul of a man; often, they will frankly accost it; but they abominate his body; and will forever cut it dead, both here and hereafter. . . . The food of thy soul is light and space. But the food of thy body is champagne and oysters; feed it then on champagne and oysters; and so it shall merit a joyful resurrection, if there is any to be" (299). With the almost Rabelaisian sense of bodily pleasure and ingestion here noted as the proper attitude towards the body, the narrator indicates Pierre's mistake in asceticizing his world and warns us of the danger of commitment to only half of the dualism, each part of which he considers necessary to achieve a synthetic understanding of life.

Language-as-Body

The language of Pierre's ascetic desire, like Ahab's, begins with an aggressive attitude towards reality, a desire to penetrate, define, and so "make fast" to the world and the inaccessible knowledge it hides. Caught within a vision that denies him his own body, he relies upon a language that futilely attempts to fill the place of that absent physicality. Yet because Pierre's world is noticeably more fictive than Ahab's, an additional element of frustration and despair enters both his conception of reality and the language with which he confronts it. No longer fully charged with the late Renaissance vitality of *Moby-Dick,* Pierre's speech seems caught within its own world's malaise: it is a dramatic language too conscious of its existence as drama, a textual utterance too certain of its own textuality.[13] Thus the only tool available to enact his bodiless desire is an equally fictive language, a language-as-body that, unlike Ahab's, must now confront a bodiless, fictive world.

Not only does Pierre's speech often strike us as less convincing and less forceful than Ahab's, but the object of its search and the very world in which Pierre lives are themselves far less palpable than the "sharkish" sea in which the white whale swims. Even so, Saddle Meadows does contain a whale of sorts, but the fleshly potency of Moby-Dick, the resurrective power of the lower stratum, is not to be found: "It was a breathless thing to see. One broad haunched end hovered within an inch of the soil, all along to the point of teetering contact; but yet touched not the soil. Many feet from that—beneath one part of the opposite end, which was all seamed and half-riven—the vacancy was considerably larger, so as to make it not only possible, but convenient to admit a crawling man; yet no mortal being had ever been known to have the intrepid heart to crawl there" (132). If not consciously drawn as a petrified whale, the Terror Stone certainly finds its metaphorical identification through bodily comparison. Not only is its shape whale-like, but it seems to "hover" above the soil as though swimming and possesses a "haunched end," a "flank" (132), a "brow" (134), and a "forehead-like summit" (134).[14] Even more significantly, however, it maintains the sort of aboriginal, "antediluvian" status in *Pierre* that the whale holds in *Moby-Dick*. Not only is it described as "belted and topped by the dense deep luxuriance of the aboriginal forest . . . like Captain Kidd's sunken hull" (132), but it also suggests Old Testament mysteries, the wisdom of "Solomon the Wise," and in "its ponderous inscrutableness" (134) seems to oppose and frustrate the desire for knowledge.

In this respect, Pierre's approach to the Terror Stone echoes the pattern of Jonah-like entrance and investigation that forms one of the major thematic components of *Moby-Dick*. Pierre "threw himself prone upon the wood's last year's leaves, and slid himself straight into the horrible interspace, and lay there as dead" (134), in an action that is clearly another in Melville's archetypal entrances into the lower body. What remains strikingly different in this case, however, is the notable absence of the death-in-life force that such encounters rely upon. Because of the fictiveness of both stone and body, Pierre must turn to language as a substitute and so futilely attempt to construct his own resurrection:

> If the miseries of the undisclosable things in me, shall ever unhorse me from my manhood's seat; if to vow myself all Virtue's and all Truth's, be but to make a trembling, distrusted slave of me; . . . if Life be a cheating dream, and virtue as unmeaning and unsequaled with any blessing as the midnight mirth of wine; if by sacrificing myself for Duty's sake, my own mother re-sacrifices me; if Duty's self be but a bugbear, and all things are allowable and unpunishable to man;—then do thou, Mute Massiveness, fall on me! Ages thou hast waited; and if these things be thus, then wait no more; for whom better canst thou crush than him who now lies here invoking thee? (134)

First of all, Pierre's speech repeats the Ahabian tendency to rely upon certain types of extra-logical mechanisms of language to shape or control the future. Here, for instance, the address to the Other also becomes a proof-demand that is self-constructed and predetermined. By assembling one conditional that encompasses the answers to all the unanswerable questions he wishes to ask, Pierre ascribes meaning to, and relies upon, an essentially meaningless event: the fall, or stillness, of the Terror Stone. In this respect, by depending upon a language constructed so as to shape the future, his action resembles Ahab's reliance upon prophecy. Pierre becomes, in effect, his own Fedallah, answering unanswerable questions in a way that reveals only a self-determined ambition.

In addition to its self-prophetic delusions, Pierre's language also attempts to supply, by means of its aggression toward the stone, the absent physicality and, by extension, the missing reality that his early world demonstrates. His words, charged as they are with the impotent's enclosed energy, attempt to vault into the physical in order to elicit a bodily response from the bodiless world. They are, in effect, the equivalent of a pre-physical, verbal taunt, a prelude to conflict that attempts by the use of words to elicit the consummative physical act. To this extent, they form Pierre's attempted seduction of the stone, just as Ahab's speeches to and about the whale fill the place of a "lover's" discourse.

For Ahab such physical contact does finally occur, but for Pierre the attempted seduction of the world's body fails because in his world no body exists except as a stony allegorization. Pierre's emergence from the interspace thus yields no true change in his psychological construction, no noticeable rebirth. He stands "haughtily upon his feet" and, we are to understand, is now convinced by his self-made delusion (135), for in this notably textual, fictive landscape, the resurrected body has become merely another trope, another linguistic entity that remains too distant, too aesthetically separate to have any palpable effect on the psychologies of the characters. The Terror Stone is a fictive whale in the "illuminate scroll" of Saddle Meadows, and Pierre's equally fictive challenge to it yields only the further artificiality of his subsequent determination.

We should not forget, however, that Pierre himself is an author of fictions, and, like the book's narrator, seems eventually locked within a mode of self-mockery that reveals him to be at least partially aware of the false faces of his world. It is this desire to self-punish, the need to adopt a tone of desperate, destructive humor, that most clearly connects Pierre and the narrator of the novel, whose changing style has preoccupied the majority of commentators. The Saddle Meadows section has come under the closest of such scrutiny in respect to the style employed and the degree to which Melville intends it as parody or non-ironic exuberance.[15] Should we accept the early chapters as parody (whether well-managed or not), however, it becomes clear that we must also recognize the desperation beneath, the clearly acerbic, unmitigated darkness of tone that allows such absurdities of exaggeration. If this language is ironic, it is ironic not in a mild or gentle manner; it is the irony of the deeply wounded, deeply frustrated quester whose undisguised voice sounds clearly in the later Pierre's defiant curses: "That morning was the choicest drop that Time had in his vase. Ineffable distillations of a soft delight were wafted from the fields and hills. Fatal morning that, to all lovers unbetrothed; 'Come to your confessional,' it cried. 'Behold our airy loves,' the birds chirped from the trees; far out at sea, no more the sailors tied their bowline-knots; their hands had lost their cunning; will they, nill they, Love tied love-knots on every spangled spar" (32). To read such a passage negatively entails accepting not only a criticism of the stylistic excesses of the sentimental novel and of Melville's own juvenilia but also a criticism of the subject matter itself, a negation of youthful love and the excesses of its sentimentality. Thus to acknowledge parody here is to admit the deep bitterness with which the narrator views his own youth and the patterns of love and infatuation that such youth often involves. The style includes a denunciation of the parodist's own past in no uncertain terms, a wounded severance of the experientially educated man from the innocent, ignorant boy.

Clearly, part of the argument that would have Melville primarily attacking Gothic romance rests upon the fact that the languages of the other characters in Saddle Meadows are equally inflated and ridiculous. After all, Lucy's speech forms a near perfect counterpart to Pierre's, with a preponderance of nominalizations and archaic, over-extended diction. Likewise, Mrs. Glendinning, while remarkably different in character from Lucy and Pierre, nevertheless sounds innocent enough at times: " 'A noble boy, and docile'—she murmured—'he has all the frolicsomeness of youth, with little of its giddiness. And he does not grow vain-glorious in sophomorean wisdom. . . . A fine, proud, loving, docile, vigorous boy. Pray God, he never becomes otherwise to me' " (19–20). Because of such parodic consistency, there is little chance to suggest that self-parody alone marks the dominant tone throughout. Instead, it is worth noting that the entire novel, no matter who or what its target and despite its relative success or failure at hitting the mark, retains a degree of self-destructive energy upon almost every page. From its formal inelegance to its stylistic anomalies, regardless of intention, *Pierre* seems a book bent on its own failure by excess and is charged with the spark of reckless self-destruction that fills Pierre himself. Thus though it is ultimately impractical to suggest that Pierre's immaturely attempted "mature book" is *Pierre* itself, we should not omit the likelihood that within this novel there exists a model of Melville's novelistic telos, a pattern of linguistic failure that haunts and dooms the narrative voice.

Beyond the book's apparently self-referential parody, the texture of the prose itself can be connected to Pierre's own language-as-body and tied to his attempt to transform language into the body that the book's world has lost. Not only do the parodic excesses of the early sections reveal the narrator's Ahabian self-loathing, but they also make use of a language remarkably aware of its own role as language, its own representational function. To this extent, representation outweighs the represented even as characters constantly confront their own fictiveness by means of a language that is attempting to become the book's reality. It is almost as if language in *Pierre* is often representing language itself and nothing more:

> This preamble seems not entirely necessary as usher of the strange conceit, that possibly the latent germ of Pierre's proposed extraordinary mode of executing his proposed extraordinary resolve—namely, the conversion of a sister into a wife—might have been found in the previous conversational conversion of a mother into a sister; for hereby he had habituated his voice and manner to a certain fictitiousness in one of the closest domestic relations of life; and since man's moral texture is very porous, and things assumed upon the surface, at last strike in—hence, this outward habituation to the above-named fictitiousness had insensibly disposed his mind to it as it were; but only innocently and pleasantly as yet. If, by any possibility, this general conceit be so, then to Pierre the times of sportfulness were as pregnant with the hours of earnestness; and in sport he learnt the terms of woe. (177)

This passage not only restates the fictive nature of Pierre's early world but also reflects the fact that in this world language is responsible for the construction of artificial relationships between the characters. Also, the style of this moment of narration, through contorted syntax and cluttered rhythms, brings attention to itself as writing. The discussion of its own "conceit" and overly officious foreshadowing equally remind us that words are the very bodily material of Pierre's world. As though to drive this point home, Melville ends the passage with a scene-closing couplet and burst of iambic verse, both heightening the self-consciousness of the language and increasing its aesthetic distance from its subject.

Only in a few of the later sections of the novel does this self-referentiality diminish—first, in book 25, section 4, the dream of Enceladus, where, as Newton Arvin was early to point out, "the strain and unnaturalness that was almost every other page of *Pierre* suddenly fall away."[16] What remains figures perhaps as the voice behind the parodist's doubletalk, bitterness concentrated to a strength able to overwhelm the shielding armor of irony: "Thus far uncovering his shame, in the cruel plight they had abandoned him, leaving stark naked his in vain indignant chest to the defilements of the birds, which for untold ages had cast their foulness on his vanquished crest" (387). The power of this image of impotence and rage, of majesty reduced to the indignity of degradation, is rendered, without deflection, in a language stripped of the unjustified bombast and cloying sentimentality of the early narrator's descriptions. For the first time in the novel the powerful feelings of indignity and failure that had given rise to the need for the initial parody have surfaced. In other words, the book's center—Pierre's incest-born impotence and the loss of his physical self—emerges from behind the parody and enables the narrator's style to meet its subject cleanly, equally, without torque or mask. The self-punishing humor that characterizes Ahabian utterance is no longer necessary because the questing voice is, at this point, encountering via dream the true root of its anguished desire.

Likewise, in the book's final pages, we are given for the first and only time in the novel a glimpse of the world that opposes Pierre's, offered in a language that itself reveals both the power of Melville's marine vision and the impotence of Pierre's landed reality: "Soon, the spires of stone on the land, blent with the masts of wood on the water; the crotch of the twin-rivers pressed the great wedged city almost out of sight. They swept by two little islets distant from the shore; they wholly curved away from the domes of free-stone and marble, and gained the great sublime dome of the bay's wide-open waters" (354). The sense of liberation so palpable in this passage originates both from the emotions of the characters and from the style of the prose, which flounders no longer in heavy nominalizations and awkward diction but instead pulses with the kind of verbal action and syntactical solidity that Melville's sea-writing so often demonstrates. Its rhythms, no longer clogged and soft, carve clean, accented paths that find sonorous balance within their own sentences. Just as the dream of impotence is connected to a stony, buried giant, so is the land itself associated with a prose texture fraught with an excess consciousness of its own representational function. Only when describing the sea does Melville's prose take on the vitality and action, the opposite of the novel's otherwise static malaise, which his fiction up to *Pierre* demonstrates. Thus in this momentary contact with a world in which lower reality exists, the book's language escapes its attempt to become its world's body simply because in such a moment the body is present, at last, in the rolling sea beneath.

With the disappearance of the flesh in *Pierre* comes a growing sense that the vitality of the body in Melville's writings is closely linked to the vitality of language. In *Moby-Dick* this connection reveals itself partially in Ishmael's troping of whale-as-book and book-as-whale and partially in Ahab's aggressive language-as-body, which like Pierre's, attempts to take the place of a denied physicality. By the end of *Pierre*, with its complete absence of the kind of qualified rebirth that concludes *Moby-Dick*, it becomes clear not only that the body is becoming increasingly more distant, less present, but that language, in conjunction with it, is growing more and more faint, despite moments of seeming revival. *Pierre* thus holds the sterile ground between the clearly conflicting dualism of mind and body that animates *Moby-Dick* and the extended trajectories of the absent body and its eventually absent or deceptive language in "Bartleby" and *The Confidence-Man*.

The Asceticism of Language

> a votary of the desk—a notched and cropt scrivener—one that sucks his sustenance, as certain sick people are said to do, through a quill.
>
> —Lamb, *The Essays of Elia*

Perhaps the most obvious and often-noted similarity between *Pierre* and "Bartleby the Scrivener" is the cityscape of brick and tombs that both the short, mysterious tale and *Pierre*'s second half share. The unnamed city to which Pierre and his entourage "escape," abandoning all hope and finding only immurement and frustration, clearly rises from the same, grassless ground of Enceladan entrapment and stony sterility that the short story's version of "Wall Street" and its almost voiceless scrivener inhabit. Perhaps of equal significance, however, is that Melville himself, though he lived the majority of his life within a city, often appears in his own letters to invoke and yet deplore this world of walls whose lifelessness seems both to fascinate and to appall. The dryness of stone, which pervades *Pierre* and which he would later find so omnipresent and disheartening in the Holy Land, continually contrasts in his mind with the fertility of arable land and a vision of bucolic and familial productivity: "The 'Whale' is only half thro' the press; for, wearied with the long delays of the printers, and disgusted with the heat & dust of the Babylonish brick-kiln of New York, I came back to the country to feel the grass—and end the book reclining on it, if I may."[17]

Grass, like water, signals movement, growth, and potency for Melville, yet its power, severely limited by season and man's own ability to destroy it with "lifeless" streets and buildings, makes it a far more fragile element for him than the resilient sea. Like the patch of turf growing at the heart of the Egyptianate Tombs in "Bartleby," grass often cautiously represents for Melville the miraculous isolation of energy—especially that of the writer—and its short and delicate lifespan. Thus the world of the city, with its life and, to an extent, its capacity for productive regeneration stunted by lack of soil, grass, or water, becomes for him a powerful image of physical and spiritual impotence, a dry bodilessness that is keyed to the oppression and failure of the writer's inspiration, energy, and desire.

In this regard, "Bartleby," like portions of *Pierre*, investigates and reveals the ascetic city-world in which the fleshly body's absence becomes the central, controlling fact of existence for the dryly uninspired scrivener. The lack of a fertile world in which to exist helps promote in Bartleby a bodiless vision that, because further deprived of the aggressive desire that has until now motivated Melville's most stubborn questers, results finally in the loss of language. Following Melville's deep connection between the potency of the world's body and the strength of the writer's inspiration, "Bartleby" gives us for the first time a "hero" to whom both body and language have become useless and impotent shadows.

That "Bartleby" is a tale about the presence and absence of the body, its domination and power to dominate, becomes immediately evident from the lawyer's initial description of the office's Dickensian inhabitants, Turkey and Nippers. Each, it seems, in unique but complementary ways, is a slave to his body and accordingly runs by its schedule. Turkey, for instance, the "pursy" elder of the two, sees his day divided by the fact that he drinks at lunch; as a result, he operates perfectly well in the mornings, but after the noon libation "his business capacities [are] seriously disturbed for the remainder of the twenty-four hours."[18] On the other hand, his counterpart, Nippers, the "piratical-looking young man of about five and twenty," appears to the narrator to suffer from a prenoon "indigestion" that further causes Nippers to grind his teeth, hiss, and even struggle with the position of his desk. The emphasis on bodily comfort, and especially on the power that bodily discomfort exerts over the actions of the cranky scriveners, comically dominates the portraits of the two Everymen of the story, whose guard-like scheduling of comfort-discomfort and overall desire to appease the body seem equally to represent their larger world's predominately physical preoccupations and establishes a notable contrast to the advent of ascetic, metaphysical Bartleby.

We should not overlook the third member of the pre-Bartleby cast, the boy Ginger Nut, whose desk contains "a great array of the shells of various sorts of nuts" (18) and who functions primarily "as cake and apple purveyor for Turkey and Nippers" (18), bringing as well "that peculiar cake—small, flat, round, and very spicy—after which he had been named by them" (18). For it becomes clear not only that Ginger Nut himself is

similarly associated with the satisfaction of bodily needs but also that the
cakes he delivers, which the copyists "gobble up" by the score "as if they
were mere wafers" (18) are in one instance strangely associated with copy-
ing and the business of creating texts: "Of all the fiery afternoon blunders
and flurried rashness of Turkey, was his once moistening a ginger-cake
between his lips, and clapping it on to a mortgage for a seal" (19). This
episode caps the lawyer's description of his office and its inhabitants
largely because it is the clearest example of the ways in which the needs
of the body become confused with, and begin to compromise, the activities of the scriveners and the law office in general. The anecdote emphasizes the precarious conflation of eating and writing by silently assuring
us not only, as Melville well knew, that some must write in order to eat
but also that the two acts, among one so dominated by the body's demands, come into inevitable conflict. In short, how one writes helps determine how one eats, and, conversely, what one ingests becomes a part
of what one writes. Furthermore, this scene forms an opposing counterpart to the disturbance Bartleby will soon create within the office not, as
does Turkey, by confusing eating with writing but by strangely refusing
the needs of the body in an atmosphere and world in which writing and
eating, physical comfort and mental production, are so vitally related.[19]

  Admittedly, some of the emphasis on food and drink, as well as its
effects on the copyists, must be attributed to the lawyer's own manner
of interpreting the behavior of his employees and the functioning of the
world in general.[20] Though the narrator fails to mention his own physical
needs—other than the vague, largely psychological reference to his "snug
retreat" (14) and gray hairs (16)—he does in fact frequently attempt to
explain behavior in terms of physical causation. Not only does he sketch
the daily life of his office as a kind of dietary experiment, citing the
sources of behavior in the discomfort and disfunction of the subjects'
bodies, but his metaphors also frequently rely upon bodily explanations
to clarify "unusual" behavior. Thus Turkey's new coat affects him and
makes him insolent "upon the same principle that too much oats are bad
for horses" (17–18); likewise, Bartleby in his initial rush to copy "seemed
to gorge himself" with no pause for "digestion" (19). Perhaps most significantly of all, much of the lawyer's attempt to understand "cadaverous"
Bartleby relies upon similar analyses of the body and its diet as explanations of human behavior: "He lives, then, on ginger-nuts, thought I;
never eats a dinner, properly speaking; he must be a vegetarian then; but
no; he never eats even vegetables, he eats nothing but ginger-nuts. My
mind then ran on in reveries concerning the probable effects upon the
human constitution of living entirely on ginger-nuts" (23). The logic of

this passage wishes to derive spiritual ailments from physical causes, to grasp at the available "evidence," itself a term that implies physicality, in order to reach a reasonable verdict. It suggests that the lawyer, if not within the story a physically dominated character himself, at least demonstrates a mind and sensibility significantly controlled by the body and its possible domination of behavior. He notes for instance that Bartleby "never went to dinner" (23), "never visited any refectory or eating house; while his pale face clearly indicated that he never drank beer like Turkey, or tea and coffee even, like other men" (28), and "though so thin and pale, he never complained of ill health" (121).

If the lawyer's mind seems dominated by physical causation as a principle of basic understanding, however, it does not follow that he himself takes an enthusiastic attitude toward physical comfort and pleasure. Instead he appears to seek a regulation of the body's desires and, in fact, hires Bartleby largely because of his "sedate" appearance and his "freedom from all dissipation" (25) and because Bartleby "might operate beneficially upon the flighty temper of Turkey, and the fiery one of Nippers" (19). Thus the lawyer does not endorse the body but, in fact, wishes to subdue it as a key to subduing its adverse effects on behavior. Because he has confined himself to largely physical explanations of possibly spiritual ailments, he has taken an attitude of cautious distrust toward the overindulgence or misuse of the body and appears to lack the ability to consider, or at least sufficiently grasp and qualify, the possible influence of emotions.

It is, of course, Bartleby himself who eventually poses the greatest test to the narrator's legalistic logic because the behavior of the pallid scrivener somehow lies beyond the bodily explanations of evidential analysis. It is in large part his inability to explain Bartleby by means of these "facts" that so irritates the lawyer's sense of snugness. For his retreat is "snug" precisely because it is not merely an office but a way of reading; Bartleby's power therefore flows not so much from his refusal to do what he is asked but from his resistance to a predominately physical interpretive mode. After all, not only does Bartleby appear bloodlessly pale and cadaverously thin, but his behavior refuses to conform to or reflect his diet: "Gingernuts are so called because they contain ginger as one of their peculiar constituents, and the final flavoring one. Now, what was ginger? A hot, spicy thing. Was Bartleby hot and spicy? Not at all. Ginger, then, had no effect upon Bartleby. Probably he preferred it should have none" (23). The lawyer's method of explanation in the case of this member of his office now suddenly fails; the nature of the substance ingested simply will not explain the character's behavior—Bartleby, whatever else he may be, is definitely not what he eats. But the lawyer's exasperated joke at the end of this passage should not be overlooked, for it is just this growing sense of Bartleby's ability to ignore or override whatever his body may or "should" be telling him that begins to make itself clear to the narrator. As an ascetic, nonaggressive seeker who has denied or psychologically destroyed his own body in search of truths that exist "through the mask" of bodily reality, Bartleby becomes, in the physically determined world of the lawyer, the truly chronometrical character who denies his own and the world's body and subsequently operates according to his own vision of purpose and reality. His is a soul lost in a world where only the body can be understood and repaired, or as the lawyer says in his moment of deepest penetration: "What I saw that morning persuaded me that the scrivener was the victim of innate and incurable disorder. I might give alms to his body; but his body did not pain him; it was his soul that suffered, and his soul I could not reach" (29). Here the lawyer understands what Bartleby has already come to embody: that some truths lie beyond the limits of physical existence and explanation. In this respect, we can begin to see Bartleby's chronometricism as involving more than just the sense of social activism and independence that Plinlimmon's pamphlet suggests; it is the chronometricality of the bodiless spirit in a physical world, of bodiless knowledge in a world of physical evidence, and finally of ungraspable language in a world of deeds, mortgages, and titles.

Because the narrator's deductive process moves from the physical to the behavioral, it is clear that his language, in stark contrast to Bartleby's, likewise emphasizes the lawyer's two "Grand Points"—"prudence" and "method" (14). From his first imprimis, with its legal, evidential flavor, he reveals both a careful habit of collecting and presenting evidence from which conclusions are then drawn and a tendency to engage in overly tortuous, casuistic self-arguments that often seem to shroud rather than reveal the truth. For instance, after praising himself for his strategy of "assumptions," the lawyer begins to doubt its efficacy and likewise partially reveals the structure of his own thinking: "My procedure seemed as sagacious as ever,—but only in theory. How would it prove in practice—there was the rub" (34). In confronting Bartleby's "Grand Point" preference, the narrator's method, divided here into theory and practice, demonstrates that the lawyer's primary function, both as a lawyer who never enters a courtroom and as the narrator of this story, is that of the isolated theorist whose plans and hypotheses are constructed largely without adequate reference to reality. Thus it is no accident that in the next line, the lawyer echoes Hamlet, for the division between thought and action, between the inaction of the narrator's assumptions and the truly responsible deeds of the man of action, unites these two characters, each of whom seems caught in labyrinths of his own construction.

On the other hand, if Ahab and Pierre can be said to employ a language that attempts to take the place of the missing body, then Bartleby, who appears to represent the penultimate example of this line of heroes, can equally be said to speak a language designed to frustrate physical contact rather than initiate it, or, more radically, to speak a language that paradoxically is not, or refuses to be, language. Bartleby's asceticism extends beyond the wounded repressions of Ahab and Pierre; his hopelessness has taken the place of their angry reactions, and, as a result, his language, the Melvillean quester's only weapon, now reflects the full loss of potency, the fully ascetic absence of desire toward which Melville's protagonists have been progressing. In this respect, Bartleby's few utterances consistently demonstrate a tendency toward unexplained, paradoxical construction that contributes to the overall subversion of communication. As the narrator notes, Bartleby begins subtly to "turn the tongues" (31) of the office members, to affect, that is, both their languages and, by extension, the logic behind those languages by "preferring" throughout "not to be a little reasonable" (30).[21]

In his other brief moments of "unwonted wordiness," Bartleby appears similarly at odds with the function of speech and tends to fall into repetitions of phrases that seem more walls than words. For instance, his responses to the narrator's survey of possible jobs are only versions of the same basic sentence, followed now by the phrase, "But I am not particular," the final repetition of which throws the lawyer into a rage. Bartleby's language then, in its unyielding refusal to reveal secrets, to engage in a mutual exchange of knowledge, or to respond in any positive fashion, suggests that he himself has become what he so mesmerically watches—a dead-wall. Only now that wall is a wall of language: repetitive, "stationary," and decidedly "not particular" about anything (41); for as the dry bricks of the city project no bodily power, no life of grass or flesh, so do Bartleby's brief speeches and his even more significant silences project his own desireless existence. Like the wall, like the building as a whole, his is a body dried of productive purpose, devoid of readable surface, and his repetitive, monolithic language simply reflects this resistance.

In this respect, the narrator's epilogue, compromised though it is by its apocryphal status and the lawyer's sentimentality, to some extent reinforces or helps justify Bartleby's linguistic recalcitrance, but in reality it tells us more about the narrator's own failure to understand Bartleby than it does about Bartleby's background. In fact, the epilogue seems further proof of the way in which Bartleby and his language force still hopeful figures such as the lawyer into supplying a "reasonable" explanation for the unexplaining and unexplainable scrivener. The lawyer, still searching for evidence, comes upon a sort of deposition, a linguistic trace of the physical act, and attempts to apply it as a cause for Bartleby's otherwise unexplained behavior; but like the wall "deficient in what landscape painters call 'life' " (14), Bartleby can only attain meaning via the lawyer's own "painting" of background.

Similarly, it is significant, and evidence of the narrator's continued misunderstanding of Bartleby, that the last service he attempts to perform for the jailed scrivener is to pay for his food. As though ironically to echo the parable of the Good Samaritan, Melville has the lawyer give money to "a broad meat-like man" to watch out for and feed Bartleby, but upon returning the lawyer finds that once again Bartleby has preferred not to dine:

> The round face of the grub-man peered upon me now. "His dinner is ready. Won't he dine to-day, either? Or does he live without dining?"
> "Lives without dining," said I, and closed the eyes. (45)

The narrator's answer, with its obvious irony, may mark a realization in his mind that Bartleby has in a sense lived without dining all along. The more overt point, however, is that the grub-man's question is answered by Bartleby's death: in short, no matter what one's commitments, whether to metaphysical truths or metaphysical despair, the body cannot live without dining. The narrator perhaps understands this notion when, after attempting to understand the silent scrivener, he finally, and for the first time, touches him: "But nothing stirred. I paused; then went close up to him; stooped over, and saw that his dim eyes were open; otherwise he seemed profoundly sleeping. Something prompted me to touch him. I felt his hand, when a tingling shiver ran up my arm and down my spine to my feet" (45). This moment, the sole physical gesture of the story, can be seen as a negative version of many such scenes of contact in Melville's early work. The touch here, so long delayed by social and linguistic barriers, is not that of Queequeg or the warm whale, nor is it the "splice" of a hand bathed in spermaceti; it is "cadaverous" Bartleby's lifelessly cold flesh, the embrace of death that can no longer lead to resurrection—the touch, once again, of stone. Whatever forces existed before *Pierre* that enabled Eros and the lower body to unite with and restore the mind have disappeared from Melville's work of this period, and the presentation of hopelessness and loss of connection to the world that the story relies upon, its sense of the failure of language to unite disparate humanity, forms the basis upon which *The Confidence-Man* will soon be written.

Bartleby sleeps his final sleep on the cusp between two worlds: one in which the hero has lost all but a resistant will and language itself refuses either to function or to deceive; and another in which questing has given in to a passive investigation of duplicity and confusion and words can do nothing but tangle, dizzy, and ensnare.

3

ISRAEL POTTER AND THE SEARCH
FOR THE HEARTH

ISRAEL POTTER, Melville's only novel written for serial publication, appears curiously out of place in the Melville oeuvre. Standing between the entombed silences of "Bartleby" and the faithless babble of *The Confidence-Man,* Melville's "Revolutionary narrative of the beggar"[1] is the muted echo of an earlier, less desperate voice. Israel, the common hero exiled from and ignored by his homeland, forced into a series of disguises and imprisonments that increase his sense of self-loss, shares, for the first time since *Moby-Dick,* traces of the Ishmaelean strain in Melville's thought, a commitment to physical comfort and metaphysical acceptance, to play and the restless search for genial warmth, which Ishmael most fully embodies. Despite its obviously ironic and often bitterly critical vision of the common man's fate at the hands of his own society, *Israel Potter* nevertheless provides not a quest for inscrutable truths but a search for heart and hearth, for the Ishmaelean center, the locus of man's only "attainable felicity."

Criticism of the novel, though limited, has revolved around questions of familial and societal authority versus youthful rebellion,[2] the fate of the common man in the wars of a thankless society,[3] the extent to which Israel's exile from, and rejection by, his homeland represents Melville's failure as a writer,[4] and the book's supposed attacks on American shallowness or Israel's inability to understand the Franklinian model of success and self-possession.[5] Few commentators have asserted the basic fact, however, that, no matter how often he is sidetracked from it, Israel's ultimate goal, that for which he leaves the domination of his father, that for which he continuously quests, is a home of his own, or, more specifically, land, a wife, and a homestead in which to enjoy the benefits of the sacredly central hearth. The search for power, for freedom from domination, and his constant need to reshape and disguise himself all follow and serve the ever-present desire for home and the demands of the body-deep heart. Thus despite the book's thinning narrative and undeniably restrained sense of novelistic construction, it nevertheless makes evident, both in the attitudes and language of its central character and in the language of the book itself, that the force motivating Melville's fiction during this respite between "Bartleby" and *The Confidence-Man* flows no longer from traces of Ahab's metaphysical desire but instead from the variably altered remnants of Ishmael's digressive, playfully critical, ultimately physical vision of life.

Nevertheless, one important qualification of the Ishmaelean vision in *Israel Potter* flows from the sense that the physicality and physical quest within the book, as well as its novelistic equivalent (the text-as-body), reveal a significant failure to consummate the Ishmaelean embrace, a notable deferral of the resurrective results of the integration of mind and body. Consequently, Israel represents to some extent both a life's devotion to the body and the failure of such a devotion, while his preferences and actions, along with the novel's very texture, reveal the book's important position in the Melville canon as the only expression after *Moby-Dick* and before the switch to poetry of the now significantly qualified Ishmaelean sensibility.

In the book's first twelve pages, the only portion of the novel devoted to the period before Israel's extended exile, Melville creates a more compact, more direct version of the longer narrative to come. Having shifted the setting from Rhode Island to his own Berkshires,[6] he introduces us to the lonely, stony landscape from which his reluctant wanderer issues and then begins the brief history of Israel's filial rebellion, at the same time consciously associating it with the patterns of the American Revolution. As Israel, by name, is the type of the wandering nation, so is his rejection of his father's authority a type of America's rebellion.[7] Yet it is important to keep firmly in mind that the source of the disagreement between father and son, that for which Israel desires freedom and autonomy, is the simple, but also sexual, urge to take a wife. Only after his father has secretly turned the girl against him does he form "the determination to quit them both, for another home and other friends,"[8] a decision that proves deeply difficult: "he lay down at the foot of a pine tree, reposing himself till an hour before dawn, when, upon awaking, he heard the soft, prophetic sighing of the pine, stirred by the first breath of the morning. Like the leaflets of that evergreen, all the fibres of his heart trembled within him; tears fell from his eyes. But he thought of the tyranny of his father, and what seemed to him the faithlessness of his love; and shouldering his bundle, arose, and marched on" (8). The "prophetic sighing of the pine," as it does for Pierre, signals in Israel both an association with the land of his birth and the emergence of a conscious sexuality, just as the trembling of his heart alerts us to both his impending homesickness and his awareness of the deep pull the land and his desire to marry exert upon him. His plan to find "another home"—that is, not just another place to live but his own freely formed family, his own hearth—combined with his perception of injustice forces him to leave the area, not as a wanderer but as a potential settler and farmer. To this end, he works first as a hired laborer and then buys his own land, builds "himself a log cabin, and in two summers, with his own hands, clear[s] thirty acres for sowing" (9). Subsequently, having traded in furs as far north as Canada, he returns "with a light heart and a heavy purse" (9) only to find not only that "he had been numbered with the dead" (9) but also that his father continues to block his marriage. Only then, in a movement that clearly echoes Ishmael's, does he turn to "the asylum for the generous distressed" (10) and become a sailor and harpooner, until, "longing once more for the bush" (11), he returns home to find "the dear, false girl" married. And so it becomes clear from this pattern of events that Israel's movements function always and only to enable him to return and establish his own home in the land in which he was born. As both the smaller and larger narratives reveal, his desire and his wanderings are physically rather than metaphysically motivated, and his search is always a deferred homecoming, always a preparation for the ultimate goal of forming a family in his native land.

In confluence with this motivation, throughout the novel Israel demonstrates both a marked bodily presence and a notable interest in things physical, in the comforts rather than the mysteries of life. We are made aware of his physical reality early in the novel by means of the catalogue of the wounds he received at Bunker Hill: "a cut on the right arm near the elbow"; "a long slit across the chest," which, after another cut, becomes the cross-like scar; "a musket-ball buried in his hip, and another mangling him near the ankle of the same leg" (14). Melville also emphasizes Israel's continual hunger (23) as well as the presence of usually unmentioned bodily functions: "The officers being landed, some of the crew propose, like merry Englishmen as they are, to hie to a neighboring ale-house, and have a cosy pot or two together. Agreed. They start, and Israel with them. As they enter the ale-house door our prisoner is suddenly reminded of still more imperative calls. Unsuspected of any design, he is allowed to leave the party for a moment" (15). It is not clear from this passage whether Israel is feigning the need to urinate or whether, seeing himself unguarded, he simply takes advantage of his otherwise honest request. Nevertheless, the presence of any such instance of direct reference to urination is highly unusual in Melville's work. In addition, only two pages later (17) Israel makes an identical request of his captors, this time, it seems, as part of a conscious plan to escape. What Melville makes clear, however, by the presence of such passages is that Israel both exists and finds significant expression of his identity within his body. Its needs, and not the demands of mental questing, largely determine his actions. Despite his wounds—which, unlike Ahab's, heal without further physical or psychological damage (14)—Israel finds temporary satisfaction in filling his bodily needs, and, on the whole, seems to want or require little more than the freedom to meet his body's demands in the manner and place of his choice.

This attitude appears forcefully in his scenes with the half-magian, half-ascetic Dr. Franklin of Melville's characterization; the encounter is yet another version of the head meeting the heart, even though Franklin's ascetic precepts, like Plinlimmon's, may not always be applicable to their creator. Franklin's removal of the brandy, cologne, sugar, and, later, the "most bewitching little chambermaid" from Israel's room emphasizes both his own "public" devotion to a mentalized existence (he leaves only the soap, a candle, the "Way to Wealth," and a guide to Paris) and, via Israel's sarcastic reaction, the wanderer's own desire for these admittedly physical pleasures:

> "Yes, but just as good as the other. You don't ever munch sugar, do you? It's bad for the teeth. I'll take the sugar." So the paper of sugar was likewise dropped into one of the capacious coat pockets.
> "Oh, you better take the whole furniture, Dr. Franklin. Here, I'll help you drag out the bedstead. . . . (51)
> "Every time he comes in he robs me," soliloquized Israel, dolefully; "with an air all the time, too, as if he were making me presents." (53)

Israel's desires are direct, rechanneled neither by a commitment to "wisdom" nor by the psychology of the frugal, and possibly due to this directness, he is likewise able to see through Franklin's gently sophistic turns of phrase and perceive as well as emphasize the physical consequences of the doctor's linguistically "sly" maneuvers. In fact, Israel recognizes and succinctly states the Melvillean conviction that an exclusive devotion to the things of the mind is liable to create a gap between language and reality precisely because such a devotion often ignores the physical consequences of the reality it describes and so is frequently forced to bridge that gap with specious or deceptive language. Thus Franklin, while cultivating a labyrinthine, technocratic mind, has, at least in the public persona through which he was widely known in Melville's time, come to represent a superficial self-discipline; nevertheless, at the same time he manages to suggest—and perhaps this is what saves him for

Melville—that this is but one of the playfully sly masks he dons and doffs in his almost magical manipulation of those around him.[9]

Israel too is capable of such adaptability, but his changes usually prove physical in origin and effect and seldom rest upon deceptive verbal constructions. Unlike Franklin's, whose personae are largely motivated by political and economic desires, Israel's various disguises come into play only in service of the desire to further his journey, to escape or enter into refuge in order to render all disguise unnecessary in the end. Nevertheless, his ability to reshape himself demonstrates his basic polymorphousness, his natural willingness to play, and his ability to avoid a monomaniacal insistence on maintaining a single, certain identity. In short, he values physical survival over the survival of his public identity and is willing to sacrifice Ahabian pride for the sake of his body's continued existence.

One of the most often noted of Israel's shape-shiftings, in chapter 13 after his resurrection from the suddenly deceased Squire Woodcock's chimney, reveals Israel "encased in a dead man's broadcloth" (75) as he pretends to be the squire's ghost in order to escape the house:

> He advanced with a slow and stately step; looked neither to the right nor the left; but went solemnly forward on his now faintly illuminated way, sounding his cane on the floor as he passed. The faces in the doorways curdled his blood, by their rooted looks. . . . Each one was silent as he advanced towards him or her; but as he left each individual, one after another, behind, each in a frenzy shrieked out, "the Squire, the Squire!" As he passed the lady in the widow's weeds, she fell senseless and crosswise before him. But forced to be immutable in his purpose, Israel solemnly stepping over her prostrate form, marched deliberately on. (76)

As several commentators have noted, the necessity of assuming other peoples' identities is a sign of Israel's exile, of the displacement of his original self, a figure for his isolation and homelessness. Furthermore, in this particular scene we are again presented with a set piece that reflects the thematic concerns of the novel as a whole, for not only does Israel take on the shell of another's identity, but he also must ignore the needs of "his" wife, or, in other words, once again symbolically sacrifice his instinctual desires, in this case to help the fallen woman; he must "step over" her fallen form and "march" on, precisely the sort of action that led to his exile in the first place. Thus it is no accident that upon emerging from the squire's house he experiences a kind of deja vu, for the narrator tells us that "the whole scene magically reproduced to our adventurer the aspect of Bunker Hill, Charles River, and Boston town, on the well-remembered night of the 16th of June" (76).

As important as such symbolic moments are in the text, what follows this particular episode, Israel's comic encounter with the scarecrow and the farm laborer, suggests that there is more to his reliance on disguise than simply the amplification of his physical and psychological exile. Just mistaken for a ghost himself, Israel initially suspects that "the gloomy stranger . . . pointing towards the deceased Squire's abode" (77) is itself a ghost—"the face was lost in a sort of ghastly blank." But after a cautious investigation and the discovery of the ocular deception, Israel proceeds to change clothes again, this time not with the dead but with the inanimate scarecrow, and so when the farm-laborer appears, he decides, with questionable logic, not to hide but to act:

> Immediately it struck our adventurer that this man must be familiar with the scarecrow; perhaps had himself fashioned it. Should he miss it then, he might make immediate search, and so discover the thief so imprudently loitering upon the very field of his operations.
>
> Waiting until the man momentarily disappeared in a little hollow, Israel ran briskly to the identical spot where the scarecrow had stood; where, standing stiffly erect, pulling the hat well over his face, and thrusting out his arm, pointed steadfastly towards the Squire's abode, he awaited the event. (78–79)

As in the episode of the squire's clothes, it is questionable both to what extent this impromptu performance is a wise maneuver under the circumstances and to what extent each episode reveals a tendency in Israel playfully to take the risk of attempting to pass himself off as another in front of unsuspecting strangers. Indeed, his feelings of guilt over his actions at the squire's (77) as well as his more freely flaunted performance at Whitehaven to procure fire for Paul Jones (102–4) suggest that Israel does indeed possess a playful streak, one that is often blended with a sense of revengeful satisfaction in his ability to dupe and make fools of his enemies. His playful barb at the horrified lighter of his pipe (" 'That was good seed you gave me,' said Israel, 'see what a yield;' pointing to the flames" [104]) confirms the perception that Israel's many disguises speak symbolically of his physical and psychological exile as well as his nevertheless metamorphic sense of himself and his relation to the world.

Both symbols are likewise readily discernible in Israel's wandering through the hierarchy of the socially modeled *Ariel* in chapter 20. After attempting to enter each "social circle" (134), from highest to lowest (both figuratively and literally), he allows the ship's officers to believe him mad and eventually, by simple self-assurance and repetition, gains official recognition for himself under the fictitious name and station he chose when he was first discovered. His ability to shape himself, to enter into and adapt to a variety of environments, projects both positive and negative visions of his life and history. As a wanderer whose chief desire is to return home, he is continually forced into deceptions that only lead him, both physically and psychologically, further from that goal. On the other hand, as a figure whose ability to metamorphose is both reliable and satisfying, he demonstrates a mind capable of flexibility and diversion, of subtlety, diversity, and, frequently beneath it all, a well-measured, well-tempered mirth.

If Franklin plays Israel's public opposite in the attitude toward physical fulfillment, then Paul Jones, the "small, elastic, swarthy man, with an aspect as of a disinherited Indian Chief in European clothes" (56), certainly forms Israel's opposite in the attitude towards self-identity. As Israel is capable of, and even prone toward, self-reshaping and the surreptitious drama of disguise, Jones revels in the flaunting of his public identity in a drama that is self-promoting and self-imposing. In marked contrast to Israel, he possesses a somewhat qualified, Ahabian vision of his relation to the rest of the world and hunts relentlessly after the vulnerable manifestations of his mental image of enemy England. His raison d'être derives from a combination of revenge and the self-assertion that inheres in revenge:

> "I would teach the British that Paul Jones, though born in Britain, is no subject to the British King, but an untrammelled citizen and sailor of the universe; . . . . (56)
> "Pretty well informed on that subject, I believe. Come along. Yes, lad, I am tolerably well acquainted with Whitehaven. And this morning intend that Whitehaven shall have slight inkling of *me*." (101)

Jones's insistence on his own fame, on the assertion of his own identity no matter the danger involved, reveals his monomania. Furthermore, his considerable desire to imprint his self onto an enemy closely associated with his youth, to attack, in essence, his homeland, suggests, with its undercurrent of self-destructiveness, an Oedipal psychology similar to Ahab's. Yet as the narrator notes, despite Paul's bravado, he possesses an "octogenarian prudence" as well (99), a tempering voice that allows him to back down before nature's more spiritual terrors such as the Crag of Aisla (97).[10]

Nevertheless, Paul Jones guards his identity in a way that suggests his resistance to any kind of blurring or melding with another. In the anecdote by which he supports his refusal to share Israel's bed in Paris, he presents an image of the Ishmaelean process of growth, the embrace of a notably other self, only to reveal his decision to avoid such a process of self-extension: " 'When, before the mast, I first sailed out of Whitehaven to Norway,' said Paul coolly, 'I had for hammock-mate a full-blooded Congo. We had a white blanket spread in our hammock. Every time I turned in I found the Congo's black wool worked in with the white worsted. By the end of the voyage the blanket was of a pepper-and-salt look, like an old man's turning head. So it's not because I am notional at all, but because I don't care to, my lad' " (62). It is hard to doubt that this recollected scene echoes Ishmael's night with Queequeg or that it likewise reveals Jones's inability to experience the kind of psychic rebirth such an encounter affords Ishmael. Jones's reaction to the blending of black and white in the blanket points to the unease such a self-blending, of which the blanket is an image, produces in him. He is unwilling to have his identity blurred, or, to extend the image, to allow his identity to age, to attain that "pepper-and-salt look, like an old man's turning head" (62).[11]

If Israel's attraction to the drama of disguise reveals a notable playfulness in his psychological construction, then his frequent symbolic resurrections may in turn provide a pattern for understanding the origin of this aspect of his sensibility. For instance, after his first capture by the British "three days out of Boston harbor" (14), Israel is "thrust aboard a hulk. And here in the black bowels of the ship, sunk low in the sunless sea, our poor Israel lay for a month, like Jonah in the belly of the whale" (15). The mention of Jonah, as readers of *Moby-Dick* well know, frequently reveals Melville's commitment to the vision of physical and psychological resurrection the biblical story entails. And yet here, despite the presence of the metaphor, few significant resurrective benefits adhere to the subsequently emerging Israel. He simply reappears, takes the place of a sick bargeman, and continues his Sisyphean journey, without a noticeable change of mind or personality.

Likewise, in the episode of the Squire's chimney, the suggestions of burial and rebirth are too strong to ignore:

> "And I am to be buried alive here?" said Israel, ruefully looking round.
> "But your resurrection will soon be at hand," smiled the Squire; "two days at the furthest." (68)

The failure of the Squire to appear "on the morning of the third day" (70) then leads Israel into a more extensive contemplation of his entombment and to a presentation of the history of this particular coffin-sized immurement:

> It seemed that this part of the old house, or rather this wall of it, was extremely ancient, dating far beyond the era of Elizabeth, having once formed portion of a religious retreat belonging to the Templars. The domestic discipline of this order was rigid and merciless in the extreme. In a side wall of their second story chapel, horizontal and on a level with the floor, they had an internal vacancy left, exactly the shape and average size of a coffin. In this place, from time to time, inmates convicted of contumacy were confined; but, strange to say, not till they were penitent. . . . Sometimes several weeks elapsed ere the disentombment. The penitent being then usually found numb and congealed in all his extremities, like one newly stricken with paralysis. (71)

The scene of resurrection now given is no longer the natural force of the sea or the physical whale but the markedly stony coffin of a group of fiercely ascetic religionists. Its purpose, far from the remolding of the self, seems to be the production of the kind of terror and hopelessness, the madness, that Pip experiences as well as a notable loss of physical sensation and control. In short, Israel, far from entering the stratum of lower reality that produces resurrection, finds himself, like Pierre and Bartleby, entombed in an ascetic trap. It is a sign of his basically self-preserving vision and lack of metaphysical desire that, despite the Squire's warnings, he soon extricates himself, though without achieving any benefits from his burial and resurrection. His is a desire to escape the entrapments of sterile exile so that he may return to the locus of fertility, the home and hearth. His resurrections, whether in the British hulk, in the Squire's chimney, or from the brick pits of London (154), produce none of the benefits of psychic rebirth because the only place in which the body and mind have a synthetic existence in this book's world is the center of Israel's home, the long-sought, always distant hearth. As a result, Israel's mild playfulness and his tendency toward self-reshaping receive no energy, nor do they originate out of his repeated resurrections. His sensibility is attuned to the physically potent rebirth, the fertile integrations of body and mind, and such ascetic snares are only delays for him, only deferrals of the life and life-force he seeks.

It is Israel's return to the hearth, the book's final resurrection, that reemphasizes the novel's bitter criticism of American fickleness—its notation of the ironies of patriotic fervor—and restates the centrality of home and hearth in the quest pattern of Israel's life. Having passed "forty-five years" as a mender of old chairs, having married and produced eleven children, ten of whom died early, Israel, white-haired and prone to hallucination, "the bescarred bearer of a cross" (167), returns to America with his only living son. Ignored, forgotten, and nearly run over by "a patriotic triumphal car" (167) as a result of the celebration of the fiftieth anniversary of the Battle of Bunker Hill, he, one of the heroes of that battle, seeks out the location of his father's homestead:

> Blindly ranging to and fro, they next saw a man ploughing. Advancing slowly, the wanderer met him by a little heap of ruinous burnt masonry, like a tumbled chimney, what seemed the jams of the fire-place, now aridly stuck over here and there, with thin, clinging, round prohibitory mosses, like executors' wafers. Just as the oxen were bid stand, the stranger's plough was hitched over sideways, by sudden contact with some sunken stone at the ruin's base. . . .
> "What are you looking at so, father?
> " '*Father!*' here," raking with his staff, "*my* father would sit, and here, my mother, and here I, little infant, would totter between, even as now, once again, on the very same spot, but in the unroofed air, I do. The ends meet. Plough away, friend." (169)

The question of why Israel has waited so long to return has both economic and psychological answers. It seems clear that in marrying and attempting to produce a family in England, he was also attempting to create a substitute home. Nevertheless, as the deaths of his progeny but one suggest, such an attempt lacked the native fertility, the symbolic American strength and purity, that a home in the Berkshires would have provided. The "City of Dis" into which he disappears not only is physically black and besmoked, but its outward decay reflects an inward sterility that compares poorly with the vision of the clean, hearty land of chapter 1. As a result, his return to the ancient hearthstone of his father is notable for the presence of arable land, for the symbolism of the plowing farmer, and for the health and verdant abundance of the area. Furthermore, the long exile that time here encircles contains added sadness for Israel not only because he realizes the passage of years but also because he sees the missed opportunities for growth and family production such an environment and such a link to the familial past could have given him. In returning to the hearth, he returns to the locus of his birth, to the body, to the land from which he sprang, and sees now the life he might have led.

The Language of Exile

Part of the pathos of *Israel Potter* for the reader who has come from *Moby-Dick* and *Pierre* issues not only from the story itself but also from the resemblance between the protagonist's inability to function in the place and manner of his choosing and the book's (and Melville's) inability to achieve the power of novelistic scope toward which the narrative as a whole seems to reach. Despite the frequently dry or reserved humorousness of the novel, we cannot help but acknowledge the weakness of novelistic construction beneath it all, the almost measurable lack of large-scale, structural strength that contributes to the fragility of the often powerful yet brief sketches. This fragmentation informs the creation of Israel, whose physical desire, despite his ingenuity and resourcefulness, is consistently thwarted, as well as the narrative itself, whose textual body seems likewise to fail to satisfy its own novelistic aims. Though Israel demonstrates an undeniable playfulness of both action and language, he also frequently appears shallow, lacking Ishmael's linguistically searching mind and sensibility, and, try though he may, is unable to consummate any of the opportunities for physical renewal consistently offered him. In a similar fashion the book itself, though composed of energetic set pieces, seems to restrain its large-scale fullness of expression. The novel and especially its textual body form a suitable image of the Melville whose novel-making, already tending toward fragmentation in *Pierre* and the now more frequent magazine stories, seems noticeably weak. Consequently, he appears left with a powerful but brief language that constructs only brilliant, small-scale textures and scenes.

Part of the shortcoming of Israel's language results from its essential differences from the synthetic and complex speech of Ishmael. For instance, the positive evidences of Israel's linguistic play—fewer, more delicate, and less important to their text than Ishmael's—proceed not from a marked psychological resurrection or reintegration but from the American's sense of fair play, plain sightedness, and congeniality. His jokes and turns of phrase carry none of the symbolic import that Ishmael's frequently do but instead arise from the occasion at hand and are usually aimed at some practical goal. Thus there is less of a distance between the ends and means of Israel's language than there is in Ishmael's. Though lacking any kind of Ahabian aggression, Israel's use of language reduces the amount of by-product resulting from the appreciation of language itself and closes the gap between word and thing: " 'Am I to steal from here to Paris on my stocking feet?' said Israel, whose late easy good living at White Waltham had not failed to bring out the good-natured and mirthful part of him, even as his prior experiences had produced, for the most part, something like the contrary result" (36). The narrator's connection between "easy good living" and the tendency toward play offers an explanation of sorts for the quietness of humor in *Israel Potter* as well as for the increasing absence or failure of humor in Melville's writing. It also consciously ties Israel's sense of play to his physical condition and suggests that experience, not heredity, is responsible for the weakening of the positive spirit in the quester. In short, the passage relies upon our assumption that Israel, were it not for the rough treatment he has received, would be a naturally playful character; as a result, in moments when such hardships diminish, he reverts to that playfulness as part of his natural condition.

Perhaps the only passage in the novel that reveals Israel in an openly linguistic playfulness that is also to some extent meditative and dilatory occurs when Dr. Franklin has left him to contemplate the "appurtenances" of his lodging:

> "I wonder now what O-t-a-r-d is?" soliloquised Israel, slowly spelling the word. "I have a good mind to step in and ask Dr. Franklin. He knows everything. Let me smell it. No, it's sealed; smell is locked in. Those are pretty flowers. Let's smell them; no smell again. Ah, I see—sort of flowers in women's bonnets—sort of calico flowers. Beautiful soap. This smells anyhow—regular soap-roses—a white rose and a red one. That long-necked bottle there looks like a crane. I wonder what's in that? Hallo! E-a-u—d-e— C-o-l-o-g-n-e. I wonder if Dr. Franklin understands that? It looks like his white wine. This is nice sugar. Let's taste. Yes, this is very nice sugar, sweet as—yes, it's sweet as sugar; better than maple sugar, such as they make at home. But I'm crunching it too loud, the Doctor will hear me. But here's a teaspoon. What's this for? There's no tea, nor tea-cup; but here's a tumbler, and here's drinking water. Let me see. Seems to me, putting this and that and the other thing together, it's a sort of alphabet that spells something. Spoon, tumbler, water, sugar,——brandy, that's it. O-t-a-r-d is brandy. Who put these things here? What does it all mean? Don't put sugar here for show, don't put a spoon here for ornament, nor a jug of water. There is only one meaning to it, and that is a very polite invitation from some invisible person to help myself, if I like, to a glass of brandy and sugar, and if I don't like, let it alone. That's my reading. (50)

Israel's mode of analysis is largely physical: he smells and tastes, using the resultant sensations as the basis for his conclusions. The pattern of investigative thought, with its occasional joke and twisting, serpentine route of inquisitive seeking, brings to mind the fluid and comedic passages in which Ishmael digresses and explains and some of the soliloquies of lesser characters such as Stubb and Pip in *Moby-Dick*. In fact, the scene can be taken as an echo, now devoid of its darker significance, of the Doubloon chapter of *Moby-Dick*. It employs a similar style of vocalized thinking as well as an emphasis on the process of interpretation. Israel, now in the relative comfort of Franklin's apartment, provides us here with a model for his mental processes and an example of his linguistic abilities. He spells out the mystery of the talismanic symbols just as does the *Pequod*'s crew, but the meaning is no longer metaphysical. The com-

forts that the items on the mantle offer and the price that will be exacted
if the offer is taken are the only considerations at stake. As a result, his
reading is, like those of the doubloon, a portrait of himself, a mirror in
which he reveals his own need to decode the paths to physical comfort.
It is also an example of his willingness to engage in the task of gaining
those comforts, to quest, by reading, for the values of physical improve-
ment and satisfaction that form the subject of his larger search.

In another instance, Israel demonstrates what may be categorized as
another "American" trait—a playfulness of conviviality, an echo of the
Ishmaelean embrace:

> "I shall be a vice to your plans, Captain Paul. I will receive, but I won't
> let go, unless you alone loose the screw."
> "Well said. To bed now; you ought to. I go on deck. Good-night, ace-of-
> hearts."
> "That is fitter for yourself, Captain Paul; lonely leader of the suit."
> "Lonely? Aye, but number one cannot but be lonely, my trump."
> "Again I give it back. Ace-of-trumps may it prove to you, Captain Paul;
> may it be impossible for you ever to be taken. But for me—poor deuce, a
> trey, that comes in your wake—any king or knave may take me, as before
> now the knaves have." (93)

This passage may mark the greatest extent to which Israel demonstrates
the fully ripe play of linguistic joy, and it is significant that it emerges
from the deferred homoerotic impulses that Ishmael, among others, demonstrates. For this dialogue, with its sense of challenge and counter-chal-
lenge in the card-playing metaphor, its productive union of two troping
voices transforming and being transformed by one another, comes closest
of all the moments in Israel's exile, and all the moments in the novel, to
the experience of Eros that Melville's "heart," and Ishmael's expression
of it, embodies. However, like all such approaches to the sacred in *Israel
Potter*, it also is far too evanescent to provide lasting comfort. The two
who, for the briefest moment of dialogue, seem powerfully connected are
joined only for that moment and only then in language. As a result, Israel's
relationship to Jones, suggestive though it is of a powerfully productive
union, does not last. He is exiled even from substitutes for the heart, even
from its voices.

It may be a matter for some surprise that Israel's companion in this
scene of linguistic sport is the notably aggressive Capt. Paul Jones. But
Jones, for all his rampant egotism's insistence upon identity, can engage
in moments of convivial enjoyment, even in the realm of speech.[12] He
forms perhaps a stronger version of that part of Israel that derives pleasure
from the residuum of bitterness that is the result of his exile. Conse-

quently, his play demonstrates, more frequently than Israel's, a sense of aggressive challenge, as though the linguistic maneuvers both forecast and reflect the physical—and, subconsciously, the erotic—maneuvers that are the issue of his motive for revenge: "Because, Yellow-hair, my boy, I am engaged to marry her to-night. The bride's friends won't like the match; and so, this very night, the bride must be carried away. She has a nice tapering waste, hasn't she, through the glass? Ah! I will clasp her to my heart" (98). The metaphor of possession, applied in this case to a ship, unites with the revenger's fantasy to reveal the pattern of Jones's mind and the ways in which language becomes for him, as it does for Ahab, a tool that in part functions sexually. In this instance, rather than probing reality with a vehicular speech, Jones reshapes the object of his desire with a playful language that enables him to overcome the obstacles to consummation. He combines the transformative power of metaphor with the destructive wishes of his vengeful desire and creates a language similar to Ahab's, though equipped with a greater degree of self-possession and control.

His counterpart in strategy and in method of ambition is Dr. Franklin, whose "sly" distinctions and qualifications frustrate the singularly determined captain. As noted above, Franklin's language, perilously close at times to the deceptiveness of the confidence-man, reveals an awareness of casuistic potential in all language, the ability of words to both transmit and obscure meaning, to discover and hide truth: "My honest friend, if you are poor, avoid wine as a costly luxury; if you are rich, shun it as a fatal indulgence. Stick to plain water. And now, my good friend, if you are through with your meal, we will rise. There is no pastry coming. Pastry is poisoned bread. Never eat pastry. Be a plain man, and stick to plain things" (45). The ascetic vision enacted here I have already discussed, but the way in which language serves that asceticism is notable largely for its attempts to redefine the desirable into the undesirable. Thus "pastry is poisoned bread"; in other words, pastry is not good for you, and yet Dr. Franklin avoids such a direct statement. Instead, as with the brandy, he metaphorizes the evil involved and transforms the object into something it is not. Dr. Franklin, the "household Plato," at least in Israel's vision, uses language in order to conceal, steal, and manipulate. He is a trickster whose trickery holds elements of play but who ultimately makes his way by putting on the mask instead of striking through it, by concealing instead of striving to reveal.

Despite the evidences of playfulness in these characters' languages, neither the generic and linguistic abundance of *Moby-Dick* nor the bitter rehearsal of psychological malformation of *Pierre* are present in *Israel Pot-*

ter. If *Mardi* and *Pierre* can be said to have transgressed on the side of overabundance, *Israel Potter* can equally be said to lack abundance, to fail either to sport a proud paunch or to worry at length over its asceticism. Both the physical body within the book and the book's body itself seem interrupted in their search for fullness, and though, as we have seen, Israel demonstrates a physical vision and quest, the ultimate object of that quest and his briefer moments of possible physical renewal are ultimately deferred. The presence of the urination scenes cited earlier as evidence of Israel's physicality is no more significant than the fact that in each of those scenes the urge to urinate is not fulfilled—each request either is a pretext for escape or inadvertently becomes one. Likewise, the most obviously Ishmaelean moment in the book, the night in Paris with Paul Jones, seems unable to become the kind of physical and psychological moment of rebirth it represents in *Moby-Dick.* In this respect, there remains an undercurrent of bodily deferral in the novel, the tendency of sexuality and sexual moments to fail to renew: "Caught in a rent of the sail, the officer slipped and fell near the sharp iron edge of the hatchway. As he fell, he caught Israel by the most terrible part in which mortality can be grappled. Insane with pain, Israel dashed his adversary's skull against the sharp iron. The officer's hold relaxed; but himself stiffened. Israel made for the helmsman, who as yet knew not the issue of the late tussel. He caught him round the loins, bedding his fingers like grisly claws into his flesh, and hugging him to his heart" (89). A more violently sexual scene can hardly be found in Melville. And yet, embedded in its language is no less than Ishmael's bodily embrace revised. The grabbing of the genitals most obviously initiates the encounter, but this advance is immediately countered by Israel's castrating response which causes the officer to "stiffen." Subsequently, after the helmsman sees Israel approaching—the "issue of the late tussel"—Israel then embraces the helmsman "round the loins, bedding his fingers into his flesh, and hugging him to his heart." Thus, in the same sort of sexual metaphorizing that appears in the earlier novels, Melville here gives us a scene in which physical contact yields not life but death and in which the Ishmaelean embrace is not a resurrective encounter with death in life but simply a death grip.

A similar subversion of positive bodily fulfillment occurs in the textual body. Though Melville does not appear to lack the ability to describe forcefully or write intensely on a small scale, on the large scale years of narrative are often inelegantly dismissed, rushed through with a degree of impatience, as though the formal qualities of the story itself no longer interest a writer who seems more concerned with a loose stringing together of set pieces.[13] Yet he does not, as in *Moby-Dick,* make such a discontinuity of genre his modus operandi but seems instead to be capable and interested in only the smaller forms his portraits and scene paintings fill. Even so, within these miniatures he achieves a distinct power: "Indeed, making due allowance for soil and era, history presents few trios more akin, upon the whole, than Jacob, Hobbes, and Franklin; three labyrinth-minded, but plain-spoken Broadbrims, at once politicians and philosophers; keen observers of the main chance; prudent courtiers; practical magians in linsey woolsey" (46–47). Here is the productive ability to rename, to synthesize disparate times and cultures into a commentary that has elements of both lightness and weight, proliferation and definition. In terms of overall juice, it is certainly drier than Ishmael at his most sea soaked, more moist than the dusty rasp of "Bartleby" or *The Confidence-Man*. At its best, it is suggestive always of the power Melville once possessed on a larger scale:

> Not long after, an invisible hand came and set down a great yellow lamp in the east. The hand reached up unseen from below the horizon, and set the lamp down right on the rim of the horizon, as on a threshold; as much as to say, Gentlemen warriors, permit me a little to light up this rather gloomy looking subject. The lamp was the round harvest moon; the one solitary foot-light of the scene. But scarcely did the rays of the lamp pierce that languid haze. Objects before perceived with difficulty, now glimmered ambiguously. Bedded in strange vapors, the great foot-light cast a dubious half demoniac glare across the waters, like the phantasmagoric stream sent athwart a London flagging in a night-rain from an apothecary's blue and green window. (123)

There is no exhaustion evident in this writing. It demonstrates a powerful sense of drama slightly undercut by its own comic sense, its own wink at the extravagance of its metaphorizing, as it paints with a degree of complexity and delicacy that reveals, if anything, a possible attraction for Melville to this kind of small-scale work, as though the fragmentation following *Pierre* may be as much the result of Melville's clearer sight of his own specific talents as the evidence of his failing energy.

What Melville manages on the small scale in *Israel Potter* does not extend to the whole, however, and as a novel it remains an echo, a sequel of sorts that feeds off the scraps of energy left from the enormous feasts of *Moby-Dick* and *Pierre*. Though it speaks of the body's need for a place of renewal and strength, for the importance of the hearth and the vision to which it remains central, the book's failure to allow that body its fulfillment suggests that it is but a resting place on the way down for Melville, a station house and boarding point of *The Fidele*, whose silent, hollow laughter can be neither reshaped nor avoided.

II

The Limits of Form

4

TOWARD DECEPTION
The Short Fiction and the Failing Body

MELVILLE'S SHORT FICTION, written in large part from 1852 to 1856, appears to have been the inevitable next step for a writer whose formal experimentation, approaching exhaustion in the form of the novel, had always led him to produce ungainly, misshapen books. Even *Israel Potter* and *The Confidence-Man*, his eighth and ninth novels respectively, now appear more directly related to investigations of the detached prose sketch, the lyric or homiletic stroke of the crayon, than to the sort of bulky, multi-generic encrustations of prose he had hitherto attempted. In fact, with *Israel Potter* it is even possible to suggest that Melville, already interested in the "Agatha" material and engaged in magazine work that had produced half a dozen stories, not only decided to publish the book serially but also planned and wrote the story with the formal divisions and space requirements of *Putnam's Monthly* in mind.[1] This strategy may not only account for the novel's episodic character, lack of cohesion, and shallow texture but may also give evidence of Melville's growing desire or need to produce smaller divisions of text.

Whatever the method of *Israel Potter*'s construction, it is clear that both the novel and the short stories written during this period share not only a sense of formal concentration but also a tendency to explore the ways in which the body continually fails to gain comfort as language becomes more and more fragmentary and deceptive. The kind of temporary psychological and physiological solution found and refound by Ishmael, sought but attained too late by Israel Potter, is systematically undermined in these tales by impotence, irony, or a language, intentionally or otherwise, inadequate to the body's true needs. From the physical wasting of Merrymusk and his family in "Cock-A-Doodle-Doo!" to the deceptively "enchanted" world of "The Encantadas," language continues as in "Bartleby" to be the body's enemy, offering in the end only obfuscation and the variations of deceit that will eventually form the fabric of *The Confidence-Man*.[2]

Runaways, Castaways, Solitaries, Grave-stones, Etc.

If it is true that the body in *Israel Potter* consists of a physical desire it cannot consummate, then the body in the contemporaneous short fiction similarly demonstrates traits of isolation and disjunction. In fact, the stories taken as a whole may be considered an irregular and uneven investigation of the ways in which the body fails to satisfy or be satisfied in a world where the disjunction between language and physical reality dominates. The narrator of "Cock-A-Doodle-Doo!," for instance, not only presents himself in a depressed state ("too full of hypoes to sleep")[3] but also dwells upon his physical condition, particularly on the connection between his mood and his body's lack of comfort. He notes his own "rheumatics" and "Dyspepsia" while listing the possible diseases from which the local children may die (270–71) and imaginatively punishes the "asses who have the management of railroads and steamboats" by declaring that he would, if made "Dictator in North America a while," "string them up! and hang, draw, and quarter; fry, roast, and boil; stew, grill, and devil them, like so many turkey-legs" (269–70). By his exaggerated presentation, Melville apparently intends to demonstrate the ugly mood of the narrator that subsequently disappears at the "optimistic" crowing of the cock. It is equally clear, however, that this teller is meant to stand as a figure dominated by the physical and that the story's tension will spring from the contrast between the narrator's own physical orientation and the aphysical, indeed defiantly anti-physical, cock crow. When the narrator's mood changes from dark to light, his interest in the body's condition does not fade. Now, instead of pondering disease or death by roasting, he suddenly feels "warmer" (271) and subsequently changes his breakfast menu from "only tea and toast" to "coffee and eggs—no, brown-stout and a beef-steak" (272). He then imagines that the railroad passengers are "going down to the city to eat oysters" (272) and receives the dun while drinking more brown-stout and reading *Tristram Shandy*. Later he similarly bemoans being served a civil-process wrapped around his cigar by noting that "it was a highly inelegant act in the constable to take advantage of a gentleman's lunching on cheese and porter, to be so uncivil as to slip a civil-process into his hat" (279), and subsequently shows interest in Merrymusk's skimpy meal (280) and the degenerated condition of Merrymusk's family (285).

Thus whatever interpretation we accept concerning the possible meaning or identification of the cock crow, it is clear that this cheering sound, a kind of language, not only affects the moods of the narrator and Merrymusk but also forms a barrier between the body and the emotions.[4] The picture of Merrymusk, with its insistence on the "long saddish face, yet somehow a latently joyous eye" (280), emphasizes the disjunction between the physical—the shabby coat, "staid, but undepressed" demeanor (280), his cold lunch—and the inner buoyancy that verges on, and soon reveals itself as, a kind of madness. In fact, it is the lunch that first alarms the narrator's sense of propriety because in seeing it his trust in the physical, his vision that we are—both physically and emotionally—what we eat, receives as great a shock as it did when he first heard the cock's crow: "From my window, where I was reading Burton's Anatomy of Melancholy, I saw him in the act. I burst out of doors bare-headed. 'Good heavens!' cried I; 'what are you doing? Come in. *This* is your dinner!' " (280). The dinner turns out to be "a hunk of stale bread and another hunk of salt beef," which the scandalized narrator replaces with "a dish of hot pork and beans, and a mug of cider" (280). The narrator's language reveals a basic conviction that to consume poor food is not only an offense against one's own body but an offense against the narrator's society, which wishes, on the one hand, to allay its guilt for its own prosperity and, on the other, to restore supremacy to the body's needs. The proof comes in the form of the narrator's confession that "it afforded me pleasure to perceive that he quaffed down his mug of cider like a man" (280) and in his notation of Merrymusk's otherwise cool reception of the free lunch. It is the workman's Bartleby-like "sullen silence" and his "calm, proud, but not ungrateful way" (280) that confuses and piques the narrator until he constructs his own explanation for this lack of geniality, this failure of good food and good drink to enliven and cheer the body and emotions of the wood-sawyer.

In fact, the story's greatest shock, akin to the discovery of the woodcutter's meal, is the revelation that the "extraordinary cock" (the phallic pun is intended) belongs not to any gentleman—that is, not to anyone who can afford good food and good drink and thus the potency that in the narrator's mind accompanies it—but to Merrymusk himself, the lower class, "unjolly" husband of "a perfect invalid," father of a "rickety," ill brood of four (280). That the head of such a diseased and physically unfit household should possess the voice of optimism directly contradicts the narrator's unconscious conviction that the body's condition is the key to happiness. Thus the improbable, dream-like ending, with its melodramatic multiple deaths at the crowing of the radiant cock, suggests a final attack both on the narrator's vision (everyone appears to die in ecstasy) and on Merrymusk's failure to recognize the importance of the physical in allowing his entire family to die prematurely, no matter what their mood. That the cock itself dies is appropriate simply because the narrator, by means of this cautionary dumb-show, has himself been converted; he now crows the language of optimism, avoids "the doleful dumps," and, we must infer, no longer allows the physical to dictate his mood, "but under all circumstances crow[s] late and early with a continual crow" (288).

There is at least one other famous cock in the Melville oeuvre, and several critics have noted a connection to the "victorious fowl" of the *Pequod*'s doubloon. However, another episode in that same chapter of *Moby-Dick* perhaps more fully foreshadows the later story's transformation of its narrator: "And I, you and he; and we, ye, and they, are all bats; and I'm a crow, especially when I stand a'top of the pine tree here. Caw! caw! caw! caw! caw! caw!"[5] Pip's madness, embodied here by the crow—black as opposed to the cock's gold—results from too much knowledge, too clear an insight; it is the dark opposite of the insanity at the end of "Cock-A-Doodle-Doo!," which in itself may be termed a sort of white madness, the result of too much light, the blindness of optimistic radiance. In each case, the commitment to the physical, to the life of the body, is lost as the character loses himself in the aphysical spaces of the mind and emotions. The narrator of "Cock-A-Doodle-Doo!" thus becomes a figure of language itself, a kind of speech whose only true potency is linguistic. He, like Pip, becomes a "crow" and comes to represent, as did the cock before him, a language that has no connection to the physical, a failed system of reference that has forgotten or dreamed away the world to which it once corresponded.

A similar failure of language to describe or even acknowledge reality underlies "Poor Man's Pudding and Rich Man's Crumbs," the somewhat heavily polemical companion pieces on poverty and charity.[6] "Poor Man's Pudding" examines the real life of the poor, as opposed to the poet Blandmour's romantic, rose-colored descriptions of it, by focusing on the meal shared by the narrator with the poor farmer Coulter and his wife. Similarly, the second tale concerns the tradition of permitting the London poor access to the leftovers of "the grand Guildhall Banquet to the princes" (297) and the frenzied rush for scraps that follows. Each piece deals once again with a "dinner," the kind of meal—whether described or, as in "Bartleby," notably absent—that continually emphasizes the body's real needs as opposed to the rhetoric of charity, sacrifice, romanticism, or noblesse oblige that surrounds it.

It is thus the test of the narrator's own body, the attempted ingestion of the "poor man's pudding," that the first sketch presents as its major evidence. Like Dame Coulter, he cannot force himself to eat the "last year's pork" that the Squire has given Coulter "on account" (293), and he can but attempt to swallow the briny pudding so naively praised by

Blandmour: "The mouthful of pudding now touched my palate, and touched it with a mouldy, briny taste" (295). It is this touch, as in "Bartleby" and *Israel Potter,* negative in its effects, that renders truth in this sketch, a reality which otherwise cannot be found or adequately described by Blandmour's poetry, for such a language, by this point in Melville's career, has lost its connection to the physical and, as a result, has clearly become more deceptive than revelatory.

The second of the sketches seems at first more interested in the threat to the narrator's own physical and social safety and the integrity of his own body than in the simple debunking of poetic or political optimism. In fact, this tale owes much to the horror of cannibalism first registered in *Typee* and foreshadows the figural terror of gestation found in "The Tartarus of Maids."[7] In addition to the contrast between the "civic subordinate's" buoyant blindness to the needs of the crowd and the narrator's stark descriptions of the same mob's violent hunger, we are presented with the kind of moment that a "life among the cannibals" usually furnishes—an outsider, caught in a swirl of "sharkishness," unsure whether or not the bestial feast will soon turn on him. Eventually the narrator's sense of the injustice and terror of the moment leads him to make comparisons to a kind of social cannibalism:

> "Yes, who knows!" said my guide, "his Royal Highness the Prince Regent might have eaten of that identical pheasant."
>
> "I don't doubt it," murmured I, "he is said to be uncommonly fond of the breast. But where is Napoleon's head in a charger? I should fancy *that* ought to have been the principal dish." (299)

The pun on "breast" contrasts upper class decadence with lower class appetite, while the potential consumption of Napoleon's head represents the sort of regicidal act suggested by the destructive energy of the crowd. More than anything else, it is the emphasis on the lower class's hunger that propels the terror and revulsion of this sketch; the sexual indulgences of the upper class indirectly rely upon the deprivation of the basic bodily needs of the mob, needs that, if left unfilled, may turn horrific and revolutionary. The alarming physical appetite, the near madness associated with the desire to possess—"The yet unglutted mob raised a fierce yell, which wafted the banners like a strong gust, and filled the air with a reek as from sewers" (301)—mark this sketch as the expression of both social injustice and the failure of charity and the language of noblesse oblige to satisfy or even clearly recognize the social body's potentially dangerous "hungers."

In a similar fashion "The Fiddler" deals with the relationship between the body and happiness by means of its presentation of Hautboy, the "short, fat" "genius" whose philosophy of "leisurely, deep good sense" appears to give him an "extraordinary cheerfulness" (264). It is difficult to say, however, whether this fragment is meant to espouse or criticize this sort of shallow jollity. The narrator, a failed poet in a miserable mood, appears to adopt by the story's end the fiddler's attitude toward fame and success, preferring a happy obscurity to an unhappy desire for notoriety. Yet the tone of the whole often gives us the sense that the tale is nothing more than an apology for resignation, a compromising dedication to "good times," after having surrendered the unhealthy ambitions of the mind: "Ah? But could you not fancy that Hautboy might formerly have had genius, but luckily getting rid of it, at least fatted up?" (265).

The rhetoric of "The Happy Failure" certainly reigns here, but significantly the question of the link between emotion and flesh, between good food and good times, again comes into question. Does happiness depend upon physical satisfaction? Or is the capacity to be physically happy the result of relinquishing obsessive quests, giving up the hunt? "The Fiddler" appears to espouse the latter sentiment, though with a twist; for at the story's end, with the narrator's purchase of a fiddle and his avowal "to take regular lessons of Hautboy," we may get not so much a picture of resignation as one of a positively revised quest. The pursuits of the mind, in this case poetry, have here been abandoned for the pursuits of the enchanting Orpheus, and the "regular lessons" may be as much a commitment to the flesh as ultimate good as it is an adoption of Hautboy's jolly acceptance of good and bad. The proof may rest in the narrator's reception of Hautboy's music:

> All my moody discontent, every vestige of peevishness fled. My whole splenetic soul capitulated to the magical fiddle.
> "Something of an Orpheus, ah?" said Standard, archly nudging me beneath the left rib.
> "And I, the charmed Bruin," murmured I. (266)

The "magical fiddle" yields the same note, it seems, as the "extraordinary cock" of "Cock-A-Doodle-Doo!," though in this case it is unclear whether or not the music of the fiddle is associated with the physical or the anti-physical. The cock crow signals the note of blind optimism and is associated with an imaginary potency, but the fact that Hautboy is healthy, unlike Merrymusk and his family, appears to attribute some positive physical powers to the fiddle. More significant, however, may be Standard's invocation of Orpheus and his dig in the narrator's ribs. The Orphic music redirects the narrator's attention toward his animal nature, and it is the convivial nudge in the ribs that quietly points to the transformation. Thus the narrator does indeed become "the charmed Bruin," his "low enjoying power" invoked and rediscovered by the music and Hautboy's philosophy, to which he is now dedicated.

Nevertheless, the nature of the physical commitment in "The Fiddler" remains complicated by the disturbing surrender of intellectual pursuits in favor of the beguiling and potentially deceptive music of the fiddle. It seems clear that "Hautboy" is more than a mere musician; in fact, each of his two remarkable names suggests the yoking of both temporal and sexual contraries. Thus as a·youth he was known as "Master Betty," while as an adult he is "Hautboy," that is, not just a musical instrument but a "high" "boy." Both names reflect the reconciliation of contraries he is said to demonstrate and further suggest that the narrator is determined to surrender his adult sexuality. Not only does Hautboy "baffle inquisition" (266), but the narrator himself suggests that he knew and understood the fiddler better "as a child": "What! Oh Standard, myself, as a child, have shouted myself hoarse applauding that very name in the theatre." (267) The ambiguity of "as a child," by which the narrator refers both to his youth and to the youthfulness of action, suggests that only the preadolescent sensibility can comprehend the essence of Hautboy's non-questing, self-pleasing enchantment. Thus Standard's sudden mention of the narrator's failed poem prompts not only a denying appeal for silence—"Not a word of that, for heaven's sake!" (267)—but also the imagistic equivalent of Hautboy's ambiguous personality: "If Cicero, traveling in the East, found sympathetic solace for his grief in beholding the arid overthrow of a once gorgeous city, shall not my petty affair be as nothing, when I behold in Hautboy the vine and the rose climbing the shattered shafts of his tumbled temple of Fame?" (267). Like Pierre's "fame-column," these "shattered shafts" recognize a degree of impotence in terms of individual understanding and achievement. The "vine and the rose," each to become significant erotic emblems in Melville's later poetry, thus suggest a renewed sexuality that eschews the aggressive desires of the metaphysical quester while resurrecting the sexual potential in the individual. In short, by renouncing the intellectual replacement of desire, the narrator is able to revitalize an earlier, less aggressive sexuality that offers the rewards of self-satisfaction and confines itself to the sexually ambiguous yet ultimately safe male "youthfulness" of Hautboy. Such a commitment remains notably anti-intellectual and anti-linguistic, producing no synthesis of mind and body, only a retreat into an infantile sexuality. After all, the narrator's inability to penetrate Hautboy's "indifferent" facade suggests that mental understanding has become difficult if not impossible for the "shattered" poet because his retreat to a safely male, precoital world is simultaneously a retreat to the pre-linguistic "music" of childhood.

While the sketches consistently investigate the body's connection to happiness, they contain yet another vision of physical reality, one that further complicates the struggle between mind and body. We see it in a brief, experimental form in "The Happy Failure," where the "Great Hydraulic-Hydrostatic Apparatus for draining swamps," at first associated with the "sphinx-like blankness" that is Melville's code for inscrutable truth, becomes upon its failure a horrific techno-body, more curse than blessing: "Then seizing the whole box, he disemboweled it of all its anacondas and adders, and, tearing and wrenching them, flung them right and left over the water" (259). The unification of the technological, the corporeal, and the horrific introduces a vision perhaps only suggested by *Moby-Dick;* for even in the cetological and "trying-out" sections of that novel the three do not unite in an image that is at once a debunked mystery, a failure, and an industrial nightmare. It is clearly important that the blow delivered to this "evil" body, the body that only mimics flesh and falsely promises the psychological rewards of renewal, delivers the obsessed uncle and allows him his humanity once again in the form of his kindness to Yorpy, the mistreated slave. It may be more to the point that this compromising recovery of sanity and kindness results purely from a denial of the serpent-filled corporeal machine, the industrial body that has threatened to destroy the humanity of the grandfather.

Melville's most famous vision of the body-as-machine appears in the "Tartarus of Maids," whose presentation of an anatomical landscape and technological female body in the form of a mountain paper-mill has been widely examined and celebrated. However, what has remained largely unmentioned by those who agree that the "piston-like machine" (328) presided over by "Cupid" does in fact represent the gestating female is the clear connection of the seedsman not merely to Melville himself or to the male principle but more specifically to the writer, the creator-gestator of language.[8] In fact, the image of the paper-mill appears earlier in Melville's writing, at a happier, or at least more active and powerful, time in his life, and though he uses it then to express a heightened potency, an overabundance of ideas, the basic structure of the comparison is the same: "P.S. I can't stop yet. If the world was entirely made up of Magians, I'll tell you what I should do. I should have a paper-mill established at one end of the house, and so have an endless riband of foolscap rolling in upon my desk; and upon that endless riband I should write a thousand—a million—billion thoughts, all under the form of a letter to you."[9] Here the nightmare of female creation has not yet overwhelmed the dream of male potency, of the "endless riband" upon which Melville's creative powers achieve unchecked numbers. It is a vision in stark contrast to the seedsman's trip for "envelopes," for though his "seeds were distributed through all the Eastern and Northern States, and even fell into the far soil of Missouri and the Carolinas" (324), there is little of the sense of joyous overproduction and limitless power that the fantasy of the Hawthorne letter suggests. Nevertheless, the basic notion that the paper-mill is somehow tied to the source of inspiration for the writer, that its ability to produce is related to the writer's ability to write, obtains in both. The significant difference springs from the fact that Melville's attitude toward such production has changed radically since the elation of completing *Moby-Dick* and the receipt of Hawthorne's praise; the sense of male intellectual companionship and soul-joining that he felt with Hawthorne has either, as in the example of "The Paradise of Bachelors," soured into a parody of convivial impotence or, as in "The Tartarus of Maids," been overtaken by a vision of female production that is neither joyous nor healthy. Similarly, the threat of "female creativity" appears with force in "I and My Chimney," in which the schemes of the wife directly attack the potency and independence of the narrator, who is "insensibly stripped by degrees of one masculine prerogative after another" (362–63). Her plan to destroy the chimney in favor of an entrance hall as well as her suggestions that the narrator "should retire into some sort of monastery" suggest that her potency has shifted from simple sexual production to a post-sexual, antiphysical desire to rule the household. Though the chimney once warmed and hatched "her eggs" (360), she now revels in an attachment to the disembodied future, "spicily impatient of present and past," (361) in direct opposition to the narrator's attempt to find contentment in a devotion to the central hearth.

In this respect, the body as technological nightmare maintains a deep connection for Melville to the problems of writing both because such production may enslave its producers—as it does the women who run the machine—and because the machine's product, paper (babies), once again metaphorically ties the body of flesh to the body of words. What apparently makes the technological body horrific where it was once ecstatic is its inexorability: "But what made the thing I saw so specially terrible to me was the metallic necessity, the unbudging fatality which governed it" (333). The ineluctable need to write, the "metallic necessity" both of the writer's desire and of his need for money, does not, by this point in Melville's career, account for, nor will it stop for, the "pallid" physical and mental state of its operator. Like the "girls"—never married, always barren maids devoted to the machine's, rather than their own, children—the seedsman's body will continue to fail within the valley; only when he is safely past the forbidding "Black Notch" will he feel the pain in his numb, frostbitten cheeks. Within the realm of inexorable production, the flesh cannot last; the dream of the "endless riband of foolscap" becomes a nightmare of erotic and linguistic failure.

The dystopia of "The Tartarus of Maids" finds even fuller extension and expression in the tartarean pages of "The Encantadas." The breakdown and failure of the body, in terms of both the social formations on the islands and the landscape itself, reflect the increasing disintegration of physical reality and help move Melville's oeuvre significantly closer to the deceptive worlds of "Benito Cereno" and *The Confidence-Man*. In fact, the body in "The Encantadas," whether individual, social, or topographical, can be said to exist as do the islands themselves, in a state of "enchantment," wrapped in the potentially deceptive and corrupting contours of a fragmenting and fragmented language. As a result, it functions, in conjunction with the landscape, as a disjuncted, unreliable signifier, just as language reinforces the gap between the unmoored landscape and the systems by which humanity attempts to understand it.

With his opening epigrammatic quotation, Melville initiates us into the nature of the world he is about to present. The description of "The Wandering Islands" stresses the danger involved in planting one's foot on land not firmly joined to the rest of the world, for the experience of a physical reality deceptive in its very foundation forever undermines one's certainty in the appearance of things. Thus landing on the Wandering Islands is, in essence, an initiatory experience, an introduction to the existence of duplicity and epistemological doubt that forever undermines the innocence of the seeker. "The Encantadas," both as sketches and as islands, therefore represent the experience of metaphysical doubt consequent upon one's discovery of illusion and deception. They embody a world that is both dead and strangely alive, present and absent, thoroughly palpable and disarmingly evanescent.

The first sketch, "The Isles at Large," with its titular pun that suggests both a survey of the group and the disturbing movement and dislocation of the land, serves to initiate us into the unreliability of the physical world. The sea that surrounds the islands holds "conflicting currents which eddy through nearly all the wide channels of the entire group" while the wind is "light, baffling, and every way unreliable, . . . given to perplexing calms" (127). Likewise, the islands themselves, because of the confusion caused by these irregular currents and winds, have given some to believe in the "apparent fleetingness and unreality" of their location

(128). On the other hand, the land itself seems transformed into a world sterile in its basic components, a body blasted and wizened, oddly transformed into a living lifelessness: "However wavering their place may seem by reason of the currents, they themselves, at least to one upon the shore, appear invariably the same: fixed, cast, glued into the very body of cadaverous death" (128). The stasis suggested by such a description is quickly underscored by its contrast with "July and August among the Adirondack Mountains" (129) and by its association with the Galapagos tortoise, "not more frightful than grotesque" (128), which quickly comes to represent the body's infernal existence in such a world. Said to be the "transformed" bodies of "all wicked sea-officers, more especially commodores and captains" (128), the turtle is associated with a sterile exile, "lasting sorrow and penal hopelessness" (129), and, in the narrator's subsequent dream, death itself.

Perhaps more significant, however, is the turtle's function in Sketch Second, in which it becomes an example of "Dame Nature's" "defects," one of the "dreadfull portraicts of deformittee" (130) that offers a strangely impenetrable appearance coupled with an antediluvian nature that strengthens its otherworldly quality. Thus "they seemed newly crawled forth from beneath the foundations of the world" and yet "hardly of the seed of earth" (131). Likewise, they represent both the failure of power— "three Roman Coliseums in magnificent decay" (131)—and, more important, the failure of a vision (perhaps attributable to commodores and captains) that forbids diversion, deception, or any sort of digressive path in the confrontation of the world: "Their crowning curse is their drudging impulse to straight-forwardness in a belittered world" (132). Nevertheless, the difference between that which they "seem" to figure forth and that which they truly are remains important to the narrator and to the sketch's interest in physical deception. Melville underlines this "seemingness" by ending the sketch with the juxtaposition of the narrator's dream of "the universal cope" against his admission that the next day "strange to say, [he] sat down with [his] shipmates, and made a merry repast from tortoise steaks and tortoise stews" (132–33). In other words, the physical experience of eating still suggests a form of knowledge that remains reliable, even if the general character of the tortoises and the islands "at large" suggest unreality and inscrutability.

Not only are the tortoises examples of the physical oddity and incongruity of the island's environment, but the majority of the fauna that inhabit these sketches also show some sort of deceptive attribute. For instance, the penguins' bodies "are grotesquely misshapen; their bills short; their feet seemingly legless; while the members at their sides are neither fin, wing, nor arm. And truly neither fish, flesh, nor fowl is the penguin; . . . " (135). The difficulty in defining the penguin's shape flows from its resistance to known categories; thus the narrator attempts to understand it primarily by negative definition, noting how it fails to embody one or another of the established formal patterns of the animal world. This resistance to definition coincides with the isles' similar recalcitrance in the face of human attempts to understand and categorize or map and capture position, inhabitants, or meaning. While not maliciously deceptive, the penguins participate in the oddity of "The Encantadas" and thereby add to the foreboding sense that in this world outer surface does not necessarily indicate inner substance, that form retains the potential to mislead.

Similarly, the human presence on the islands demonstrates both physical decay and the failure of the body to fulfill itself in a world hostile to physical existence and hospitable to the unscrupulous acts of corrupt politics. Perhaps the best-known example of familial breakdown occurs in Sketch Eighth, "Norfolk Isle and the Chola Widow," in which the title character is stranded after her brother and husband die in the surf: "the ill-made catamaran was overset, and came all to pieces; when, dashed by broad-chested swells between their broken logs and the sharp teeth of the reef, both adventurers perished before Hunilla's eyes" (154). The manner in which the raft "came all to pieces" reflects the fact that the social group in question likewise fragments at this moment. Hunilla's position, seated on "a lofty cliff, a little back from the beach" (154), figures forth her isolation and the now metaphysical distance between her and her family. After her husband's body has washed up on the beach, her embrace of the corpse is, once again, a negative, unproductive coupling in which flesh fails to communicate to the spiritually absent other. The "encirclingly outstretched" arm, both ironic and pathetic, the speechlessly locked jaw, and the bridegroom clasp of the "lover-husband" (154) all provide us with the sickening knowledge of human separation. The body, in other words, fails both because nature is malignant and because the limits of physical reality are heightened in a world that continually breaks apart.

If nature conspires against the fruitful embrace, then humans themselves, especially the social outcasts attracted to the sparsely inhabited islands, frequently promote their own separations through deceptive activities and self-centered perspectives. For instance, Oberlus of Sketch Ninth, "Hood's Isle and the Hermit Oberlus," represents both the island world's blighted physical reality and the landscape's accompanying treacherousness. His own body appears to be "the victim of some malignant sorceress; . . . beast-like; . . . nose flat; countenance contorted, heavy, earthy;

hair and beard unshorn, profuse, and of a fiery red" (163). Physical reality in this case does indicate an inner malady, and yet Oberlus's propensity for deception, his desire "to prove his potency" (165) by seizing and enslaving sailors, is not readily evident from this description. Instead he appears trapped and penalized within a typically Melvillean psychodrama: the curse of the powerful mother is responsible for his sexual and physical distortion, and the absence of a father intensifies his longing for power at the same time that it increases his sense of isolation and epistemological anguish.

Despite his "ursine suavity" (166) and initial failure to capture the negro sailor, Oberlus does succeed in snaring a functional body politic over which to rule, but only after reaching an understanding of the power of duplicity: "Warned by his former failure in kidnapping strangers, he now pursues a quite different plan. When seamen come ashore, he makes up to them like a free-and-easy comrade, invites them to his hut, and with whatever affability his red-haired grimness may assume, entreats them to drink his liquor and be merry" (166).

As though in parody of the political process, Melville offers a model of the tricky campaigner, plying the voters with drink only to enslave them and proclaim himself "Emperor Oberlus" (167). It forms an echo of sorts to Sketch Seventh, "Charles's Isle and the Dog-King," in which the Creole establishes himself as ruler of the island but protects himself from his unruly subjects by employing a "body-guard of dogs" (148). More important, he too lures sailors away from their ships and incorporates them into the island population, suggesting that the politics of the islands, in echo of the instability of their enchanted world, reflect the distance between appearance and reality and specifically emphasize the potentially hazardous results of both natural and man-made deceit.

"The Encantadas" ends with a sketch ("Runaways, Castaways, Solitaries, Grave-Stones, Etc.") that surveys the fragmented physical and social remains existing among the islands. Thus we read of a man, "lost upon the Isle of Narborough," who was "brought to such extremes by thirst, that at last he only saved his life by taking that of another being" (171). He kills "a large hair-seal" and "throwing himself upon the panting body quaffed at the living wound; the palpitations of the creature's dying heart injecting life into the drinker" (171). That this sort of embrace, vampiric and primal as it is, is the only sort of physical connection made in this world becomes clear from the sketch's subsequent examples of broken relics and remnants of other attempts at survival as well as its final image of graves and gravestones left by the those who have piteously failed to keep the body alive.

"Try a *Section* of It—That Will Do Just as Well"

As a primarily disjunctive world, "The Encantadas," in conjunction with Melville's other tales, consistently turns away from metaphysical questing toward linguistic failure or deception. The language of Ahab and Pierre, having by this time failed to produce the physical response of the inscrutable, devolves in these stories into variations of duplicity and silence even as the stories continue to warn of the dangers of such a language. The loss of faith in the power of words to discover hidden truths extends itself into a condemnation of linguistic illusion that is, at the same time, a self-punishing attempt to reveal the deceptiveness of all language.

Both "Cock-A-Doodle-Doo!" and "Poor Man's Pudding and Rich Man's Crumbs" deal specifically with the disastrous physical consequences of too great a belief in the powers of language to transform. Ahab's Faustian utterance of the baptismal "blessing," with its clear belief that the words themselves evoke the devil in place of the trinity, fails to apply either to the "triumphant thanksgiving of a cock crow!" (271) or to the benignly harmful "poet" Blandmour's mouthing of romantic sentiment. In each case the magic of language, indeed the capacity for magic in the very worlds of the stories, has disappeared, lost perhaps with Pierre's final curse and not to appear again until Billy Budd's ascension.

This loss extends even more profoundly to "The Tartarus of Maids" where not only is the seedsman, a figurative maker of language, given a glimpse of the "blankness" of industrial rhetoric—"Yours is a most wonderful factory. Your great machine is a miracle of inscrutable intricacy" (334)—but more specifically the language of love, itself constructed primarily of willing self-delusion, comes under ironic scrutiny: "More tragical and more inscrutably mysterious than any mystic sight, human or machine, throughout the factory, was the strange innocence of cruel-heartedness in this usage-hardened boy" (331). The "usage-hardened boy" is, of course, "Cupid," the ironically presented voice and figure of love, and it is precisely the mixture in him of innocence and cruelty, the unconscious potential for harm that Melville asserts. The "cruel-heartedness" of which the seedsman speaks shows itself in Cupid's "pure ignorant drollery" (331) and flippant language in the face of the debilitating conditions of the factory. In other words, in this story, the poetic trappings of love, its language, rather than love itself, are blind.

Of all the tales (excluding for the moment "Benito Cereno") "The Encantadas" shows the clearest commitment to an investigation of a world in which language, like the landscape of the islands themselves, fails to maintain a firm connection between signifier and signified, fails, in other words, to participate in a system of reference that is reliable and free of misdirection and deception. In fact, language within the sketches has two apparent functions or modes of being: it exists either as part of the islands' otherworldly unreliability ("enchantment"-as-illusion) or as a powerful force akin to prophecy and curse ("enchantment"-as-malediction). In subordination to these two categories, it sometimes becomes the negative form of a productive, communicative medium—as reptilian hiss, avian cry, or disjuncted, forlorn human attempt to contact and reconnect fragmented society.

The language of nature is the narrator's first concern in outlining the islands' receptiveness to the newly landed. As evidence of their "emphatic uninhabitableness" (126), he notes that "no voice, no low, no howl is heard; the chief sound of life here is a hiss" (127) and cites in the process the familiar voices of a pastoral nature (human, bovine, canine) in order to contrast them to the reptilian language of the fallen landscape. Likewise, he registers the "screaming flights of unearthly birds heightening the dismal din" (127), as though to emphasize the unceasing presence of a noise that threatens to produce chaos through its dissonance and alterity. Most significantly, nature's hostile "speech" functions as part of the overall depiction of the landscape as cursed, a world that is at once the victim of malediction and the locus of linguistic failure. The notion of a "spellbound" world (128), a landscape caught in the constricting folds of a prophetic language, suggests that language, while clearly impotent in terms of human connection and social formation, may in fact maintain a degree of power unseen in Melville's work since *Moby-Dick*. And yet, it is equally significant that this power flows from neither the productive speech of Ishmael nor the reductive, questing language of Ahab; instead, such an ability to damn resurrects the spectral world of Fedallah and his ensnaring utterances of prophetic trickery. In fact, to extend the parallel, it is even possible to suggest that "The Encantadas" gives us an equivalent in landscape to the very condition of Ahab himself: sexually blighted, uncommunicative, and, most important, "enchanted" by his own monomania and the gnomic speech of the Parsee.

The enticing whispers of Fedallah thus find some degree of echo in the language we encounter throughout the sketches. Perhaps the first example of the disjunction between word and thing comes in Sketch First in the description of the islands' history of geographical "movement." As the narrator notes, mariners once thought "that there existed two distinct clusters of isles in the parallel of the Encantadas," probably because of "the difference in the reckonings of navigators produced" by tricky tides and shifting winds (128). In other words, the science of navigation, itself a referential system similar to language, has failed to assure the accuracy and solidity of the connection between its own signs and the reality it is purportedly describing. A similar example is given in Sketch Fourth, in which "Cowley's Enchanted Isle" is said to have appeared in a variety of positions on the compass and in a variety of shapes to those who first recorded an encounter with it. Furthermore, the narrator goes on to equate this "self-transforming and bemocking isle" with both the pirate Cowley and the similarly named "self-upbraiding" poet, noting that "that sort of thing evinced in the naming of this isle runs in the blood, and may be seen in pirates as in poets" (142). In short, the deceptiveness of reality, of language, and of human behavior spring, it seems, from a similar source, each evidence of the epistemological difficulty inherent in the world of the sketches.

Still other, more treacherous examples of deceptive language exist among the socially disjuncted islands. At the end of Sketch Seventh, for example, the narrator relates an episode that occurred off Charles's Isle, in which the lookout of the ship on which he served spotted a light coming from the shore. The contrast between the captain's knowledgeable interpretation and the gullible reaction of the third mate serves to emphasize the need to recognize potential deception. The signal, if the captain is correct, is of course a lure, a sign that purportedly asks for help but whose true referent is death or imprisonment. It is an inversion of another such displaced sign, the promise given by the Frenchman to return for Hunilla. In each case, the language openly proffers a sign of connection, of consummation of the social bond, only to hide the deepest treachery, a betrayal that lies at the heart of the story's world and that is responsible in some respects both for the islands' damnation and for the fragmented character of the physical, social, and textual reality the reader encounters.

The language of deception and fragmentation also appears on the formal level in the tales. If "Benito Cereno" and *The Confidence-Man* give us Melville's most complete look at all levels of textual deception and fragmentation, then the smaller tales that surround these works reveal an increasing tendency to experiment with the fragment as a formal and symbolic problem. Among the stories, the most obviously unique in form are "The Encantadas" and the series of so-called diptychs: "Poor Man's Pudding and Rich Man's Crumbs," "The Two Temples," and "The Paradise of Bachelors and the Tartarus of Maids." "The Encantadas," a series of "views" or sketches, clearly functions as a travelogue that both echoes Melville's earlier, factually based novels and foreshadows his 1857–59 lectures, "Traveling" and "The South Seas." Perhaps of more significance, however, is that the poetic epigraphs drawn from Spenser, Thomas Chatterton, William Collins, and Beaumont and Fletcher have generic as well as thematic connections to the text. For instance, the largely imagistic character of the sketches, their tendency, as in Sketches Second and Third most obviously, to structure themselves around the presentation and exploration of a single picture, suggests a lyric mode of observation and meditation that Melville had practiced before in his novels but that he now appears to elevate to the status of method.[10] Even the openly narrative sketches such as "Norfolk Isle and The Chola Widow" appear to participate in the intense, and perhaps more sentimental, patterns of the poetic ballad—the concentrated, imagistically told tale of suffering—than does anything Melville had hitherto written: "The panel of the days was deeply worn, the long tenth notches half effaced, as alphabets of the blind. Ten thousand times the longing widow had traced her finger over the bamboo; dull flute, which played on, gave no sound; as if counting birds flown by in air, would hasten tortoises creeping through the woods" (157). Here is a prose narrative language only a step away from the verse of its epigraph:

"Black his eye as the midnight sky,
White his neck as the driven snow,
Red his cheek as the morning light;—
Cold he lies in the ground below." (151)

Only the rhythm of the verse separates these two indirect descriptions of emotion; each evokes a complex of feelings and a perhaps excessive degree of pathos by listing details that in themselves project psychological and emotional descriptions of character.[11] Admittedly, this method is never alien to prose, but in this particular instance the concentration of the sketches as well as their visual and balladic feeling seems to emphasize Melville's increasing poeticism and his employment of tighter forms. In fact, we might consider the possibility that Melville's generic method in "The Encantadas," in both the narrative and the descriptive sections, is only minimally different from that he will later employ in *Battle Pieces* in such narratives as "The Scout Toward Aldie" and such lyrics as "Shiloh."

The diptychs too, for all their generic inventiveness, appear to echo, if not extend, a form more important to the history of the lyric poem than to the short story. We know, for instance, that Melville knew and quoted from Milton's early ode-like companion poems, "L'Allegro" and "Il Penseroso."[12] However, to note the apparent likeness of these exercise poems to Melville's similarly structured two-part sketches is not to suggest that

the poems are sources, generic or otherwise, for the stories but rather to
direct attention to the presence of a generically "poetic" predecessor to
the dualistic form. Whether we call these stories companion pieces, after
lyric poetry, or diptychs, after sacred painting, it is clear that our attempts
to describe their form may help us understand them more clearly as participating in a visual, concentrated, static genre, meant to reflect off and
form a dialectic between opposing "points of view" or opposing objects
in view. Theirs is a form that owes more to imagistic juxtaposition and
reader-responsive dialectic than to pure narrative and has more in common with the abrupt mosaicism of lyric poetry than with the linear constructions of prose fiction. Admittedly the overall condensation of genre
in this period of Melville's writing takes place gradually, and such creeping poetic formalism appears unevenly throughout the tales. Nevertheless
its presence is undeniable even in such a "story" as "Jimmy Rose," in
which Melville unexpectedly and innovatively employs, in what is otherwise a diluted character sketch, a balladic refrain.

Though the formal question of exactly why Melville gradually quit
writing longer prose narratives must remain the subject of speculation,
we can be sure that writing and the difficulties and possible failures of
composition—as well as issues of genre—persistently maintain a place in
his mind during this period. For instance, not only does "Bartleby" demonstrate its well-known connection to the problems of inspiration and
creative desire, but a number of the other stories have likewise been read
as at least partially commenting on the struggle to produce successful
texts. "The Happy Failure," "The Fiddler," and perhaps "The Paradise
of Bachelors and the Tartarus of Maids" all participate in that strain of
Melville's fiction making that seems unable to write without internally
commenting upon the process itself. The presence of such internal maps
has long provided critics with tantalizing models for the books in which
they appear, and the short fiction seems to have its own share of hidden
mirrors. Even such a sketch as "The Happy Failure," which possesses no
purely textual model, can be seen to comment on the writer's task in
general and perhaps on the benefits of generic shifting as well: "Do, do
now, dear uncle—here, here, put these pieces together; or, if that can't
be done without more tools, try a *section* of it—that will do just as well.
Try it once; try, uncle" (260).

The uncle of this passage is the mildly monomaniacal inventor of "a
huge, shabby, oblong box, hermetically sealed" (254), which he calls his
"Great Hydraulic-Hydrostatic Apparatus for draining swamps"; his test
of the device—over which he has labored for ten years, approximately the
same amount of time Melville himself had been writing—proves a com-

plete failure. The nephew, at this moment clearly the voice of calm against the uncle's despair, suggests a briefer scope to the project, an admission of limitation, and encourages a turn to smaller tasks. The story can be and has been read as a commentary on Melville's famous statements in letters to Hawthorne concerning writing and failure, but this particular passage hints at a more specific notion of the possibilities for one who may have perceived himself to have had trouble "putting the pieces together" because he lacked "more tools."[13] In fact, it is possible to see the uncle and the nephew as different parts of a single self: one determined and over-ambitious, the other more reserved, a voice of artistic compromise. In this respect, "The Happy Failure," with its message that happiness comes from freeing oneself from obsession, may in fact parallel Melville's own sense of his situation in the aftermath of *Pierre*. It is ultimately the nephew's advice "to try a *section* of it," to move toward smaller, more focused forms, that he appears to have followed.

Finally, with the increasing interest in the aesthetics of fragmentation and the benefits and pitfalls of deceptive language, Melville's work of the late 1850s moves by means of an investigation of Ahabian desire and physical unfulfillment into perhaps its darkest stages. Throughout the tales, there is an increasing sense of mingled frustration and surrender, as though the final utterance of the supremely tortured and immured Pierre had unraveled into the series of small investigations of failure that this period contains. The space between the blithe miscues of *Israel Potter* and the infernal separation and criminal malice contained in "The Encantadas" is filled with half-starts and stops, characters who give up or hold out weakly against disintegration, as well as authorial attempts to shrink the space of thought, to miniaturize, control, and so understand such half-living characters and their worlds. It is an investigation of life perhaps as broken as the reality it attempts to depict, and it prepares the way for the inverted realities of "Benito Cereno" and *The Confidence-Man*.

5

INVERTED WORLDS
"Benito Cereno" and *The Confidence-Man*

BEYOND THE INITIAL fragmentation of *Israel Potter* and the short fiction, the trajectory of Ahabian desire and language after *Moby-Dick* continues to increase both the level of its metaphysical frustration and its tendency to convert and invert language into an agent of deceit. Melville increases his interest in the ways in which his characters fail to communicate as well as the manner by which language itself ensnares those who fail to account for its potential duplicity. For example, in "Benito Cereno," his most thorough investigation among the short stories of linguistic trickery, Melville presents a world more intensely duplicitous than any offered in "The Encantadas" while placing within its bounds as potential reader one of the least cautious characters in his oeuvre. Yet such an inverted world, a textual construction in which even the reader is deceived, only prepares the way for the metaphysical vacuity and linguistic maziness of *The Confidence-Man*, itself the last major incarnation of Melville's reversed realities; for it presents a universe in which even the figure of Christ, forlorn and silent in the pages of "Bartleby," becomes a potential trickster, a mute con artist preaching with dubious tone the virtues of "confidence." That this resonant term, omnipresent on the pages of its dizzying book, is itself employed with dark irony alerts us to the April Fool's world to which Melville and his seekers have come. No longer hoping to grasp and embrace the contours of a distant meaning, they now search only to seduce and destroy.

The Master's Deception

The psychological and physical hazards of bodily ignorance find their most complete examination among the shorter tales in "Benito Cereno," the powerful narrative in which the "innocent" Captain Delano's refusal to acknowledge darkness, both in sexuality and behavior, nearly costs him his life. The contrast upon which the story plays between Delano's figural blindness and the very real potency and physical threat of Babo and his slave crew appears early in the metaphorical opposition of the "white noddy, a strange fowl, so called from its lethargic, somnambulistic character, being frequently caught by hand at sea" and "a dark satyr in a mask, holding his foot on the prostrate neck of a writhing figure, likewise masked."[1] That the first stands for Delano is hard to doubt; the second, however, remains ambiguous. While it is tempting to consider the dominating satyr as Babo, the carving nevertheless constitutes part of the heraldic device of the ship's and slaves' owners, and so the meaning of the device must be more general. Instead of an individual metaphorical counterpart to Delano's "white noddy" benevolence, we see a wider representation of domination embodied in masked figures that suggest, despite their opposition, the sort of ambiguous symbiosis that inheres in patterns of domination and submission. As in all such relationships, it is difficult to distinguish master from slave, good from evil, because the two are, within the complicated matrix of the relationship, one.[2]

In this respect it becomes clear that Babo and Benito Cereno form a deeper, more powerful riddle than Delano can begin to solve. Babo, a slave who becomes a master, also becomes during the story the substitute for Benito Cereno's diseased and traumatized body; the two, in effect, produce one duplicitous figure, upon which the existence of each clearly depends. Frequently described as Benito's "body servant," Babo, within the context of the story and within the psychological context of their inverted relationship, physically blurs with Benito—"Sometimes the negro gave his master his arm" (52)—and becomes the captain's voice by telling Benito what to say and at times speaking for him. Admittedly, this unification occurs within the context of the deception, but there is a sense in which the deception, like the very masquerade upon which slavery originally depends, becomes at least as real for the players as the "truth." Thus Benito's final inability to recover from his experience, his avowal that "the negro" casts his shadow over him, further suggests that the separation of Babo and Benito is primarily the cause of Benito's soulsickness. Apart, not only does Benito lose even the semblance of bodily potency—"And that silver-mounted sword, apparent symbol of despotic command, was not, indeed, a sword, but the ghost of one. The scabbard, artificially stiffened, was empty" (116)—but both effectively lose their voices, unable or unwilling to speak without the other. Even in death they are, in a sense, united:

> Some months after, dragged to the gibbet at the tail of a mule, the black met his voiceless end. The body was burned to ashes; but for many days, the head, that hive of subtlety, fixed on a pole in the Plaza, met, unabashed, the

gaze of the whites; and across the Plaza looked towards St. Bartholomew's church, in whose vaults slept then, as now, the recovered bones of Aranda; and across the Rimac bridge looked towards the monastery, on Mount Agonia without; where, three months after being dismissed by the court, Benito Cereno, did, indeed, follow his leader. (116–17)

The destruction of Babo's body, minus the head, hints perhaps at the deeper sexual fear that the slave has been able to evoke in the Spaniards. Even more significantly, however, is the ambiguity of the final sentence, in which it impossible to say whether Benito Cereno is "following" Aranda, his ostensible "leader," or Babo, his once master and slave.[3]

Given the complexity of this psychological knot, it is little wonder that the "singularly undistrustful good nature" (47) of Captain Delano is unable to penetrate the scene that greets him aboard the *San Dominick*. It is also clear that the sort of charitable benevolence that characterizes Delano does in fact result, at least partially, from his presence on a ship called *The Bachelor's Delight* and from his own probable bachelorhood. In other words, like the Templars of "The Paradise of Bachelors" and the narrator of "Bartleby," Delano participates in a line of Melvillean characters who have lived lives sheltered from both evil and sexuality;[4] such characters frequently remain, in fact, what they often dream of being—happily innocent boys: "What, I, Amasa Delano—Jack of the Beach, as they called me when a lad— . . . I, little Jack of the Beach, that used to go berrying with cousin Nat and the rest; I to be murdered here at the ends of the earth, on board a haunted pirate-ship by a horrible Spaniard?—Too nonsensical to think of! Who would murder Amasa Delano? His conscience is clean. There is some one above. Fie, fie, Jack of the Beach! you are a child indeed; a child of the second childhood, old boy; you are beginning to dote and drule, I'm afraid" (77). This figural moment of regression not only reveals a simplistic theology in which the "some one above" sees to it that only the "bad" are murdered but also indirectly pronounces more truth concerning Delano's character than he himself is aware. The insistent repetition of his boyhood nickname, with the addition of "little" in two instances, gives a momentary glimpse of his secretly innocent self, while the final words of the passage unknowingly pronounce the truth even as they unconsciously attempt—by invocation—to suppress it.

That sexual innocence should coincide with innocence of evil in Melville's work should be no surprise to those familiar with his series of sexually wounded questers whose adoption of, or flirtation with, darkness coincides with their introduction to sexuality. As the early books frequently deal with just such encounters and their results, so do the tales, especially "Benito Cereno," attempt to show the results of avoiding such contact with the lower stratum. In this respect, Delano's blindness and impotence clearly extend to his vision of the body while on the *San Dominick:*

> His attention had been drawn to a slumbering negress, partly disclosed through the lace-work of some rigging, lying, with youthful limbs carelessly disposed, under the lee of the bulwarks, like a doe in the shade of a woodland rock. Sprawling at her lapped breasts was her wide-awake fawn, stark naked, its black little body half lifted from the deck, crosswise with its dam's; its hands, like two paws, clambering upon her; its mouth and nose ineffectually rooting to get at the mark; and meantime giving a vexatious half-grunt, blending with the composed snore of the negress. (73)

As a counterpart to the "Grand Armada" chapter of *Moby-Dick,* this moment reveals a number of contrasts to Ishmael's resurrective, fully integrated vision of death-in-life.[5] While the "maternal circles" in which the whales mother their young project a similar warmth and beneficence, they are nevertheless perilously surrounded by palpable dangers of which Ishmael is fully aware. Delano, on the other hand, in a remarkably similar situation, remains completely oblivious to the death that surrounds his observation of the primal moment of infantile sexuality and, as a result, his response—"There's naked nature, now; pure tenderness and love, thought Captain Delano, well pleased" (73)—while accurate in sentiment, nevertheless reveals his own basic innocence of the darker aspects of bodily reality. Having failed to encounter death, he remains incapable of comprehending its reality until it is almost too late: not until he sees the "dagger" in Babo's "snakishly writhing" (99) hand do the "scales drop from his eyes." In short, only the violent gesture of the "body servant" against "the heart of his master," a negative version of Christ's healing touch, can perform the "miracle" of allowing him some degree of vision. Yet, probably because he merely watches rather than participates in this experience, his initiation into the lower stratum proves short lived, for he remains unable to fathom Cereno's melancholy and boyishly cites "the blue sea, and the blue sky" (116) as cures for the doomed Spaniard's "shadow."

In addition to its basic investigation of the relationship between master and slave and the problem of evil, "Benito Cereno" also has the most to say of any of the short fiction about the deceptiveness of both word and fact. Not only is the basic mechanism of the story built around the deception of Delano and the reader, but the language of slavery and the resultant silence of the enslaved also play a significant role in the story's duplicitous technique. After all, slavery's language entails more than simply Delano's condescending vision of the slave as "shepherd's dog" (51); it concerns the ways in which speech, via pointed ironies, is able to cripple and ultimately silence the voices of the enslaved.[6] Such ironies depend upon a shared secret between master and slave, a secret that the one in power wishes to conceal in order to consolidate strength but that the one enslaved wishes to tell in order to deprive his dominator of that power. The pole of tension is the uninitiated, "innocent" outsider for whose acceptance each party struggles. Thus the secret that the master and the mastered ultimately share—and that Melville here attempts to reveal—is the understanding, conscious or unconscious, that there is no basis for one person's domination of another except the possession of power. In "Benito Cereno" Melville helps us to understand this aspect of domination by inverting the typical order; the facts that Babo and Benito alternately attempt to conceal or reveal illuminate the structure of mastery in which the terms "master" and "slave" are revealed to be only place-markers for "powerful" and "powerless." In this respect "Benito Cereno" is ultimately more than a story about slavery in America; it is an examination of all slaveries, whether racial, political, or psychological.

The linguistic result of this structure appears in the contrasting voices of slave and master: the first strives to seduce the outsider into belief while the second hopes by meaningful silence to initiate in the reader a critical vision of the master's voice. For instance, the doubleness of Babo's speech, in which each utterance reveals and conceals its true meaning, functions to deceive and convince Delano and, at the same time, to reassert Babo's mastery over Benito. Likewise Benito's responses are prompted by Babo's commands, for the one "enslaved" can only speak, if at all, with the voice of the master: "But it is Babo here to whom, under God, I owe not only my own preservation, but likewise to him, chiefly, the merit is due, of pacifying his more ignorant brethren, when at intervals tempted to murmurings" (57). The doubleness of this speech remains largely powerless, for though it is similar to Babo's in irony, it is forced to produce that irony within the context of the master's created drama. Benito Cereno has no voice of his own; only in silence, by the look in his eyes, does he speak for himself.

That Babo succeeds in seducing Delano is evident not only from the story's action but also from the extortion from Benito of the Faustian signature: the admission of confidence or faith that consummates the relationship between master and slave, seducer and seduced:

> It was a moment or two before the Spaniard sufficiently recovered himself to reply; which he did, at last, with cold constraint:—"Yes, Señor, I have trust in Babo."

> Here Babo, changing his previous grin of mere animal humor into an intelligent smile, not ungratefully eyed his master. (67)

The "intelligent smile" is meant not only to unmask the seemingly "animal" Babo but also to signal the reward of his successful entrapment of Delano. He now, in fact, possesses two slaves and maintains that possession almost exclusively by linguistic means.

Babo's control over Benito's voice seems also to extend to Benito's body, which, whether because of fear or because of a kind of physical impotence, will not allow Benito to exceed the linguistic limits set by Babo's drama. This physical barrier to speech, usually a cough, suggests that the enslaved body, like the enslaved voice, becomes impotently the property of another—that, in fact, the body of the master subsumes the slave's body, becomes it in a way that furthers the possibility of a union between the two. The body that fears its own destruction may not be capable of overcoming that fear, just as the body that has become corrupted through its own previous role as master may not now be able to overcome its new role as slave, even though it is to some extent its own creation.

Finally the consistent presence of such physical debility and disease in the short tales of the 1850s both underscores the perception of Melville's weakened novel-making power and strengthens its connection to the systemic ailment of the body in this section of his oeuvre. Even more significant, language itself, beginning with its starvation in "Bartleby" and extending to its manifestation as cough in "Benito Cereno," appears equally infected with a germ that threatens its disintegration and silence. If Pierre and Ahab finally employ a linguistic substitute for the denied body, then the short tales note both the sickness of that body and the consequent debility of a language that attempts to understand either physical or metaphysical reality. What remains, therefore, what survives the double-death of master and slave at the end of "Benito Cereno," is the language of appearance, a syntax of surfaces. The speech into which Babo is forced by the binding relationship of master and slave becomes the speech of *The Confidence-Man*, and at the same time the diseased body of Benito Cereno, consumed by the engine of its own making, populates the decks of the *Fidèle*, participating once again in the drama of seduction.

Talking Wounded

The revision of form that occurs in Melville's work of the late 1850s, his turn to more controlled or controllable tasks, continues in his ninth novel, *The Confidence-Man*. Largely a set of variations on the theme of social faith, this compilation of conversations and tales presents a remarkably fictive world which, like *Pierre*'s Saddle Meadows, both senses and plays upon its existence as fiction. Unlike *Pierre*, however, the later novel toys with the relative deceptiveness of its characters, presenting as part of its fabric the misleading narratives these characters concoct as they attempt to convince their victims within the book and us as readers to believe in them. This repetition of the pattern of seduction—the attempt to consummate a relationship via the convincing or evocative power of language—becomes one of the book's basic structural components and indicates Melville's continued pursuit of large-scale structural fragmentation and the attenuations of Ahabian desire. Though the metaphysical pursuit finds its highest expression in the final pages of *Moby-Dick*, it is after *Pierre*, the short fiction, and especially "Benito Cereno" that such a search is reduced to an impotent and paradoxical desire to elicit and destroy "confidence" wherever it is located. No longer can the metaphysical quester hope to seduce the inscrutable into physical revelation; at best he can employ his now purely linguistic body in repeated, false rehearsals of the divine seductions he once attempted.

Coupled with the confidence-man's fictive reality, we find here both an impalpable "landscape" or physical setting and a body that is presented either as a misleading mask or as evidence of the broken and diseased world that reflects the quester's inner condition. Thus the deceptive and fragmented form of the novel finds its reflection in the deceptive and fragmented bodies aboard the *Fidèle*, while the book as a whole projects the failure of social and linguistic faith even as it attempts to seduce its readers into a confidence in its own constructions. In this respect, rather than presenting a reducible allegory of satanic soul-takings, *The Confidence-Man* reveals itself to be a book about the seduction of faith in a fictive world of bodily and linguistic decay.[7]

The world of the *Fidèle* shares with sections of *Pierre* the distinction of being among Melville's most completely fictive "landscapes." Each, despite various claims to the negative, presents a world in which the physical body that had been so much the center of books like *Moby-Dick* and even *Israel Potter* no longer exists in substance as flesh. Instead, the *prima materia* of these worlds, their foundation and irreducible matter, is the "stuff" of words, of writing and talking, of textuality and fiction. From the book's first sentence, in which the man "in cream colors" appears "suddenly as Manco Capac at the lake Titicaca," we realize that the setting of this novel of appearances and disappearances is of little concern to Melville.[8] Very few words are spent on description of anything other

than the superficial trappings of the various passengers and those few
details of the ship needed to give each dialogue the semblance of a location.[9] In fact, the first attempt to describe the landscape places us more
in the realm of distant legend—"The great ship-canal of Ving-King-
Ching, in the Flowery Kingdom" (8)—than it does on the currents of
the Mississippi. Similarly, the other brief visions of the shore or river waters are equally evanescent, as though all background for the book's voices
is seen through gauze or partially intuited by a nearsighted eye. Physical
scenery passes in a blur, either "rapidly shooting" or "seen dimly" (8),
and only the shapes of amorphous "crowds," "bluffs," and "shot-towers"
(8), the largest units of descriptive cognizance, present themselves to the
narrative vision.

The other "major" descriptive passages of the landscape similarly stress
the unreality rather than the concreteness of this book's world. Both in
their generality and in their figurative connections to the fictive, such
"settings" offer us a consistently twilit universe regardless of the ostensible time of day: "The sky slides into blue, the bluffs into bloom; the
rapid Mississippi expands; runs sparkling and gurgling, all over in eddies;
one magnified wake of a seventy-four. The sun comes out, a golden huz-
zar, from his tent, flashing his helm on the world. All things, warmed in
a landscape, leap. Speeds the daedal boat as a dream" (77). This sparkle
and gurgle is the most Melville gives us of the water, once so significant and powerful an element in his books' worlds, while the land, always
problematic and important in his earlier works, here simply "slides" by as
though exhibited under glass. No colors appear except the sun's gold;
what "things" it warms into leaping we have no way of knowing or seeing. Only the final sentence confirms what we have been too long sus-
pecting: that this book is in fact, like the speeding boat, a construct, a
"daedel" mechanism moving through the blurred figures of a dreamed
world.

If the world in *The Confidence-Man* begins to betray its fictiveness by
means of its impalpability, however, then the individual body reveals its
own deceptive nature through the repeated appearance of diseased or
crippled characters. Of those aboard the *Fidèle* who appear either sick or
wounded, there are two primary groups: first, an assortment of passengers
who either participate in the presentation of a society in decay or bear
the marks of previous seductions; and second, those confidence-men who
bear "false" wounds in order to deceive.[10]

Of the passengers, those who are both diseased and gullible, whose
physical suffering forces them into strained acts of faith, serve as objects
of prey and scorn to the confidence-man even as they remind us that the

Fidèle's humanity tends toward spiritual and physical failure. They carry the disease that often seems to inhabit the very air, a "Cairo" fever (129) of failed contact with the lost sources of spiritual health. The "shrunken old miser," for instance, whose dignity and health have been compromised by a commitment to material rather than spiritual values, is "eagerly clinging to life and lucre, though the one was gasping for outlet, and about the other he was in torment lest death, or some other unprincipled cut-purse, should be the means of his losing it; by like feeble tenure holding lungs and pouch, and yet knowing and desiring nothing beyond them; for his mind, never raised above mould, was now all but mouldered away" (58). The equation in this passage of "mould" with money, flesh with the decay of materialist values, reinforces the presentation of the individual who has sold life for lucre and whose body, approaching the static lifelessness of the money it so feverishly hoards, nears failure. Thus the mind "never raised above mould" has finally infected the body and so brought about a reversal of what has been for Melville a positive dialectic. Instead of the body's subsumption and resurrection of the often ethereal mind, here we have a mind, itself poisoned by a blind materialism, further tainting and finally destroying the flesh that was once the locus of its salvation. In this respect, the miser's subsequent seduction in chapter 15 simply reaffirms his failure to invest in some degree of transcendence, for even to the end he attempts to buy back the health that his devotion to money has stolen from him.

In contrast, the majority of the diseased or wounded victims aboard the *Fidèle* reveal varying degrees of such materialism combined with a cynicism or distrust whose strength depends upon the depth of their wounds. This list includes the man with the "wooden leg," the "invalid Titan," the "soldier of fortune," and the famously fictional Colonel Moredock. Though the histories of these characters are variously incomplete, they all enact essentially the same pattern: each has encountered a type of "confidence-man" in his past and now bears the scar of the wound to which his former trust made him vulnerable. Thus the body bears the evidence of seduction not because it was the target of the seducer but because it represents the social disjunction, the breaking up of the communal body that the failure of linguistic and social faith enacts. These characters are not only fragmented themselves; they are in fact the fragments of a world no longer connected by the invisible and vulnerable ties of social confidence, and they themselves reflect, ultimately, the splintering of the book's own form.

As the first of these walking wounded to appear, the "gimlet-eyed, sour-faced" (12) man with the wooden leg helps establish the basic type.

Not only does he demonstrate the darkness of his cynicism in the episode with Black Guinea, but there is also the suggestion that he wishes to revenge an earlier blow. The narrator hints, for instance, that the "shallow unfortunate" could be "some discharged custom-house officer, who, suddenly stripped of convenient means of support, had concluded to be avenged on government and humanity" (12), while the "cripple" himself suggests that he may have been the victim of another kind of confidence. In telling the story of "a certain Frenchman of New Orleans" (30) who, having married a woman of a "liberal mould," fails to spot the most obvious signs of his cuckoldry, the cynic may in fact be rehearsing another version of his own loss of faith.

Whatever the nature of his history, however, it is clear that his incomplete body reflects both a physical and a confidential impotence, for the "seeds" he sews carry none of the resurrective power of *Moby-Dick*'s "sperm." In fact, they are nothing more than the seeds of doubt: "Look you, I have been called a Canada thistle. Very good. And a seedy one: still better. And the seedy Canada thistle has been pretty well shaken among ye: best of all. Dare say some seed has been shaken out; and won't it spring though?" (15). That the seeds of life have been transformed into the seeds of disbelief, the grass growing at the heart of the pyramid into the Canada thistle, speaks of the body's failure in this book not only to cohere but also to produce anything more than that which destroys and deconstructs.

A slightly less cynical version of the impotent appears in chapter 17. The "invalid Titan," who emerges with "a puny girl" "of alien maternity" (85) from the dusky road to board the *Fidèle*, not only projects the physical fracture of a previous seduction but also demonstrates, in suitably Ahabian fashion, that his outward condition ("slanting his tall stature like a mainmast yielding to the gale, or Adam to the thunder" [86]) mirrors his inward pain as symbol and evidence. Like the wrinkles in Ahab's forehead, the "dusk giant's" pains are physical only in effect; they cannot be cured by medicinal means because they originate beyond the realm of the body. The only cure for metaphysical pain—as Melville has suggested in *Pierre* and "Bartleby"—will be metaphysical in substance, and the characters aboard the *Fidèle* who suffer from physical defects help reinforce the underlying notion that the loss of social and linguistic faith, the failure of language, creates an unbridgeable distance between the bodily self and the metaphysical cure that is its only salvation.

Similarly, the "soldier of fortune," whose history presents both a failed judicial process and the social disjunction such corruption reveals, notes that his lack of "friends" was ultimately responsible for the disease in his legs. As is true for Bartleby, the "Tombs" becomes his only home because, in effect, no one will "pay his bail" or vouch for him. Thus the condition of his body flows directly from the failure of social connection, for seduced into a belief in social values, the "steady, hard-working cooper" (96) discovers not only that others do not share those values but also that his own faith, his own capacity for belief in both justice and language, is responsible for his condition. As a result, he himself becomes a minor confidence-man, not a version of the book's central figure, but a transitional figure between faith and faithlessness. Knowing that the world continues to dream chronometrically even as it acts horologically, he provides the language it wishes to hear, the story that it literally pays for, while saving the bitterness of worldly truth for his own self-torture.

In addition to the variously disabled and seduced passengers, there exists a central, representative figure for the wounded-seduced in *The Confidence-Man:* the Indian-hater par excellence and his representative, Colonel Moredock, one of the many internal, doubly fictive characters in this book of telescoping tales. Much of the criticism of the novel centers upon this figural character, the type he represents, and whether or not his attitude toward "Indians" represents Melville's, presents a negative example, or provides some broader comment on "heroic" questing.[11] Yet fewer readers have focused upon Moredock's similarity to many of the passengers of the *Fidèle,* especially in light of the description of his youth and early history. He is more than a mere fictional type constructed in opposition to the confidence-man; like the other cynical and wounded victims who precede him, he opposes the seducer only because he has already been defined as victim. His raison d'être derives from the desire not only to revenge the original wound but also to punish himself for initially falling victim to faith. What distinguishes him from the other wounded passengers is that his wound, like Pitch's, is not bodily; nevertheless, his history suggests that the psychological scar left by his early life has overwhelmingly affected his attitude toward the physical world.

Both Moredock and the Indian-hater par excellence are said to take the path of monomaniacal revenge because of youthful trauma, and it is precisely the occurrence of such an event "in youth or early manhood" (149) that produces its misanthropic power. The blow, whether to his own or to the social or familial body, produces a powerful impression because the victim is still an infant, close to "mother's milk" (149), whose bones have yet to harden and whose consciousness has yet to form. Thus in this presexual, semiconscious state, he feels the "signal outrage" (149) as it strikes at his early conceptions of faith and protection, of bodily integrity and social union. As a result, like his true model, the young Pierre, he "makes a vow" and "with the solemnity of a Spaniard turned monk" "takes leave of his kin" (149) and hits "the ascetic trail," "a monk who apostatizes to the world at times" (150). In other words, the Indian-hater's seduction by social faith, the destruction of his belief in the goodness of others, has the effect of turning him against both society and his own body. He becomes, like Pierre, an ascetic quester, his sexuality "wounded" by the destruction of his early illusions of maternal and communal protection. Consequently, he "apostatizes to the world at times," attempts, like Ahab and Pierre before him, to seduce meaning from the invisible, to elicit a response from "the forest primeval" (149). His search therefore becomes more than a hunt for "Indians"; it grows into a search for the meaning of his early wound, the reason behind the failure of confidence. In this respect, his "racial" hatred is more deeply directed at himself and is fueled by the perception of evil in all people. He has learned too early and too suddenly that all people, including himself, are potentially "Indians" and that trust, whether placed in language or in the body, is thus impossible and ultimately dangerous.

Melville's main purpose in the Indian-hater section is thus to present a negative picture of ascetic enthusiasm and to use the Indian attack as a metaphor for the presence of treachery in all people and in nature itself. In this light the Indian is less the member of a malevolent race than an arm of dangerous nature; he is akin to the panther (145) and, in the context of another Melvillean world, the shark: " 'Queequeg no care what god made him shark,' said the savage, agonizingly lifting his hand up and down; 'wedder Fejee god or Nantucket god; but de god wat made shark must be one dam Ingin.' "[12] As we have learned, the shark in *Moby-Dick* represents what Ishmael calls "sharkishness," a voraciousness that inhabits both man and nature and that informs much of what may be called evil or cruel in human activity and natural processes. That the shark should be defined by a "savage" as "one dam Ingin" more than suggests that, like such notions as "savagery" and "sharkishness," "Indianness" can be applied both to nature and to people. Just as we are presented in *Moby-Dick* with representative white "savages," so in *The Confidence-Man* are we given multiple shapes and colors of "Indian."[13]

Colonel Moredock himself demonstrates the Indian-hating principle and also provides an example of the effects that an early psychological wound can have upon attitudes toward the body and society. Like the Indian-hater par excellence, John Moredock "was just entering upon man-hood" when the massacre of his mother and siblings left him "in nature sole survivor of his race" (153); as though to emphasize the change in his attitude toward the physical, he receives the news while eating: " . . . as the tidings were told him, after the first start he kept on eating, but slowly and deliberately, chewing the wild news with the wild meat, as if both together, turned to chyle, together should sinew him to his intent. From that meal he rose an Indian-hater" (153). The transformation from bucolic repast to symbolic last supper both echoes Pierre's sacramental dinner with Isabel and emphasizes the metamorphosis of unconscious, physical action (eating for nourishment) into conscious, metaphysical action (symbolically eating for revenge). By this means Moredock changes his previous, youthful devotion to the physical body into a bodiless quest; it is the meal itself that helps to cement his new identity.

The major difference between Moredock and the Indian-hater par excellence is that the colonel maintains both a family and a convivial relationship with his community while nevertheless remaining an Indian-hater. Like Pierre's Christian-militant grandfather, Moredock blends within himself the "lion and the lamb" and demonstrates the principle that "nearly all Indian-haters have at bottom loving hearts" (154). In other words, though less of an ascetic than the Indian-hater par excellence, it is clear that Moredock shares with his ideal prototype the same basis for action, whether in love or in hate; both, like the other wounded passengers aboard the *Fidèle*, have been victims of their own capacity for love, of their own ability to trust in the bonds of their communities. In the Indian-hater par excellence this foundation of love, now scarred, produces an ascetic devotion to the hunt for those truths that underlie treachery and his own failed trust in humanity. In Colonel Moredock, who after all "was not an Indian-hater *par excellence*" (152), the early blow produces both a less intense metaphysical quest and a powerful desire to reform and reconstruct the familial and social body where possible. His "hate" and his distrust he confines to "Indians"; his questions he reserves for the "religious" trail.

Aside from the genuinely wounded passengers, there remains a second group that shows various degrees of physical debility. Among the shape-shiftings of the confidence-man three either physically or symbolically "wounded" figures emerge: the deaf-mute, Black Guinea, and John Ringman. With the exception of the deaf-mute, who appears more as a figure of impotent desire for faith than an actual confidence-man, each of these characters employs his debility as a tool in his seductive drama, a sometimes tacit, often overt piece of evidence of his own previous seduction and, more importantly, of his apparent physical reality. Black Guinea, for instance, "a grotesque negro cripple" with "something wrong about his legs" (10), makes use of his condition not simply to beg coins from the passengers—certainly the most minor of the confidence-man's games— but also to pave the way for the confidence-man's other guises by convincing the world of the reality of his wounds and, by extension, the reality of his body. To prove the wound is to prove his innocence as victim; to prove his bodily reality is to seduce the passengers into the kind of social and epistemological faith that the later manifestations of the confidence-man both elicit and destroy.

Black Guinea's lack of an evidential body becomes clear from the passengers' request for "any documentary proof, any plain paper" or, failing that, "some one who can speak a good word" (13) for him. In other words, in this predominately textual world, where the flesh that remains is fragmented and corrupted, the confidence-man can produce only textual "proof" of his "condition"; only by self-referentiality within a closed fictional system, essentially citing himself as reference, can he verify his existence. Thus, as though in acknowledgment of his true nature, the passengers, themselves also more voice than flesh, ignore the most obvious manner of detecting fraud—the physical investigation suggested by the genuinely wounded "man with the wooden leg." Instead, their faith in appearances totally lost, they now believe only in the word, whether written or spoken, even though, as we come to understand, it too can be counterfeited.

Similarly, in the history of John Ringman, "the man with the weed," we get textual support for one of the confidence-man's disguises. The story of his "castration"—"a judicial blasting of his private reputation" (63)—at the hands of the "cactus-like" Goneril helps establish him as one of the (false) wounded-seduced, the possessor of an erotic wound rendered by the "mysterious touchings" of his wife. The similarity between Goneril's "evil-touch" (61) and the mesmerizing powers of Ringman himself in the episode with the sophomore suggests that Ringman is less the victim than the student of such "wonderful" and enigmatic actions. Indeed, it is he who wishes to "touch" the passengers for money and belief; in this respect, the story of his own victimization attempts to establish his position as victim, to explain the obvious sign of the weed, and to place him on an equal footing with the broken-spirited society of the *Fidèle*. After all, in the predominately fictive world, the world of surface-distrust, it is the fiction that establishes one's being, the story that weaves one's "character" into the fabric of society.[14]

Sounding the Hollows

If indeed the world of *The Confidence-Man* is the most fictive Melville produced, if it lacks either the palpable flesh of *Moby-Dick* or the illusion of palpability to which Pierre falls victim, then it becomes clear that the

Ahabian vision of language as weapon is no longer viable. As in *Pierre*, the fictiveness of the universe precludes any response from beyond "the mask." Yet unlike Pierre, who still believes such a consummation is possible, and unlike Bartleby, who has lost both desire and hope for connection, the confidence-man understands that his world is a fiction even as he retains vestiges of Ahabian desire. In consequence, he elicits and yet destroys what traces of metaphysical faith he encounters. What had been Ahab's self-cutting despair has apparently blended with Bartleby's catatonia to produce a remarkably detached, almost scientific spirit and style in which the seduction and destruction of faith are carried out. The confidence-man has become, in the most Melvillean sense, a truly "heartless" mind, free from flesh and subject only to the cool inversions of a profoundly impotent desire.

His first appearance as the Christ-like "man in cream-colors" both establishes his desire to find genuine faith and provides us with an image of his linguistic reality. This pallid figure, an extension of Bartleby, "unaccompanied by friends" (3), desirelessly pursues "the path of duty" (3) and begins a task much like an author's: he writes upon a blank surface what are clearly words of hope but, because of his dumbness, can provide no context or authority for the language he offers. Like Bartleby's, his phrases repeat with only minor variation, offering a "shield-like" wall (5), rather than a connection, between himself and the world. He therefore represents the absence of the author in relation to his audience and the failure and powerlessness of Christly principles in the world we are entering. Most of all it is his "lamb-like" (6) chronometricality, his physical and linguistic passivity that set the tone for the book as a whole. In other words, not only are we entering a world that would ignore or distrust Christ himself, but, more significantly, we are coming into contact with the final stages of Ahabian language and desire, reduced now to a few scriptural quotations scribbled on a slate by a passive deaf-mute.

Yet whatever our conjectures about his connection to the confidence-man's other guises, the positive nature of the deaf-mute's quotations cannot be denied. After all, one of the book's basic ironies relies upon the paradox that useful and powerful truths, whether uttered in deception or in earnest, retain their power even as they potentially mislead. Similarly, in his other shapes, the confidence-man often demonstrates an altruistic hope for the survival of charity and confidence among humanity. The "man in gray" (chapter 7), for instance, who reveals his extravagant plans for charity, the herb-doctor who applies to himself his own medicine (89), and the cosmopolitan who argues for friendship and charity (chapter 39) all show degrees of genuine desire for confidence even though, at other moments, they appear to take advantage of such belief. In short, even in the most obvious of deceptions it is impossible to see pure negativism in the confidence-man himself; he desires faith as he destroys it, and this paradox underlies all of his deceptions.

Nevertheless, it is the desire to destroy, the remnant of Ahab's destructive aggression, that makes the confidence-man the notable and treacherous figure he is. The best example of his method comes in the cosmopolitan's scene with the barber, in which—after arguing extensively for the value of confidence and finally resorting to mesmerism—he pulls his carefully woven rug from beneath the barber's incredulous feet:

> "Stay, sir—the—the shaving?"
> "Ah, I *did* forget that. But now that it strikes me, I shan't pay you at present. Look at your agreement; you must trust. Tut! against a loss you hold the guarantee. Good-night, my dear barber."
> With which words he sauntered off, leaving the barber in a maze, staring after. (237)

The cosmopolitan's pleasure, thin and dark though it is, derives from the cinch in the circular logic with which he finally ties the baffled barber. He both produces confidence in the barber and takes it away, deriving from the process a seemingly unemotional benefit that echoes, in a paler form, Ahab and Pierre's self-punishing humor and dark word-play.

Similarly, the basic structural principle of the book bears out the notion that the confidence-man is a kind of experimenter whose questing energy has been diverted from finding answers to snaring those who believe that an answer is possible. In repeated scenes we meet with a linguistic structure that, like Ahab's, mirrors the actions of the body. In this case, however, in place of Ahab's aggressive verbs, we are introduced to the confidence-man's teasing game of flirtation, retreat, and seizure. We see, in other words, the sexual snare remade in words that weave and encircle before they attack and are presented with an advanced type of bitter play that ends in the sting of the seduction.

The earliest full-scale encounter in the book can serve as a structural model for those that follow. In it, the man with the weed accosts "with the familiarity of an old acquaintance" (18) one Mr. Roberts, who is gradually persuaded, despite his protestations to the contrary, to hear Ringman's "story" and finally "put into the stranger's hand" a sum of money. The basic structure of the event is thus composed of an encounter, a one-sided conversation that usually leads to the essential narrative, followed by the acquiescence of the hearer and the consummative act of belief, sometimes followed by its physical sign, the surrender of money or name. In each case, language elicits the response of belief; in other words, not only has language replaced the body in its erotic activity, but also the physical response of the inscrutable, once the desired result of the quester's seductive speech, has been replaced by the acquiescence of basic *human* faith in language. No physical consummation is necessary, only the admission of "confidence" that, once given, helps to destroy that faith in the giver and yield a cold return to the clinical confidence-man.

As if to emphasize such distanced eroticism, Melville repeatedly shows us how each successful snare produces a sudden chill in the confidence-man that in turn leads to the sort of post-coital despair that contributes to the victim's loss of confidence: "Assistance being received, the stranger's manner assumed a kind and degree of decorum which, under the circumstances, seemed almost coldness" (21). This moment immediately follows the "stranger's" acceptance of the money and further hints—by such diction as "coldness," "not over ardent," "chastened" and "self-respect" (21–22)—at the sense of restraint and desirelessness that the success of the encounter has produced.

The latent sexuality of the repeated encounters also appears in the way Melville describes the words and actions of the seducer as well as in the reactions of those who are the subject of the "stranger's" strategy. In chapter 8, for instance, "a charitable lady" is beset by the agent for the "Seminole Widow and Orphan Society." The exchange echoes the common demand for physical proof in an unconsummated relationship:

> "That you have confidence? Prove it. Let me have twenty dollars."
> "Twenty dollars!"
> "There, I told you, madam, you had no confidence."
> The lady was, in an extraordinary way, touched. She sat in a sort of restless torment, knowing not which way to turn. She began twenty different sentences, and left off at the first syllable of each. (44–45)

The notable pun on "touched" both establishes the way in which the language of the confidence-man becomes a substitute for the physical act and reveals the underlying eroticism of an argument so persuasive and ensnaring that it can in fact "touch" the listener emotionally and "physically" via the exchange of money.

The secret of the confidence-man's linguistic "touch" ultimately lies in the way he brings into question the victim's confidence in his or her own goodness. The syntactical, inquisitorial seduction he practices requires as its target an innocent conscience and unmarred confidence not only in the continuity of social good but in the spotlessness or potential for redemption in the victim's own self-image. Thus his sentence, while superficially dizzying, in the end presents the shadow of Ahab's stabbing syntax, an aggression of language aimed at the fragile self-conception of the poorly experienced passenger. In this respect, even the seemingly "wounded" and apparently critical Pitch—though adequate to defend himself against the confidence-man's "punning with ideas" (125)—finally feels the "touch" not because of an analogy but because of a direct compliment to his own moral nature (128). The "Missouri bachelor," who until this point has shown little of the inexperience evident in Melville's other bachelors, not only momentarily loses his language in response to this clearly "touching" statement but also quickly returns the confidence he has received and expresses faith in the boys he had hitherto known as rogues. The exchange of confidence, in other words, like the exchange of money for goods, reflects the consummative pattern of gesture that underlies the confidence-man's seductions. His language, from its frequently broken syntax to its analogical method of argument, reflects his preparation of the victim for this gesture, the sort of disarming and overbearing talk that is both a drug and a type of foreplay. Even more, its disjunctive phrasing, its intensity and awareness of its own wordiness have the effect of leveling all language in the mind of the victim, of reducing language to a meaningless babble, a magical, "cabalistical" chant that finally prevents the listener from responding critically. In short, the passengers' sensitivity to the subtleties of language is destroyed even as those subtleties are turned upon them.

Just as the *Fidèle* contains both the genuinely and the falsely wounded, the book as a whole demonstrates a genuine lack of coherence even as it employs its own fragmentation as part of an argument to convince us as readers to believe in it. As a broken textual body, the book fails to cohere on many levels. Not only is its basic structure founded upon the repetition of conversation and seduction, but within those conversations smaller generic forms, mostly stories, continue to assert their own integrity in a way that frequently makes them more memorable than the debates in which they appear. The story of Goneril (chapter 12), the soldier of fortune's tale (chapter 19), the chapters concerning Colonel Moredock, the story of Charlemont (chapter 34), and the story of China Aster (chapter 40) all contribute to the large-scale fragmentation of the novel by virtue of their individual integrity. In other words, because they maintain relatively tight narrative structures, they are easier to remember and easier to grasp than the book itself. They thus reveal the softness of the book's overall structure and contribute to its breakdown simply because they tend to break free from their contexts.

Admittedly, the book's final sentence—"Something further may follow of this Masquerade" (251)—has frequently been cited as evidence that Melville either left the book incomplete or understood that its structure was infinitely open.[15] Whatever the case, however, it is clear that by the end of the novel we experience little sense of progression, little narrative arc, despite what some have seen as the apocalyptic quality of the final chapter. That the book ends with the close of the April Fool's Day on which it began gives it little real tension or texture within that time frame; indeed, time itself within the vertiginous text is difficult, if not impossible, to measure or perceive. Part of this difficulty may be due to the narrative style, which, like the voice of the confidence-man himself, frequently prefers to muddy rather than clarify.[16] Such a style recalls Melville's own depiction of Benjamin Franklin in *Israel Potter,* for that character's "slyness" relies upon a similar mazing of syntactical direction, in which qualification and double-negation produce a degree of baffled acquiescence. In short, one tends to be lulled asleep by repeated confusions. The consistent encounter with such clotted prose only contributes to the striking clarity and direction that the enclosed stories maintain, thereby reinforcing the book's overall failure to incorporate its materials into a graspable form.

At the same time, the strength of these shorter forms suggests that, as in the short fiction and "The Encantadas" especially, Melville is furthering his investigations both of the fragment and of the ways in which lyric spatiality can help structure a "fragmented" text. After all, if the diptychs mosaically spark meaning within the framework of their admittedly spatial juxtaposition, it is also possible that the pieces of *The Confidence-Man,* while maintaining their independence, similarly form tensions and countertensions in the spaces of discussion between them. In this respect, *The Confidence-Man,* as though in echo of its own doubleness of language, may paradoxically be said to both fall apart and cohere, to exist as pieces of a temporal narrative while operating as a spatially arranged entity. Similarly, it is possible to suggest that for the first time in the Melville oeuvre the fragmented social and physical body under investigation since "Bartleby" has taken on a purpose and function within the matrix of the text itself. In this book about the deceptiveness of both language and body, fragmentation becomes, paradoxically, part of the very argument for the book's wholeness, an argument that carefully echoes the confidence-man's own seductive ploys. Just as the characters aboard the *Fidèle* are asked to have "confidence" in the integrity of an obviously fractured social body, so are we as readers asked to believe in the integrity of a fictional body, despite its obvious failure to incorporate its elements.[17]

Such arguments for "consistency" begin in chapter 14, where the inconsistency of human nature is cited in order to support the sudden reversal of character in the previous chapter. Though the merchant who exclaims that "Truth will *not* be comforted" is himself not a disguised confidence-man, the arguments begun in chapter 14 and continued in chapters 33 and 44 have the effect of apologizing not only for the inconsistency of human character but for the inconsistency of the confidence-man and, by implication, of the book itself. The greater the distance placed between the fictional and the represented world, no matter how valid the symbolist arguments in chapters 33 and 44, the more room the confidence-man can enjoy in which to reverse his positions. The book itself thus becomes the confidence-man's double, both betraying its fragmentation and offering it as a symbolic representation of the true nature of society, an integral, "whole" picture of a fragmented world.

That Melville was able, after the turn to shorter forms in the 1850s, to make fragmentation a potential asset rather than a liability speaks for his growing interest in smaller forms as well as his own aesthetic investigation of the nature of both bodily and linguistic disintegration. Even as the last embers of Ahabian desire turn to ashes in the pages of *The Confidence-Man,* he is already engaged in the transformation of his failing novelistic powers into a mastery of smaller forms. Indeed, far from the collapse into silence usually attributed to his work after *The Confidence-Man,* his turn to poetry marks the next logical step in a career that finds artistic nourishment in the aesthetics of fragmentation and the possibility of reformation that poetic form and poetic language can offer.[18] In addition, the dialectic of mind and body, now exhausted in the fleshless world of the confidence-man, will find in the notion of poetic form, the bodiedness of meter and stanza, and in the social and moral dialectic of the Civil War both a new identity and a new vigor. Out of amoral deception will arise a sense of moral value; out of fragmentation, the potential for social and linguistic rebirth.

III

Reshaping the Lost Debate

6

THE FISSURE IN THE HEARTH
Battle Pieces

A S EARLY AS "Fragments from a Writing Desk" and continuing through *Mardi, Moby-Dick,* and the short tales, Melville demonstrates a notable affinity for the short or shortened form. Even his largest constructions frequently attain their novelistic fullness not by elaborating characters in an intricately planned, generically unified action but by assembling a wide variety of genres under the tenuous arc of a questing plot line. Through this tendency toward both large and small scale fragmentation, even in his most noteworthy prose, Melville reveals one of his deeper connections to the romanticism he nevertheless frequently distrusts: "Romanticism, as Friedrich Shlegel said in his *Athenäums-Fragment 116,* was an eternal 'becoming' that had as its chief characteristic that it 'nie vollendet sein kann'—can never be completed. Schubert's 'Unfinished Symphony' participates in this characteristic no less certainly than does Keats's 'Hyperion' (and even the 'heavenly length' of Schubert's great C-Major Symphony implies a sense of incompleteness in its reaching and longings.)"[1] In other words, the romantic search for the infinite, like Ahab's quest for bodiless truth, contains the inevitability of incompletion or fragmentation, for regardless of the length of the text or work, such a reach beyond both physical and textual boundaries assures that each will remain unfulfilled. Thus even *Moby-Dick* retains an unpolished, imbalanced quality due in some part to its "purposeful" failure to integrate its smaller forms, the result on the one hand of Ishmael's recognition of his overwhelming subject matter and on the other of the romantic voice the book often speaks.[2] The subsequent dominance of that voice in *Pierre,* "Bartleby," and *The Confidence-Man* helps to increase the fragmentary qualities of those texts and so gradually leads Melville toward the incompletion and linguistic failure that Ahab's questing ultimately produces. The increasing presence of shorter forms in the later work therefore suggests both that Ahabian desire is breaking down Melville's ability to produce larger texts and that Melville's interest in the fragment is beginning to move into a new, increasingly productive stage. In short, by the time he begins to write brief tales and especially lyric poetry, to organize and develop the smaller form for its own sake, Melville has begun to combine Ahab's romantic longing with Ishmael's recognition of the fragment as a viable form. He has begun to investigate his own ability to resurrect a playful, formally contained body language that delights in its own sounds as much as in the meanings it transmits.[3]

Given this shift of genre and voice, it is not surprising that the tension that once fueled *Moby-Dick*'s dialectical fires reemerges in somewhat different guise in the lyrics. In *Battle Pieces*, for instance, the very palpability of the fleshly body in battle cuts against Melville's frequent attempts to allegorize that body into a highly formal, social dialectic that expresses his moralistic vision of civil war. Perhaps of more significance, however, is the way this renewed and reformulated tension finds reflection in the very form and language of the poetry itself. The torque placed upon the Ishmaelean impulse toward rhyme, meter, and the playful, bodied language of poetic speech results from the continuing presence of the sort of metaphysical questing that inevitably produces fragmentation. Thus the ruggedness of Melville's verse is not only, as Newton Arvin and others have suggested, intentional and purposeful, but ultimately expressive of Melville's continuing reformation and reinvestigation of the conflict between mind and body.[4]

With his continued interest in the dialectics of form versus disintegration, wholeness versus fragmentation, Melville apparently took notable interest not only in the politics and consequences of the Civil War but also in its ramifications as an image of the struggle in which his own work had participated for many years. *Battle Pieces*, his first published book of verse, records his reactions to the social and political complexities of the conflict along with his investigations of the ways in which the individual and society—the wounded soldier and the wounded nation—struggle to remain whole. By envisioning the battle for union as the dialectic between head and heart transformed into a contest between good and evil, order and chaos, he was able to invigorate his vision of the war with his own personal literary and individual concerns.[5] The resultant, unresolved tension within the nation, the consequent fragmentation of the individual and familial bodies, and the qualified unification of social and political form create a powerful source for Melville's continued interest in the viability of form and the uncertain results of the desire for individualism.[6]

The physical body of *Battle Pieces*, though clearly more palpable than that of *The Confidence-Man*, suffers neither from the kind of textual replacement and psychological repression that dominates the novel nor from the erotic deferral and distance that occurs in *Israel Potter*. Instead, it participates in patterns of individual fragmentation and corporeal destruction that result from the ultimately negative physical contact of war. Like Israel's grappling fight with the British boatmen, the battle scenes of *Battle Pieces*, as the title itself suggests, reveal the ways in which the violent embrace destroys and dismembers the individual body, transforming it into a figure for the equally broken nation. Just as the work itself is constructed of "pieces" that may or may not cohere, so are the individuals in this world frequently fragmented within the context of the struggle for social wholeness. In this respect the individual body becomes the ironic casualty in the attempt to reform or retain the integrity of the social body; the genuine wound to the flesh both reflects and, the poetry hopes, ultimately heals the symbolic wound to the country.

Significantly, Melville begins his examination of the dynamics of this relationship in the book's first poem, "The Portent." This brief lyric depicts the hanging of John Brown as both a parodic crucifixion and potent mystery that foreshadows the violence and sacrifice of the coming conflict. The tension between law and conscience as well as the distance between a passive and an active christology appear in the hanging figure whose wounds remain unhealed and who neither promises nor exemplifies resurrection. The individual body displays its physicality in the open wounds that reflect the "stabs" within a country whose "Christ" comes not in peace but in war and whose "law" must destroy him.[7] As though to double the irony, it is here the law, the force that strives to maintain the unity and integrity of social form, the force that in part drives the Union armies, which must, in effect, sacrifice an enemy of the Union even if that figure follows a "chronometrical" path. In this respect the impulse toward union is qualified from the beginning by its own internal tensions between practicality and idealism; the figure of John Brown not only forecasts or "portends" the war but also hangs in the center of the minds and hearts of those who will fight it—a violent, bloody "savior" whose mysteriousness flows ultimately from the inscrutability of death rather than the revelation of divine sacrifice.

A similarly sacrificial quality informs "Lyon," a description of the battle of Springfield, Missouri. Its ostensible hero, freed from the paradox of lawless lawfulness that envelopes the prewar Brown, offers both body and courage to lead his inexperienced soldiers into battle and as a result is awarded an unqualified ascension into heaven rather than a tonally complex death on earth. The poem's idealizing voice—frequently undercut by the sing-song verse and overly inspirational tone—contrasts the increasing destruction of the bodies of Lyon and his men with their similarly increasing courage, as though the spiritualization of the flesh were to some degree both responsible for and the result of their willingness to disregard the safety of their bodies. Thus a conjunction appears between the earthward bleeding of the soldiers and the heavenly appearance of "the Leader," who leads his "Star-browed" horse "Orion" (25) as though in opposition to seemingly malign Fate. This otherworldly quality extends to Lyon's courage as well, for his fearlessness is not benign or passive but "bitter" (25), as though to indicate his acceptance of negative physical facts and his ability to transcend the distasteful limits of the flesh. The separation of spirit from flesh and the depiction of Lyon as a "seer" (27) suggest that courage in the face of physical danger liberates the hero from bodily existence even before death occurs. The body remains as evidence of his bravery, its wounds the proof of transcendence because the acceptance of the wound signals Lyon's ability to sacrifice the flesh in favor of spiritual health. Even more important, however, despite the sacrificial nature of the poem, is the sense that the heaven to which Lyon ascends is after all an Old Testament paradise, a Zion of "prophets" and "armies," and not the pacifistic reward of Christ. In this civil war world, in which John Brown is the only "Christ," the nature of sacrifice has come to be individual and heroic—it is the death of the servant of an angry God in a "holy" war.

The destruction of the soldier's body also forms part of a process through which the individual is subsumed by the collective body of the army itself. In "Donelson," for instance, the expansive description of a winter siege offers an increasingly horrific, carefully ironic picture of the tension existing between the single body and its larger extension. Though soldiers are slowly and consistently dismembered and destroyed, their absences are quickly filled so that the fight between two armies, the duel of two giant bodies of men, can continue. Likewise, the poem's chorus, a group of city residents reading battle reports on a public bulletin board, forms a smaller version of the body politic that similarly displays its inner tensions and individual differences, even to the point of absorbing the individual grief of those whose relatives have died in the fight.

The poem begins with a description of the crowd whose organization in the harsh weather forecasts the commands and maneuvers of the troops about which they have come to read:

> About the bulletin-board a band
> Of eager, anxious people met,
> And every wakeful heart was set
> On latest news for West or South.
> "No seeing here," cries on—"don't crowd"—
> "You tall man, pray you, read aloud." (33)

The anonymous command not only structures the group around the tall reader but also suggests a delegation of function within the group in which individuals perform as parts of the whole. The acquiescence of the group allows the distribution of information and enables the efficient functioning of the larger entity, providing, on a small scale, an example or echo of militaristic maneuver. Nevertheless, the next scene in which the crowd figures reveals some of the frictions within their daily gathering and begins to suggest that individualism will not always yield to the public good, especially when visions of societal goals differ. First a "cross patriot" pessimistically avers that the battle " 'Twill drag along—drag along" (39). This assertion meets quick response in a "stripling's" cheer for Grant, which in turn is taken up by the crowd and ultimately responded to by the sneering Copperhead, whose cynical but level-headed vision of war offers no heroes and forecasts doom for the country as a whole:

> "Win or lose," he pausing said,
> "Caps fly the same; all boys, mere boys;
> Any thing to make a noise.
>   Like to see the list of the dead;
> These '*craven Southerners*' hold out;
> Ay, ay they'll give you many a bout." (39–40)

The figure of death here speaks an unpatriotic truth, debunking the glory of heroism and debasing the nature of the individual sacrifice, neither of which the crowd, committed to patriotic rhetoric, will allow. Thus like the country as whole, they too attack their disturbing neighbor. Allowing weapons to replace the binding power of dialectic, they purge the dissenting element in their system with "a shower of broken ice and snow" (40).

The Copperhead's prophecies predictably become fact, and with the posting of the following two installments the crowd encounters an even more severe uncertainty within themselves. Each individual finds himself forced to contemplate the pitiless reality of a nature that offers no solace to the wounded and no answer to the "mysteries dimly sealed" between "right and wrong" (44). Furthermore, as the suffering of individual soldiers appears in the daily dispatches, so do the individual readers begin to feel the combatants' isolation in the midst of battle and subsequently to question the nature of the fight that demands such sacrifice:

> The storm, whose black flag showed in heaven;
> As if to say no quarter there was given
>   To wounded men in wood,
>   Or true hearts yearning for the good—
> All fatherless seemed the human soul. (44)

In other words, the facts of conflict, like the facts of nature, make little real distinction between "true hearts yearning for the good" and their counterparts. The individual, whether scaling the cliffs at Donelson or standing in the sleet before the "wafered square" (47) of bulletin board, seems "fatherless," uncared for by God, nature, or society, while the structure that knits together crowd and country, family and fighting unit, is threatened with disintegration by the lawlessness of battle. Even when news of victory eventually arrives, the tension within the public remains. The division and inner conflict of the crowd dissolve into reuniting handshakes, purgative tears, and communal, genial bowls of undiluted punch (51–52). Yet this social reformation remains qualified by the "others" whose husbands, sons, and brothers appear on the endless death list, the river of names that reminds us that the communal joy of victory, the restatement of social unity, arrives only after and because of the destruction of individuals and families, now unable to join hands or gather together.

It is precisely this paradox of communal victory and individual loss that invests the battle reports with both vivid detail and horrific reality. The tension between the fighting "we" and the fighting soldier continually appears in the language describing the skirmishes and sorties up the bluff:

> Each wood, each hill, each glen was fought for;
> The bold inclosing line we wrought for
> Flamed with sharpshooters. Each cliff cost
> A limb or life. But back we forced
> Reserves and all; made good our hold;
> And so we rest. (35)

Both the careful use of passive voice and the subtle impersonality of "*A limb or life*" suggest that the "we" that rests at the end of the day remains unified and continuous despite the loss of its own, partially expendable "limbs." The death of the single soldier remains insignificant: "*Their ranks all riven/Are being replaced by fresh, strong men*" (48). Only in his relation to the whole, as a percentage of the total of which he is a part, do his integrity and existence have value. Provided that the army accomplishes its objectives without losing too large a percentage of the whole, the individual may be dismembered without a reflecting wound in the social form. Thus Melville enumerates such "personal" wounds with the accumulative energy of cataloger, providing visions of the maimed (36, 48), the frozen (38, 43), and the "captain of the gun" "cut in two" by a cannonball (42). The overall effect tends to undermine both the victory and the moral stance—"*The spirit that urged them was divine* (49)—upon which the triumph bases itself by stacking against it the shattered bodies of the individual soldiers on both sides. The crushing movement of the social "we" as represented by the armies—like the mechanization Melville deplores in "A Utilitarian View of the Monitor's Fight"—presents the ironic coupling of enormous efficiency and mass effort with individual human destruction.[8] The great assent up the bluff of "Donelson" no doubt provides a picture of heroism, but it is a heroism caught within the mad, ineluctable movements of a giant apparently bent on the destruction of its own human members.

The singular effects of this self-mutilation appear most forcefully in "The College Colonel," in which the tension between self and community is painfully resolved in favor of sacrifice and the undefined "truth" that suffering reveals to the prematurely wise victim. The poem provides a tableau of the effects of physical destruction and emotional strain, emphasizing the abandonment of the body to a vision that, like Pip's, isolates the viewer from participation in society. The "Indian aloofness" (120) on the young officer's brow suggests that he has experienced something similar to John Moredock's youthful encounter with violence, the sudden perception early in life of the cruel possibilities of human nature. His inner self, now aged "a thousand years" (120), thus reacts coolly to the patriotic fervor of the crowds who clearly fail to understand the effects of battle on the individual:

It is not that a leg is lost,
    It is not that an arm is maimed,
It is not that the fever has racked—
    Self he has long disclaimed.

But all through the Seven Day's Fight,
    And deep in the Wilderness grim,
And in the field-hospital tent,
    And Petersburg crater, and dim
Lean brooding in Libby, there came—
    Ah heaven!—what *truth* to him. (121)

The conflict between individual physical integrity (the preservation of the self) and collective success (the preservation of the Union) here moves to a new level of complexity by introducing a deeper struggle within the individual. The loss or partial destruction of his own body, though doubtless not without effect, here fades into the overwhelming perception of the "truth" of human reality, a spiritual experience that takes place both in "the Wilderness grim" of battle and in the scenes of suffering caused by the fighting itself. The poem provides, in essence, the description of a spiritual and psychological experience that takes place in the uncivilized, godless world of lawless destruction, and it is the power of this experience, whose stunning depth overwhelms the ironies of self-sacrifice, that enables it to reveal the paradox of individual heroism.

In a like manner, poems such as "In the Prison Pen"—with its vision of the individual's fate in diseased confinement—and "Magnanimity Baffled" suggest that a significant amount of Melville's attention in this collection, despite its larger allegorization of the conflict, focuses on the single soldier's terrible position in the narrower context of battle. Despite the larger issues of "right and wrong" that the poems frequently invoke, it is the effect of that moralistic clash upon the physical and emotional life of the individual that provides the book's central focus. "Magnanimity Baffled," for instance, provides perhaps the most succinct vision in *Battle Pieces* of the failure of human contact and the negative facts of combat. As though offering a reconciliation scene between two quarreling friends, the poem, despite its overt sentimentality, manages to create an atmosphere of tenderness, to "touch" the reader with the revelation of the reality of such a "quarrel":

> "Brave one! I here implore your hand;
>   Dumb still? all fellowship fled?
> Nay, then, I'll have this stubborn hand!"
>   He snatched it—it was dead. (156)

The offer of the hand, the unifying gesture that is both social and productive in *Moby-Dick*, attempts to convert the negative "touch" of battle into the positive embrace of peace. But this moment of final contact, as in "Bartleby's" climactic scene, becomes one of horror, the perception, on the one hand, that the genial embrace is lifeless and, on the other, that the language of peace, indeed the language of diplomacy and grace, cannot overcome the negative act that precipitated the need for such an address in the first place.

Admittedly, the soldiers who fight these battles are not always the victims of larger, uncontrollable social movements, for though Melville frequently elicits a tension between the fate of the individual and the impetus of social duties, he also depicts the ways in which the failure of individual responsibility and maturity can lead to similarly unfulfilling results. For instance, "The Scout Toward Aldie," the longest and most purely narrative poem in the volume, offers the story of a young officer killed not because he is a member of a larger organization but because his own immaturity and inexperience have prevented him from questioning the rhetoric of heroism. The legendary and seemingly omnipresent Mosby, the Confederate guerilla leader, haunts the young officer's imagination in the shape of his own dreams of martial renown. Mosby's is the form that the challenge of life and nature assumes in order to test his strength of character and ability as a commander. What becomes clear, however, is that such a vision is founded upon only rumor and speculation. The young officer is, after all, "green," and unlike "the maimed ones or the low" (188) has never seen or encountered a "Mosby"—that force, that perception of the sharkishness in man and nature, which once met, in whatever form, leaves the survivor scarred and wise:

> The Leader lies before his tent
> Gazing at heaven's all-cheering lamp
> Through the blandness of a morning rare;
>   His thoughts on bitter-sweets are bent:
>   His sunny bride is in the camp—
>   But Mosby—graves are beds of damp! (189)

Each stanza enacts the process of the poem itself by establishing the blithe mood of the "bridegroom" leader only to dampen it with the concluding couplet in which Mosby's name always appears. Here the presence of the bride, like all the other "facts" concerning the officer, maintains a double meaning, for each scene is presented as though from two vantage points: first, the blindness of the inexperienced "boyish" (189) commander; second, the dark insight of the speaker who sees through Mosby's deceptions. In this respect, the bride is both a symbol of youthful potential and an evocation of ironic loss, a procreation never to come, the marriage bed that becomes a forest grave.

Besides the stanzaic pattern in which optimism is perpetually defeated, the narrator provides a number of emblematic scenes or characters that serve to counter the physical and emotional enthusiasm of the scouting party. Thus as the column leaves it passes the hospital, and though the riders feel strong "on their horses free" and "the tendoned thigh" "tingles" with life (190), it is the wisdom of the "cripples," those who have lost such "boyishness," that resonates most deeply throughout the episode. As though seeing themselves, the wounded do not speak; only the caws of the crow give ironic voice to the scene (190). The wounds of the hospitalized soldiers reach beyond the mere physical; their very visions of heroism in war, of adventure and bravery, have dissolved because Mosby does more than simply threaten the lives of those who encounter him: he radically alters their perceptions of life by allowing them to escape with a glimpse of death. Despite his legendary status, he stands for the real, the fact of physical pain or destruction, and continually dissolves the airy dreams of valor that fill the minds of his inexperienced enemies.

In similar opposition to the young officer is the older, more experienced major, whose silence and laconic comments offer a cool counterpart to the dangerously hot-blooded and premature decisions of the younger colonel:

> The Young Man talked (all sworded and spurred)
> Of the partisan's blade he longed to win,
>   And frays in which he meant to beat.
>   The grizzled Major smoked, and heard:
>   "But what's that—Mosby?" "No, a bird." (197)

The portrait of an immature war mentality grows sharper here by contrast to the "grizzled Major" who wisely and meditatively smokes rather than offer empty rhetoric. Likewise, and perhaps because of his lack of delusion, he demonstrates a clearer consciousness of the world around him, which, through his steadier eyes, seems less the haunted, decayed "wilderness" of the bugaboo Mosby than a palpable natural environment, neither full nor empty of danger.

The subsequent narrative in which the young officer fails to recognize the infiltrating Confederates, including Mosby himself, suggests that the desire for blood and fame he represents is both responsible for and, at the same time, a product of the movements of war. His death likewise reemphasizes the partial complicity that the individual maintains in his own destruction, whatever the tendencies of the larger forces in society. The damage to the individual body proceeds from the desire to preserve social form and from the blindness of the individual who sees self-sacrifice as something other than the reality of death:

> The Major took him by the hand—
>   Into the friendly clasp it bled
> (A ball through heart and hand he rued):
> "Good-by!" and gazed with humid glance. (221)

Once again, the "friendly clasp" fails to fulfill itself as useful embrace because the body, medium of such contact, has failed to survive the mind's desire. The ball has penetrated both heart and hand or, in other words, struck at the two significant points of human physical and emotional connection: the hand through which the "splice" of disparate lives is initiated, the heart that imbues that handshake with meaning even as it cements the emotional bond of the touch. Thus by poem's end not only is the friendship between soldiers lost but the bride has become a widow, and the young colonel is buried "where the lone ones lie" (224).

In order to balance his presentation of the tension between the individual and society, Melville provides a number of individual poems that focus more upon the delineation of larger issues and less on the effects of those issues on particular soldiers. These verses (the list includes "The Conflict of Convictions," "Apathy and Enthusiasm," "Dupont's Round Fight," "Battle of Stone River, Tennessee," "Gettysburg," "Look-out Mountain," "The Armies of the Wilderness," "A Canticle," and "America") consistently transform the battles they describe and the war itself into a moral and spiritual dialectic, a "conflict of convictions" and ethical visions, that echoes both the dualistic nature of the combat itself and the remaining components of Melville's interest in the struggle between head and heart. That dialectic, in part overborne and virtually silenced at the end of *The Confidence-Man,* reappears not as a primordial struggle within the individual but as a basic ethical conflict between the forces of law, order, reason, and beneficence and the opposing "sins" of exploitation, disruption, and treachery. Nevertheless, the underlying principle of the dialectic—that conflict should yield a productive synthesis rather than a unilateral victory—continues to assert itself in Melville's vision of the war. The horrible embrace of right and wrong, North and South, brother and brother has the potential to yield a new, more permanent bond that transcends both old orders and recent conflicts.

As an addition to the tension between individual and community, Melville sometimes portrays this dialectic as a figurative social body, a national mother or wounded whole that displays the rent social sinews of the nation. Such a presentation echoes the wounded individual at the same time that it demands that the reader understand the war's larger implications. No matter how tragic or poignant the destruction of the individual may be, it is ultimately the wound to the irreplaceable national idea that now demands attention and concern. The individual body is thus, once again, subordinated to the integrity of its social counterpart; the soldier is destroyed and partially forgotten within an increasingly Manichean vision of the larger, more significant conflict.

The first of these moral schemata, "The Conflict of Convictions," presents the new dialectic as a contest between hope and despair, a God-centered versus a godless world. Two voices—each employing a Miltonic conception of the coming war and each apparently unaware of the other's presence—speak rigidly of their opposing visions, providing us with a clear sense of the mutual intransigence of the mental and spiritual underpinnings of the discord. The disagreement extends beyond the simple presence or absence of religious or social faith. It comes to include a profound gap in relative conceptions of the relationship between physical and spiritual reality and so reflects the tension between the war of issues and the war of peoples, the strain between mind and flesh.

This essential difference appears openly in stanza three, in which the positive voice presents its response to the opening description of Satan's strength and Christ's weakness:

> The terrors of truth and dart of death
>   To faith alike are vain;
> Though comets, gone a thousand years,
>   Return again,
> Patient she stands—she can no more—
> And waits, nor heeds she waxes hoar. (15)

The social quietism of faith, which "can no more" but stand and wait, suggests a vision of the world in which ideal reality outweighs, by its sheer longevity if nothing else, the importance and strength of physical events. The motions of comets, like the actions of "meteoric" John Brown, cannot affect the patience of this bodiless ideal simply because the two exist in separate spheres; even age has little influence because faith, simply by not "heeding" the effects of reality, can, within its realm, overcome them. The implications of such an argument, as well as the unbridgeable distance between the two stances, become clear when the negative voice couches its reply as an appeal to the undeniable movements of physical reality or "strong Necessity" that "Surges, and heaps Time's strand with wrecks" (15). Thus the voices do not so much disagree as mutually exclude each other, the positive vision citing the eternal nature of idea, the negative wielding the fact of social conflict and the perpetual presence of "necessity."

The more serious implications of the positive voice's idealism appear in stanza eleven, in which the motions and actions of physical reality are not only dismissed as misleading but subsequently offered as worthy of destruction in favor of the new ideality:

> The Ancient of Days forever is young;
>   Forever the scheme of Nature thrives;
> I know a wind in purpose strong—
>   It spins *against* the way it drives.
> What if the gulfs their slimed foundations bare?
> So deep must the stones be hurled
> Whereon the throes of ages rear
> The final empire and the happier world. (17)

The paradox of sacrifice appears clearly in the image of the wind that "spins *against* the way it drives," while the apocalyptic vision of a world destroyed in order to rise again as "The final empire and the happier world" has a similarly Christian tone, an attitude toward the physical that clearly disregards both its value and its potential powers while offering it as victim of spiritual progress. In short, the conflict of convictions is at this point a struggle between a godless materialism and a dangerous spiritualism, each, Melville seems to suggest, equally frightening world views that, together or apart, spell disaster for the nation.

The final stanza suggests the terrible position of the prewar nation that finds itself subject to such voices:

> YEA AND NAY—
> EACH HATH HIS SAY;
> BUT GOD HE KEEPS THE MIDDLE WAY.
> NONE WAS BY
> WHEN HE SPREAD THE SKY;
> WISDOM IS VAIN, AND PROPHESY. (18)

"THE MIDDLE WAY," apparently an enigmatic silence, a refusal to reveal or conform to a single vision, is thus the way of the future and of truth, the ineffable and unmeasured space between the physical and the ideal. The poem intends an ominous, prophetic tone, and its Jobian ending reinforces the smallness of mankind and the inconsequential nature of his visions, no matter what attitudes he expresses. The overwhelming sense that all physical matter is at this point moving toward its own destruction helps us clarify the peril in which the individual, the single soldier in battle, will come to be placed. The larger concerns will crash around and through him, destroying his body while claiming to have rescued his soul.

A similarly imagistic, though less allegorical, description of individual and national suffering appears in "Shiloh," the evocative "requiem" that depicts slain bodies in the stunning silence of the battle's aftermath. The poem begins by establishing the strangely distant yet comforting relationship between nature and man in this civil war world. "The swallows fly low," the "April rain" momentarily solaces the wounded (63), and yet such imagined sympathy between the "forest-field" (63) and the dying and dead men upon it yields no more benefit to them than does the obviously hollow church—it "echoes" rather than answers their prayers and cries. In fact, despite the poem's skillfully rendered atmosphere of mourning, there is a clear if subtle note of the failure of God or nature to render lasting solace to the fallen bodies, and the mourning sounds of the verse—"While over them the swallows skim, / And all is hushed at Shiloh" (63)—may bemoan the lack of such aid as much as it expresses grief for the fallen combatants.

But if the soldiers are ultimately isolated from the assistance of God or nature, there is the suggestion that they have come closer to their enemies. Having discovered by means of their wounds the reality and importance of the physical body ("What like a bullet can undeceive!" [63]), they are now able to ignore the larger, ideological issues that moved them to fight. As a result, they befriend their wounded enemies and ironically "embrace" those whom they themselves have injured. In other words, the violence itself, a negative form of contact, enables the true embrace by exorcising the commitment to ideology that originally prompted the fighting. The individual body, like the nation it metaphorizes, can rejoin, Melville suggests, but only after and because of the purgative conflict. Yet the cost of such "therapy" is nothing less than the loss of the belatedly rediscovered body, sacrificed in pursuit of perilous ideals.

By contrast, "America," perhaps the most allegorical poem in *Battle Pieces*, once again depicts the country as a quarreling family and maternal body internally wounded by fraternal strife. Presented as a psychic history of the country—from auspicious beginning through the trauma of self-mutilation to the victory of law and triumph of maturity—the poem offers an apocalyptic dream, the vision of the poetic voice that appears to grasp both the form and meaning of the events it has recounted. As in "Apathy and Enthusiasm," we are again presented with a fatherless family in which the children are initially happy in the warmth of a youthful mother (160). That the father seems forever absent from such symbolic groups apparently reflects Melville's own background even as it suggests a more intimate, maternal locus for the national idea:

Valor with Valor strove, and died:
Fierce was Despair, and cruel was Pride;
And the lorn Mother speechless stood
Pale at the fury of her brood. (160–61)

At this point the brothers appear as allegorical representations of emotional states, and their conflict, fraught with the ambiguity of intrafamilial struggle, silences the mother's "language"—the binding argument that defines her as national idea. This loss of speech reappears frequently in *Battle Pieces* and serves to remind us that the failure of language generally means the birth of war, the work of words becoming the "speech" of weapons. Thus the "speechless" mother recedes into a coma to dream the primordial vision of an essentially cruel and threatening universe:

The terror of the vision there—
    A silent vision unavowed,
Revealing earth's foundation bare,
    And Gorgon in her hidden place. (161)

The evocation of Gorgon, a clear threat to the potency and growth of the national idea, suggests that what the mother sees is a potential reflection of herself, the form she may assume should she fail in the face of strife. The dream also allegorically suggests that the true nature of the Civil War, especially the battles themselves, comes closest to the kind of horror represented by the castrating vision of Gorgon, for seeing and comprehending the horror of one's own fratricide may in fact equal the confrontation of the Gorgonian element in the self.

Thus the mother's resurrection yields a figure without "trace of passion or of strife—":

A clear calm look. It spake of pain,
But such as purifies from stain—
Sharp pangs that never come again—
   And triumph repressed by knowledge meet,
Power delicate, and hope grown wise,
   And youth matured for age's seat—
Law on her brow and empire in her eyes. (162)

The picture of national regeneration through the perception of internal evil, the realization that the conflict exists within the nation and within each individual, offers a synthetic result to Melville's dialectical processes within the volume. The conflict, he seems to hope, will purify and help give new life to the wiser, more fully integrated national consciousness. The "death" brought about by war, the figurative sleep of the mother, will yield a new birth that heals the national concept even if it destroys the individual in the process.

A War of Words

If the forces of romantic desire attenuated in the pages of *The Confidence-Man* find new life in *Battles Pieces,* they do so both in the investigation of a fragmented formality and in the overreaching heroic patriotism of the potentially shattered individual. Each such fundamental strain within the collection not only helps renew Melville's concern with the conflict between flesh and spirit but also reformulates the linguistic debate by setting formality against the desire to reach beyond restraining limits. The consistent energy that upsets or possibly destroys the poetic line, stanza, or structure clearly recalls the seemingly ineluctable, Ahabian desire that has so often formed the source of such self-destructive impulses. In this respect, these early lyrics not only present fragmented forms that reflect the disintegrating world and its conflicting linguistic visions but also employ individual forms and lines that embody those tensions and so provide a contextual rationale for Melville's "unwieldy" verses.

The impulse toward disintegration in the collection revises Melville's earlier interest in spatial form into both an exploration of concrete lyric formality and the creation of even smaller, more concentrated "formal" fragments. The "Verses Inscriptive and Memorial," for instance, reflect the damage that the war has inflicted and attempt to gather the remnants of the shattered society that the volume depicts. The section contains sixteen poems, most of which briefly speak in epitaph, as though carved on the gravestones of those who died in the earlier pages of the book. The majority of these poems are thus attempts to provide closure and moral purpose to the lost lives of the dead and the psychological wounds of the living. Nevertheless at the same time they linguistically "stand for" the absent bodies of their subjects. Like the desire to carve language into the permanence of stone, to give presence and voice to the silent dead, these poems address the distance between the dead and the living, now bridgeable only by language. The gathered fragments thus arrange the missing into a larger form at the same time that they reflect the palpable gaps in the clearly wounded body of the nation.

For instance, "On the Men of Maine, killed in the Victory of Baton Rouge, Louisiana" begins by noting the distance between the soldiers and their homes, revealing the difference between North and South and weakly attempting to bring together the disparate states of Maine and Louisiana under a national embrace:

> Afar they fell. It was the zone
>   Of fig and orange, cane and lime
> (A land how all unlike their own,
> With the cold pine-grove overgrown),
>   But still their Country's clime. (168)

This argument seems forced against the simple statement of the climatic and floral differences that assert themselves as facts equal to those of the soldiers' deaths. Likewise, the syntactical and rhythmic emphasis on "Afar" indicates that the subject of these first few lines is the anxiety created by the double absence of those who die away from their homes. The poem's second half thus attempts to take up the challenge of the first half's ending by offering a structure of sacrifice and gain that will reclaim the distant dead and simultaneously strengthen the national vision by assuring that the dead did not, after all, fall on "foreign" ground. The example of the fallen, praying with their last breath for the preservation of

Union (168), becomes an attempt at union itself: the language of the dying transcends the distance between Maine and Louisiana even as it offers
a challenge to those who doubt the assertion that such far-flung areas can
exist under a single government. The tension between physical distance
and emotional connection gives the poem its energy and reemphasizes its
place in the collection as both a "piece" of the whole and a reminder of
the separateness of those pieces. It is, like the soldiers, a fragment in its
position in the "national" volume and, at the same time, a component
straining to justify its meaning and purpose.

What is perhaps more significant than the connection between the soldiers and the fragmented sections of the volume, however, is the simultaneous presence within the poetry itself of a struggle between unity and
violation, form and anti-formal energy. Such "awkwardness" of verse has
long been attributed to Melville's supposed lack of poetic skill, and yet it
is clear that the basic energies of his aesthetic interests require such a
rough and struggling meter and such seemingly uncomfortable stanzaic
forms to help express the abiding dialectic between form and disintegration that informs the very content of the poems.[9] In "The Conflict of
Convictions," for instance, not only do we hear a debate between opposing visions of human reality but we feel in the texture of the four stress
lines and in the irregularity of the stanzas and rhymes the volatile nature
of Melville's material and his difficult and at times uncertain attitude towards it.

This sort of metrical and formal maneuver, at once awkward and meaningful, pervades the early poetry to the point that it is often difficult
to imagine that Melville can, in fact, construct an elegant line, but such
lyrics as "Shiloh" reveal if not metrical perfection then a delicacy of verse
whose ventures into roughness are brief and meaningful.[10] Just as in the
majority of these poems, Melville makes use of metrical *regularity* as the
emphasizing exception rather than the rule and yet does prove capable of
following the more traditional path of introducing anomalous variations
into an otherwise euphonious construction.

Whatever the ultimate reasons for the relative suavity or roughness of
Melville's early verse, it is clear that his conception of language during
this period has come to include a conflict between metaphysical yearning
and the limitations and variations of form. *Battle Pieces* offers a surprising
struggle between the author's language and the function of words within
the battle poems themselves. Language undergoes a remarkable inversion:
the Ahabian conception of speech as the vehicle that replaces bodily absence reappears both in the war cries of the charging brigades and in the
"mouths" of the rifles and cannon that "speak" against the men and cities

before them. A sense of the perversion of debate emerges, the failure of speech to perform its normal duties, leaving weapons to take the place of words.

A similar vision of the "word" of war appears in "The Swamp Angel," a personification of the "great Parrot gun" firing during the bombardment of Charleston. The gun's dooming "far decree" and "scream that screams up to the zenith" are contrasted with the "wails and shrieks" of the victims, their former mockery of the "coal-black Angel," and their vain calls to Michael "(The white man's seraph was he)" (109). The righteous rhetoric of the anti-slavery North has become the mighty righteousness of the "speaking" black cannon whose "Afric lip" (107) damns the once scornful inhabitants of the city.

The apparent omnipresence of bellicose screams and screaming weapons, however, ultimately cuts against the overarching effort of *Battle Pieces* to recover via language a sense of social connection and social form. The same impulse that cites the silence of the victorious troops at Vicksburg informs the voice of the historically silent Lee as he fictionally exorcises the struggle he seemed to embody. Likewise, Melville's own "Supplement" speaks directly of the failed "symmetry" of his book and of the failure of events to "round" "themselves into completion" (259). Thus the larger rhetoric of *Battle Pieces* attempts by a keener devotion to form and by sense of the function of tragic structure to rebuild and repair, to employ a more rigidly regulated language in the hope of giving form to the formless aftermath of the Civil War.[11] That it fails seems perfectly clear to Melville as does the sense that in the struggling roughness of that failure some sense of the doubleness within himself and the nation does appear. In fact, he seems in the end to see the nation and his book as versions of Ishmael's "man . . . [who] takes this whole universe for a vast practical joke" and "bolts down all events, all creeds . . . never mind how knobby; as an ostrich of potent digestion gobbles down bullets and gunflints":[12]

> With certain evils men must be more or less patient. Our institutions have a potent digestion, and may in time convert and assimilate to good all elements thrown in, however originally alien. (269)

Though this passage from the supplement employs a more collective moral vision than Ishmael's grimly comic perception of nature's malice, each presents an image of incorporation that sees form as a body that, knit together, attains a symmetry no matter how contradictory its parts. It is Melville's vision in *Battle Pieces* both for America and for his obviously knobby, lead-filled book, and it is finally appropriate that the image recalls Ishmael, whose spirit, changed though it is, resurfaces in the book's pages.

7

CLAREL AND THE SEARCH FOR THE DIVINE BODY

But ah, the dream to test by deed,
To seek to handle the ideal
And make a sentiment serve need:
To try to realize the unreal!

Despite the apparent differences between *Battle Pieces* and *Clarel,* the distance between the personal and social civil war that the earlier collection offers and the exploration of Western religion found in *Clarel* is neither great nor troubling. Though ten years stretch between their respective publications, each book participates in the important revitalization of Melville's interest in large-scale constructions and in the productive tensions that animate his earlier work. Having found in the Civil War patterns of social, familial, and personal division—as well as an important dialectical struggle between form and dissolution—Melville emerges from *Battle Pieces* with enormous energy and a surer sense of the sources of his creative power. Now free from the strictures of a historical subject, he turns once again to a more personal and biographical investigation of the problematic relationship between mental and physical fulfillment. In service of this revised goal, he consequently shifts the locus of his search, transforming the dialectic between flesh and spirit—or, as in *Battle Pieces,* between form and content—into an attempt to understand the relative benefits of mental and physical fulfillment in light of the paradoxical presence-absence of Christ's mystical body. In other words, if Christ, the underlying "object" of the poem's quest, represents the incarnation of divine spirit—the metaphysical become physical—then the attempt to locate evidence of his reality becomes, in effect, the search for a body that has already ascended into spirit and so ceased to exist as physical reality. The result of this paradox is a newly created tension within the older head-heart dialectic, for the figure of Christ, suggesting as it does a miraculous resolution of the dualism, serves finally only to deepen the mysteries of human reality.

In order to intensify rather than relax the argument, Melville places at its center not an experienced quester but a figure whose understanding of both mental and physical fulfillment is tentative and largely hypothetical. Clarel, like Pierre before him, draws most of his experience from books and clearly lacks both sexual maturity and the ability to balance or harmonize a restless intellectualism with emerging erotic desires.[1] In this respect, his search for physical verification of spiritual fact, his quest for the Christly body, also becomes a search for the validity and meaning of his own attempt to gain fulfillment through sexuality. Caught within the radical paradox of the mystical body, Clarel searches for evidence of Christ's reality even as he searches for an understanding of the relationship between physical and spiritual existence in himself. Yet he finds only a deeper involvement in and frustration with this modified, Christianized dialectic, the paradox of which ultimately prevents either physical or mental comfort.[2]

Around this unmoored, undecided youth moves a various cast of characters who nevertheless fall into relatively clear categories according to their attitudes toward the body. Among the numerous minor figures in the poem, Clarel encounters both a significant number of religious or philosophical ascetics and a nearly equal contingent of Dionysian revelers. In fact, the supporting cast in the poem can be easily divided into those who deny the value of bodily experience and those who rely upon the physical as the central source of their existence. The poem's other major figures, including Clarel himself, unfold within this very concrete manifestation of the book's dialectic, each attempting some synthesis of the two philosophical alternatives. Thus it is finally the conversations of these major figures set against the divided background of the minor characters that form the substance of the poem and provide us with a linguistic correlative for the dualistic framework. The poem itself, like the characters it presents, offers a vision of language that struggles between tortured metaphysical address and various degrees of playfulness, and the central characters who debate the viability of the spiritual world they physically seek likewise attempt to construct the absent body of Christ in that very language. The poetry thus becomes, in effect, the missing body, for though it finally fails to locate the remnants of the mystical flesh, it does give us, in content as well as style, a solid picture of the paradox of its absent subject.

Dead Sea, Missing Body

Perhaps the most frequently noted characteristic of both Melville's experience of the Holy Land and its depiction in *Clarel* is the lifelessness and desiccation of the land itself, the palpable sense of physical blight with its intimation of lost promise and waste.[3] The landscape of the pilgrimage, the place through which Clarel and others will seek traces of divine presence, presents an image of bodily loss, a world whose physical aspect, much like the landscape of "The Encantadas," reveals a profound inability to invigorate either its own soil or those who dwell or walk upon it. Lifelessness and impotence pervade the poem's world, and Melville's descriptions of it continually emphasize the omnipresence of stone and the feeling of entombment found in *Pierre* and "Bartleby":

> Behold the stones! And never one
> A lichen greens; and, turn them o'er—
> No worm—no life; but, all the more,
> Good witnesses.
>
> .   .   .   .
>
> Their mount of vision, voiceless, bare,
> It is that ridge, the desert's own,
> Which by its dead Medusa stare,
> Petrific o'er the valley thrown,
> Congeals Arabia into stone.[4]

The familiar opposition in the first passage between green and its stony absence informs us of Melville's primary perception of this world's bodily foundation. Similarly, the specific mention of the absence of any "worm" or life beneath the stones suggests that this landscape likewise maintains no regenerative properties, no ability to reanimate flesh through the ingestion and reformation that the worm provides. It is a world beyond productive decay, separated from the cycles of natural rebirth in which the figure of Christ traditionally participates. Likewise, the second passage recalls the psychological and sexual petrifaction or castration Melville so often presents in the figure of Medusa and thus suggests that this landscape embodies the essential reality of a flesh rendered unproductive through psychological terror. The power connected with Mrs. Glenndinning in *Pierre* and Goneril in *The Confidence-Man*, for instance, here shows itself not so much in a single figure but in the negatively "touched" surface of the once-divine landscape.

Just as the land itself exists in a cadaverous state beyond decay, its indigenous inhabitants and their architecture also reveal a physical decay and disease that the landscape seems to promote. The Jerusalem of the book's beginning contains "Dismantled, torn, / Disastrous houses, ripe for fall—" (70) and a populace that "Harbors like lizards in dry well" (70). Melville compares these inhabitants to the outcast, impoverished, and criminal beings of the world, as though the holy city, instead of the site of resurrection, had become nothing more than an elaborately built tomb, a place for the physically beaten to await their end. With his picture of Emim Bay, once "armed, and, happily, mounted well," entering Jerusalem "maimed, [and] disfigured" (71), Melville alerts us to the distance between past and present, between the Jerusalem that Christ entered and the city of Emim Bay and Clarel—a place of violence and demythologized death, where the individual body tends its unhealing wounds or succumbs to disease. Beyond its sepulchral associations, the city itself is also figuratively connected to the body, but only in order to emphasize Jerusalem's production of waste in the form of both refuse and diseased humanity. The description of the "dung-gate" (77), for instance, suggests an anatomical metaphor in which the body of the city discharges through this anal opening both the physical waste produced by its inhabitants and the "scum" (77) among its population. Not only was the imprisoned Christ supposedly forced to pass through this gate, but the location also becomes within the poem the "birth" site of Margoth, the iconoclast who produces roughly the same deflating effect upon the visions of the holy city as does the sight and smell of the dung-gate. Each, by different means, effectively and factually debases the belief that the pilgrim treads on "holy" ground.

But perhaps the most devastating and convincing evidence that this city and its environs fail to provide evidence of heavenly blessing or fertility appears in the poem's reaction to and description of the Dead Sea. For Melville, who has so clearly relied upon the death-in-life powers of water to feed his life and writing, the very notion of a "Dead Sea" deeply intensifies the horrific lifelessness and lack of regenerative power this world presents. It is as though in seeing this image of doom, this evocation of the destruction of Sodom and Gomorrah, he is also contemplating his most personal image of vital dissolution, for the scene seems less an example of Ishmael's "ungraspable phantom of life" than some equally mysterious phantom of death:

> No gravel bright nor shell was seen,
> Nor kelpy growth nor coralline,
> But dead boughs stranded, which the rout
> Of Jordan, in old freshets born
> In Libanus, had madly torn
> Green from her arbor and thrust out
> Into the liquid waste. (231)

Though the verse acknowledges that "beauty inextinct may charm/In outline of the vessel's form" (230), it is more for the purpose of pointing out the differences between "Fair Como" and this sea and shore now overrun by "horror." This world has lost its fertility; stripped of any ability to provide productive physical or spiritual solace, it is a place of unmiraculous death.

It is to such a world and landscape that the student, Clarel, comes in order to conduct his search. From our first vision of this brooding young man it is clear that he possesses less experience than education, less contact with the life of the flesh than that of the mind. Thus his initial experience of the legendary land yields two important disturbances within his ability to understand what he sees. First, he quickly begins to realize that the world described in his books does not necessarily coincide with the one before his eyes—that, by implication, the ideal realities pictured in theological texts may not exist in the physical forms before him. Second, his uncertainties about the reliability of books, which began even as he toured "Latin lands" (5), suggest that his understanding of all aspects of life, given his limited experience, is now open to the same subversion:

> So he, the student. 'Twas a mind,
> Earnest by nature, long confined
> Apart like Vesta in a grove
> Collegiate, but let to rove
> At last abroad among mankind,
> And here in end confronted so
> By the true genius, friend or foe,
> And actual visage of a place
> Before but dreamed of in the glow
> Of fancy's spiritual grace. (6)

This description plays not only upon Clarel's delayed introduction to raw experience but also upon the uncertainty within the composition of a self that has had little chance to test what the mind has attempted to grasp. In fact, the first line suggests that until this point Clarel has, in fact, been nothing more than a *mind* that has remained virginal, a condition that must equally apply to his descriptively elided body. In short, Clarel lacks both a depth of mental experience that will temper and complete his reading and an initiation into bodily reality that will feed and help reshape his thinking. Like Pierre, he has lived thus far in a fictive garden, and the encounter with the rougher edges of human existence will continue to tax his flimsy epistemology.

In this light, Clarel's "pilgrimage" becomes a double search for the "body" of theology, on the one hand, and for his own bodily reality, on the other. He comes to Jerusalem to test the ideal against the real, but he also comes, as do all who visit historical sites, in hopes of receiving from the very physical matter of the place some connection to "absent" histori-

cal or theological truth. His is the psychology that infuses relics with the
presence and meaning of absent people or times. Yet what he ultimately
seeks—physical proof of the metaphysical, a response from Pierre's Terror
Stone—cannot exist because such a vision remains bound in this place to
the mystery of Christ, the spirit made flesh, the resurrected and ultimately
ascendant body. Thus Clarel seeks the missing body of Christ in the landscape, in historic sites, relics, and even in the bodies of those with whom
he travels. At the same time, however, he begins to find his own physical
self and to test its discovery within the context of his new relationships.
That Christian theology in many ways insists on the problematic nature
of this sort of search contributes to the futility of Clarel's religious quest
even as it frustrates his own sexual one. He remains caught within a contradictory dualism, and the process of his search, as well as the very texture of the poem, continually reflects the difficulty of his position.

For instance, his initial encounters with the holy sites of Jerusalem,
despite Nehemiah's example of faithful interpretation, become a series of
disconcertions and disillusionments. The vision of Olivet "Distinct, yet
dreamy in repose, / As of Katahdin in hot noon, / Lonely, with all his
pines in swoon" (11) and the "locations" of the passion evoke only outbursts of struggling disbelief—"Olivet. Olivet do I see? / The ideal
upland, trod by *Thee?*" (11)—and complex emotional and intellectual reactions that reflect the confusion of the "earnest" mind. Unlike the complete cynics who note only the irony of such "holy" places surrounded
"By pedlars versed in wonted tricks, / Venders of charm or crucifix" (15),
and even more unlike the hermits who care for these sites (13), the seeking
mind of Clarel finds itself somewhere between iconoclastic disdain and
the blindness of faith; he searches the grounds with an uncertain sadness,
unable to accept their connection to the absent God and unwilling to
surrender his hope that such a god may, in fact, still be present:

> "—Nay, is He fled?
> Or tranced lies, tranced nor unbewept
> With Dorian gods? or, fresh and clear,
> A charm diffused through the sphere
> Streams in the ray through yonder dome?
> Not hearsed He is. But hath ghost home
> Dispersed in soil, in sea, in air?
> False Pantheism, false though fair!" (18–19)

The distance between the ugliness of the smoke-filled tomb and the vision
of the rapturous faces of those who tended the fallen form of Christ leads
the young thinker to attempt an explanation, via Greek theology, that

will account for Christ even as it discounts this particular scene. It is an attempt, in some respect, to remove the figure of Christ from its associations with the God of the desert and place it in the more humanistic atmosphere of Hellenism. And yet, even as he undertakes the explanation, Clarel realizes its casuistic basis and ends his small, inner debate in the same place he started. Even more significantly, however, his encounter with the physical site of Christian event yields, at least for the moment, neither faith nor denunciation but an inner struggle to bridge the gap between reality and spirituality by means of a language that, as the poem develops, consistently seeks to reconnect physical evidence with its ostensible spiritual identity:

> What object sensible to touch
> Or quoted fact may faith rely on,
> If faith confideth overmuch
> That here's a monument in Zion:
> Its substance ebbs—see, day and night
> The sands subsiding from the height;
> In time, absorbed, these grains may help
> To form new sea-bed, slug and kelp. (79)

The question asked forms one of the fundamental statements of the poem, for the attempt to find in an "object sensible to touch" evidence enough to believe in the monuments of Zion does, in fact, form the basis of Clarel's search. Even in this passage he attempts to involve the lifeless landscape before him in the processes of regeneration by suggesting that the dissolution of the soil "may help / To form new sea-bed, slug and kelp." But what remains is simply the confused question, the desire to see it positively answered, and the problematic voice that wishes, as though in re-creation of Christ, to bring flesh and spirit together.

The result of Clarel's early tourism is an intensification of the split between past and present, scripture and scene. He becomes intensely aware of the difference between that which has seized his imagination in books and that which purports to be the reality behind such words. In fact, the further Clarel investigates the holy sites, the more he appears to realize that should a spiritual reality exist for him, it does so not in the rocks and desert and broken lives he sees before him but in the very language of the texts he has previously studied. And yet, such a celebration of "Those Paschal words" (83) fails ultimately to satisfy both because of the language's distance from reality and because of the difficulty for Clarel and others who attempt to enact the vision it creates. In this respect it is significant that upon their exit from the "upper room" where those

words seem potentially powerful, Clarel and Nehemiah encounter not another vision of Christ's legendary presence but a human "horror":

> Clarel shrank:
> And he, is *he* of human rank?—
> "Knowest thou him?" he asked.—"Yea, yea,"
> And beamed on that disfeatured clay:
> "Toulib, to me? to Him are due
> These thanks—the God of me and you
> And all; to whom His own shall go
> In Paradise and be re-clad,
> Transfigured like the morning glad.—
> Yea, friend in Christ, this man I know,
> This fellow-man."—And afterward
> The student from true sources heard
> How Nehemiah had proved his friend,
> Sole friend even of that trunk of woe,
> When sisters failed him in the end. (83–84)

The shocking distance between the revery of Saint John's loving words
and their enactment by Nehemiah underlines, on the one hand, the split
in Clarel's mind between his reading and his first-hand discoveries, and,
on the other, his own failure to incorporate the paschal vision into a practical ethic. The sight of Toulib's "disfeatured clay" disrupts his dreamy
remembrance of charitable ideas and forces him to come to terms with
the world before him and its relationship to theology. Nehemiah's ability
to apply Christian doctrine and believe in the prospect for spiritual and
physical transformation challenges Clarel's intellectualism with the simplicity and undeniable reality of his actions.

A similar juxtaposition of potential reverence and irreverent fact occurs
much later in the book. While in Bethlehem, the pilgrims visit the supposed site of the Nativity and with silent respect view the "semicircular
recess" that holds "A silver sun" "set in plummet-line exact / Beneath the
star in pavement-tract / Above" (429)—the marker of the "exact" point
upon which Christ was born. But their quiet visit is soon disrupted, first
by the sight of "A band of rustics" (429), some with missing hands, and
then, somewhat later, by an ass that "violates" the container of holy water
at the shrine entrance (437). Such a scene recalls Ahab's legendary insult
to the calabash even as it asserts the power and undeniable presence of
physical fact in the face of idealistic vision. The religious attempt to transform the physical water into symbolic substance, to, in effect, partially
deny its reality as water via symbolic utterance, holds no validity for the
ass, whose motivations are purely physical. Thus the effect of the scene is

not necessarily to debunk the symbolic meaning of the water but to ridicule those who insist upon denying the water its physical reality in favor of an exclusive symbolic meaning.

Clarel's search for evidence of the divine body does not confine itself to a tour of dubious locations, however. Perhaps of more importance and certainly of greater influence are his early encounters with Nehemiah and Celio.[5] Nehemiah, while clearly offering the strongest visible example of the Christian life, simultaneously evokes the absent god and invites a criticsm of "chronometrical" devotion by sometimes acting the fool. He functions as both wise man and idiot and continuously makes clear the close ties between these two roles. His initial appearance to Clarel thus exhibits all the drama of an incarnation, as though this fatherly pilgrim had appeared in response to the younger man's crisis:

> Nearer he drew
> Revealed against clear skies of blue;
> And—in that Syrian air of charm—
> He seemed, illusion such was given,
> Emerging from the level heaven,
> And vested with its liquid calm. (26)

Nehemiah's otherworldliness applies, at least by impression, to his ethereal body. He appears to emerge not only as a result of Clarel's prayer but as though directly sprung from the scripture-filled mind. Furthermore, Nehemiah's offer of the biblical "guide book"—"Without a guide where guide should be? / Receive me, friend: the book—take ye." (27)—merely reinforces the sense of separation between the world of the scriptures and modern Jerusalem. For Nehemiah's "guide" refers, of course, to another place and time and is ultimately useful only as a key to the inner world not yet fully glimpsed by the young Clarel.

If Nehemiah's faith and actions demonstrate his resemblance to Christ, however, then his frequent repetitions of spiritual truths, uttered as though to avoid thought, make him both liable to criticism and frequently useless to Clarel's troubled mind. For instance, his ability to see past Toulib's deformity also leads him to taste the polluted Jordan. In each instance the physical reality at hand is either devalued or ignored in favor of a symbolic vision: the deformed beggar is thus whole; the dirty, unpalatable river "sugar sweet" (212). Yet as Melville's previous pictures of transcendental idealism have shown, the willful insensitivity that values symbolic "sweetness" over actual bitterness may protect the soul, but it does nothing for the survival and happiness of the body. Such a vision perversely overturns natural fact and argues, with the "triumph" of paradox, that black is white and white black. Even so, the dreamy, transfigurative description of Nehemiah's death suggests that, whatever the objections to his thinking, his verifiable goodness and virtue do not fail to lend his life a degree of transcendent power. In his behavior he remains the most notably sanctified member of the pilgrimage, and his absence severely darkens the poem's second half.

On the other hand, his counterpart, Celio, recreates the absence of Christ while offering a distant companionship, if not guidance, to the mental seeker. Thus while following Nehemiah in search of divine contact, Clarel is also conducting a similar "pilgrimage" to the "holy" sites of Celio's "passion," only to discover that, like Christ, Celio has left tantalizing words and an unresponsive grave. The failure to effect a true connection with Celio reinforces the poem's attempt to delineate the unfulfilled spiritual and physical desires of the quester. Still, the search for the missing Christ—the figure who, at least in imagination, fully integrates spirit and flesh—leads Clarel toward such attractive figures at the same time that it prevents him from fully accepting them as viable substitutes.

Given Clarel's lack of sexual experience, this early search, as well as its expansion throughout the volume, quickly becomes a youthful investigation of the value of physical and emotional contact with those he encounters. In other words, the search for physical connection to the divine body joins, in effect, a desire to locate Clarel's own capacity for physical and emotional fulfillment—to find his own body—and to test that capacity within his emerging relationships. Thus the early identification with Celio involves Clarel's newly emerged desire for feminine sexuality even as it reveals a degree of narcissism. The voiceless meeting of the two not only suggests a version of "love at first sight" but, because of this epiphanic tone, also alerts us to the probability that each is seeing in the other his own vision of a passionate, secret self:

What look, responsive look is seen
In Celio, as together there
They pause? Can these a climax share? (48)

. . . .

Think ye such thoughts? If so it be,
Yet these may eyes transmit and give?
Mere eyes? so quick, so sensitive?
Howbeit Celio knew his mate. (49)

The language of these passages is not only sexually tinged, but furthers the distance between these apparently mirrored sensibilities by evoking physical contact in order to emphasize its absence. Theirs is a meeting of minds that have moved away from the distinguishable sides of dualistic debate to find wordless, untouchable sympathy in the tenuous middle ground of doubt. Their "romance," brief and unconsummated though it is, not only haunts Clarel with its untested promise of intimacy and spiritual support but also curiously infiltrates his emerging feelings for Ruth, the two potential "lovers" mingling in a difficult combination of physical and mental desire:

> But every thought
> Of Ruth was strangely underrun
> By Celio's image. Celio—sought
> Vainly in body—now appeared
> As in the spiritual part,
> Haunting the air, and in the heart. (65–66)

In part because Celio is a hunchback, the sense of separation between spiritual and physical selves within him grows particularly strong in Clarel's mind. The physical and emotional contact that Clarel sought with Celio yields to Clarel's physical desire for Ruth, and yet the spiritual consummation that does, in fact, occur between Clarel and Celio appears to block a similar, bodiless intimacy with the feminine. Thus in somewhat typical Melvillean fashion, Clarel finds deep personal connection more accessible with a male, despite the brevity of the incident and perhaps because of its negative physicality, than with a female whose attractions appear to be predominantly physical. Whatever formula this mixture finally follows, it is certain that Clarel's difficulties in regard to these potential "mates" reflect his similar efforts to unite fact and faith within his search and so come to terms with the paradoxical composition of the figure of Christ.

Though Ruth's appearance and Clarel's sudden attraction to her clearly echo his brief relationship with Celio, these discoveries also open a more significant area of investigation in Clarel's search for his own sexuality. The notion that Ruth may offer a fulfillment that will replace the need for spiritual certainty gradually becomes a part of the poem's dialectic, joining its force to the examples of other characters who have found contentment in the physical. In fact, at first sight Ruth evokes in Clarel a vision of preconscious, Edenic pleasure. Like her predecessors from the early novels, Ruth attracts in part because she manages to combine tropical sensuality with much more "civilized" features—in her case, the "Hebrew profile" that apparently balances the "pagan" aspects of her appearance (54). Even more significant than her association with "Red budded corals" and palm-fringed "Indian reefs" (54) is the evidence in her "tell-tale flush" of "June in some far clover land" (54). Having migrated from America to Jerusalem, she retains for Clarel some evidence of her birth in the far more verdant and, by implication, more potent land of his own birth. In other words, much as the idea of Christ combines spiritual strength with the palpability of flesh, so does Ruth bring the fresh flush of American life into harmony with the austere but potential spiritual vigor of the holy lands.

Ruth's evocation of America depends in part upon her virginity and her close ties to her mother, Agar. The image of home and hearth they present strengthens Clarel's desire not so much for Ruth herself but for the construction of his own familial center, Ishmael's commitment to the "wife, the heart, the bed, the table, the saddle, the fire-side, the country":[6]

> Clarel, bereft while still but young,
> Mother or sister had not known;
> To him now first in life was shown,
> In Agar's frank demeanor kind,
> What charm to woman may belong
> When by a natural bent inclined
> To goodness in domestic play:
> On earth no better thing than this—
> It canonizes very clay:
> Madonna, hence thy worship is. (120)

Clarel, whose sexual innocence extends to his lack of any feminine contact when young, is attracted not simply by the combination of maternal warmth and budding sensuality in Agar and Ruth but by the paradoxical combination of virginity and maternity. The "virgin's eyes" (76) of Ruth, "Pure home of all we seek and prize" (76), in combination with the "domestic play" of Agar help to form an image, equally evocative of Christ and the Virgin Mary, in which sexuality is paradoxically coupled with innocence, spirit with flesh.[7] In short, these women together form a potential substitute for the absent figure of Christ by means of their very presence as opposed to Christ's all too obvious immateriality.

Despite the pleasing duality of the women themselves, however, it becomes clear that for Clarel they ultimately fall on the side of flesh rather than spirit. In other words, the solution they offer eventually opposes the austerity and asceticism of those committed to purely spiritual fulfillment.[8] Thus late in the text, after his encounters with numerous ascetics, it is no surprise to find Clarel expressing his willingness to give up the search for divine truth in favor of the more tangible satisfactions of his own emotional and physical desires: "No life domestic do ye own / Within these walls: woman I miss" (376). Yet he cannot ignore the arguments within himself that such desire and its rewards may too greatly lack a spiritual reality. In fact, this struggle continues until Clarel, still unsure of the true import of his decision, determines to "let fate drive" (485) and mentally commits himself to a "domestic" life with Ruth.

Like the structure of *Israel Potter*, however, the pattern of the poem's movement undercuts productive union by assuring that Clarel's retreat into the precincts of intellectual male companionship helps destroy his opportunity for both female attachments and physical fulfillment. The poem's tension between flesh and spirit manifests itself in its similar opposition between the implications of male and female lifestyles: the masculine element—with few notable exceptions—offers an aphysical, philosophical life, while the feminine brings an active sexuality and emotionalism that, whatever its spiritual associations, opposes such male intellectual questing.[9] The death of Ruth and Agar thus suggests not only that the life they offered remains unreachable for Clarel but also that his failure to accept the ascetic life coincides with his failure to consummate the physical. Each vision within the poem runs on a parallel, coterminous track, thereby assuring that the dialectic remains unresolved and Clarel's search for synthesis fails.[10]

In only a few cases does Clarel attempt to violate his division of the world into masculine spirituality and feminine sexuality. In the episodes with Celio, for instance, there are hints that a possible physical connection may have discovered a source of contact suitably "pure," and yet the fact of Celio's deformity seems partial evidence that the poem works against such a meeting. More significant, Clarel seems for a moment to discover in Vine a solution to the strain between physical and spiritual commitment as well as to the corresponding conflict of the sexes. Not only does Vine look "So pure, so virginal in shrine / Of the true unworldliness" (225), but he arouses in the younger man a desire for "communion true / And close" (225). Clarel thus comes near to an awkward theory of an aphysical sexuality based upon a "masculine-feminine" union of minds:

> Divided mind knew Clarel here;
> The heart's desire did interfere.
> Thought he, How pleasant in another
> Such sallies, or in thee, if said
> After confidings that should wed
> Our souls in one:—Ah, call me *brother!*—

So feminine his passionate mood
Which, long as hungering unfed,
All else rejected or withstood. (226–27)

Such language is largely responsible for the critical argument that Vine
stands for Hawthorne to Clarel's Melville. Whatever the biographical basis
for the relationship, it is clear that to Clarel the potential exists for a type
of union that would provide an equivalent to the male-female relationship. Clarel assumes the feminine stance and thus reformulates his previous division of male and female, spirit and flesh, into a vision of male
union that comes near to integrating body and mind.

The prospect proves evanescent, however, and quickly evaporates in the
face of Vine's unresponsiveness:

But for thy fonder dream of love
In man toward man—the soul's caress—
The negatives of flesh should prove
Analogies of non-cordialness
In spirit.—   (227)

In imagining Vine's thoughts, Clarel reveals his own answer to his own
advance. He thus offers "The negatives of flesh" not only as a barrier to
all spiritual understanding but as an analogue of the spiritual barriers between men. In other words, while women apparently offer the potential
for physical and emotional fulfillment, men, despite the purity of the
philosophical encounter, remain apart both mentally and physically. Any
attempt to move beyond debate to some more intimate understanding
fails in part because of the physical barrier between them. In this respect,
in the search for his own sexuality and its connection to his spiritual quest,
Clarel finds himself caught between an intellectually poor but physically
rich relationship with Ruth and an intellectually rich but physically impossible union with Vine. In understanding that intellect can progress
only so far, he is led back toward a realization of the importance of each
half of the dialectic. In the search for Christ *and* contentment, Clarel
remains uncompromising and so unsuccessful in his desire for a synthesis
of mind and body.

"Then Keep Thy Heart"

The contour of Clarel's overall search becomes clearer when we allow
the poem's multitude of supporting characters to emerge in contrast to
his changing positions. These partially programmatic figures, whether
they appear briefly or at length, fall easily into three categories: ascetics,

either religious or philosophical; Dionysians, or those otherwise attuned to the pleasures of a physical life; and the few tenuously independent seekers, like Clarel himself, who struggle to synthesize these two extremes. Each character Clarel encounters thus acts as the representative of a potential vision and language that he can measure, try on, or critically oppose. He becomes, in essence, the largely silent but observant center of a series of encounters and debates that variously embody the dualistic movements of his own mind.

As though in correspondence to Clarel's initial encounter with the stark landscape, the various religious and philosophical ascetics who populate the poem offer a vision of spirituality that sees the flesh as enemy. Like Ahab and Pierre before them, they fear both the deceptiveness and the limitations of the body and consequently devote themselves to the avoidance of physical reality and the intensification of their mental or spiritual lives. Aside from Nehemiah, Clarel meets several spiritualists through the course of his journey, among them the Syrian Monk, who in penance for the "sin of doubt" reenacts Christ's period of temptation in the desert. Likewise Salvaterra, the Franciscan guide to the Church of the Star, has forsaken "the charm / Val d'Arno yields" (425) for "this dull calm / Of desert" (425) and has effectively ruined his health through ascetic fervor: "the cheek austere / Deepening in hollow, waste and loss" (428). The strongest negative example of the physical and psychological dangers of the ascetic life appears at the monastery of Mar Saba in the form of the "celibate" whose encounter with Clarel becomes a turning point in the younger man's journey. Hoping to gain some insight or guidance from the priest concerning the sources of spiritual truth, Clarel confesses to him his own desire for "domestic" life and contact with women, only to receive in return the monk's continued silence and a book of celibate teachings that contains "Renouncings, yearnings, charges dread/Against our human nature dear" (376). The overall effect of the encounter is to suggest that denial of the body, as in "Bartleby," becomes for some a denial of language, a failure to encounter the world either physically or linguistically, and so Clarel is left in unconvinced and unenlightened contemplation of the "Silence and the Dead" (378).[11]

As Melville has repeatedly demonstrated in his earlier works, however, the ascetic vision is not confined to religious enthusiasts.[12] There consequently appears in *Clarel* a collection of characters whose avoidance of the body parallels that of the spiritualists but whose devotion centers on the powers of the mind rather than God. Celio, whose tortured body and romantic language echo Ahab's, is the first in this group of metaphysical questers. Like some of Melville's earlier characters he demonstrates a con-

nection between a wounded flesh and a negative attitude towards the
body (37). Separated from both feminine love and mental companionship,
he distorts the physical world into a reflection of his own, self-loathed
form. Yet unlike Nehemiah, whose vision of spiritual life compensates for
the failures of reality, Celio fails to believe in the transfiguring power of
Christ and so desires an ideal reality free from Christian pattern:

> This world clean fails me: still I yearn.
> Me then it surely does concern
> Some other world to find. But where?
> In creed? I do not find it there.
> That said, and is the emprise o'er?
> Negation, is there nothing more? (38)

Such a tenacious inability to commit to faith recalls Hawthorne's description of Melville prior to his Middle Eastern trip, and yet, in this passage
at least, Celio has not yet made up his mind "to be annihilated."[13] Rather
he continues to posit a distant, masked world that contains the certain
truth he cannot reach because of the limits of his physical form.

Similarly, both Mortmain, the disillusioned Swedish idealist, and Ungar, the wounded half-Indian and former Confederate officer, reflect varying degrees of monomania and metaphysical discontent.[14] Ungar especially comes to represent the madness of physical pain that leads to bodily
denial and to a distortion of the search for truth. He embodies both the
desolate, postwar South—"the immense charred solitudes" (401)—and
the more general bitterness of the defeated individual who cannot survive
in his native land. His is an attitude toward the world that appears to be,
in part, a result of genealogy: he is the son of an English Catholic immi-
grant and a "wigwam maid" (403), a combination that apparently divides
his very self, for he possesses "An Anglo brain, but Indian heart" (403).
In other words, his ability to reason often finds itself subject to a powerful emotionalism—"A bias, a bitterness—a strain / Much like an Indian's
hopeless feud / Under the white's aggressive reign" (402)—that contains
both resistance to tyranny and self-destructive pride. That he fights in the
Civil War because of a fatalistic vision of himself rather than a desire to
protect the institutions of the South is evident in his opposition to slavery,
and yet he stands as one of Melville's strongest critics of the potential
abuses and corruptions of democracy. Most significant for this discussion,
however, is his refusal to drink wine (407) and his vision of physicality:

> "Now the world cannot save the world;
> And Christ renounces it. His faith,

Breaking with every mundane path,
Aims straight at heaven." (454)

Such a separation of the unredeemable physical world may echo the thought of the religious ascetic, but Ungar's denial of reality reveals a far less hopeful vision of spiritual reward. In fact, in this passage he attacks Derwent's compromising religiosity more because of its lack of mental integrity than because he hopes to offer a more accurate vision of Christ's purpose. Instead, his notion of worldly evil overwhelms belief in the Christian rebirth: "What's implied / In that deep utterance decried / Which Christians labially confess— / *Be born anew?*" (462). As a result, his tortured hatred and denial of the physical world is coupled with a similar doubt of the validity and beneficence of spirit.

In marked opposition to the ascetic spokesmen are a similar number of less thoughtful but clearly more content travelers who make a point of pursuing physical and emotional pleasure. The pair of "Beyrout" financiers, for instance, show the least intellectual and most simplistic appetites among the book's physical revelers: "Scarce through self-knowledge or self-love / They ventured Judah's wilds to rove" (137–38). Glaucon constantly sings mindless but playful songs and thinks Homer is a fig-dealer he once knew, while the corpulent banker, his mules loaded with excellent wine, worries only about his rapidly deteriorating physical comfort. In fact, the pair soon decides to abandon the journey, return to the comforts of civilization, and avoid the greater difficulties to come.[15]

Another somewhat similar Dionysian appears at the monastery of Mar Saba. A purveyor of "stores" and a "mellow," "jovial" drinker of wine, the Lesbian stands out among the melancholy, gaunt pilgrims and monks both by virtue of his personality and through the evidence of his physical form. The contrast between his physical and psychological health and the bleak lives of the Mar Saba monks appears directly in the notation that the jovial man is not, like the ascetics, "broken" "with fast and prayer" (298). Furthermore, his general physical appearance distances him from his surroundings not only because his leg is plump and his cheek bright but, perhaps more significantly, because his "fleecy beard" and ruddy face evoke both spring and all it implies as well as the "lax Paradise" and Dionysian past of the Hellenic isles (298–99). The Lesbian's connection to the Hellenic past also strengthens his commitment to physical enjoyment by lending it a mythological and philosophical basis; his actions appear, in other words, as more than the shallow hedonism of the Levantine banker and Glaucon. He acknowledges that "Life has its trials, sorrows— yes" but asserts that "blessedness / Makes up" (301) and in his singing and drinking offers a vision of pleasure based upon the body's, rather than the mind's, contentment.

Though other characters sometimes criticize the Lesbian's insistence on joviality, it is clear that he operates within the poem as a serious, if not conscious, critic of asceticism and religious questing in general. His tale of the sailor at masthead whose cap is taken by a "demonic" bird functions as more than a mere echo of Ahab at odds with nature. It is a picture of the solitary man's dangerous symbolization of nature: "he deemed it was the devil" (364). The nearly fatal consequence—the sailor's fall from the mast—is due in large part to his apocalyptic reading of the bird and its purpose. Just prior to the sailor's fall "the bird tore at his wool cap, / And chanced upon the brain to tap" (363–64), an image that suggests the mental nature of the sailor's distress. Indeed, even after the incident, he requires "some good vicar" to "unravel / The snarled illusion in the skein" in order to get "back his soul again" (364). Thus a revised theological interpretation becomes the cure for a dangerous reading, and yet the point of the Lesbian's tale is that such a cure would be unnecessary had the sailor seen the bird as a bird rather than a devil.

The final and, in the context of Clarel's journey, most convincing Dionysian in the poem likewise evokes connections to a pre-Christian paradise. The Lyonese—a French Jew who, as Bezanson notes, "has run over to Bethlehem to see its traditionally pretty girls"—argues with Clarel on behalf of a less tortured, more sensual existence.[16] More significantly, however, his arguments echo the evocations of his own appearance:

> Rich, tumbled, chestnut hood of curls,
> Like to a Polynesian girl's,
> Who, inland eloping with her lover,
> The deacon-magistrates recover—
> With sermon and black bread reprove
> Who fed on berries and on love. (474)

This striking image connects the Lyonese to Melville's familiar world of liberating, primitive sensuality. Clarel's attraction to him is thus both partially sexual and increasingly infused with a sense of intellectual and emotional commitment to the values of physical satisfaction. Though he doubts the Lyonese's direct appeals to instinct—"Come, look straight things more in line, / Blue eyes or black, which you like best?" (473)—he finds himself convinced more by the speaker's healthy beauty and its contrast to the withered figures he has met along the way. The criticism of mental and spiritual questing thus arises not so much from the mind but from the presence of the body itself, the surest positive evidence to the wavering Clarel of the efficacy of the Dionysian vision.

Of the other minor characters there remain a few whose visions of the world enable them to escape a wholesale commitment to either spirit or body. For instance, both Elder, the unfriendly Scottish Presbyterian, and Margoth, the Jewish geologist, ally themselves less with the ascetics' denial of reality than with a scientific commitment to engage and explain the physical by mental means. Each thus becomes, by virtue of his faith in science, an outspoken critic of all interpretations that allow for the activity of spirit. In this respect, Elder apparently desires to "disenchant the Land Divine" "by square and line" (135), while Margoth misses no opportunity within the text to disturb or ridicule the unscientific reactions and emotions of his fellow travelers. He, more than Elder, becomes the dark, bitter voice of modern, apostate science laughing at the faith of those who ignore both reality and the scientific explanations of miracles. In fact, it is due to the parodic tendency of his character that he is associated with the "dung-gate" at which Clarel and Nehemiah first meet him and hear his mockery of the city of David. He insists upon the hard, geological reality of all spiritual sites and refuses either a mental or emotional capitulation that might spare their feelings. As a result, he provides both a materialistic critique of errant spiritualism and a bitter self-parody of the heartlessness of science.

By contrast, the most evenly balanced characters in the supporting cast are those who demonstrate a patient endurance of trial coupled with a refusal to overindulge either their bodies or their minds. The two Arab guides, for instance, by means of their evident physical prowess and close association with the land, reveal a functional, earthly vision of life that seems to originate from their supposed primitivity. Djalea especially evokes the image of Queequeg, for like the Polynesian he is "rumored for an Emir's son / Or offspring of a lord undone / In Ibrahim's time" (154) and similarly demonstrates a primitive acceptance of the mysteries of reality (281). Also, his sense of both physical and linguistic economy significantly contrasts the restless conversation and endless debate of the pilgrims; he is apparently capable of maintaining a passive, mediative connection with the land that understands its terrors without being overwhelmed by them.

In a similar fashion, the aging timoneer, Agath, demonstrates both patience and a willingness to suffer in order to understand. His face is "weird and weather-beaten" and "fine vexed / With wrinkles of cabala text" (307), and he speaks less to debate than to tell cryptic and ironic stories of failure and survival. Most important, like Israel Potter and

Daniel Orme, he "bears a cross," his in the form of a crucifix tattooed upon his forearm. Even so, such a mark pushes him neither toward nor away from body or spirit; he remains patiently and mysteriously between, a sufferer who partially embodies the very uncertainty and mystery of the world.

The remaining major characters in the poem—Rolfe, Vine, and Derwent—demonstrate some degree of the balance between mind and body that Djalea and Agath carefully maintain and, in their attempts to remain true to their own visions, offer the clearest examples for Clarel of the kind of energy and activity necessary to avoid overcommitment to a single idea. Of these, Rolfe provides the best example of intellectual honesty coupled with a sure sense of the value of belief and the significance of physical life. His personality demonstrates both a large capacity for empathy and compassion and a clear sense of the rewards and limits of mental and spiritual questing. Despite his own difficulty with absolute faith, he nevertheless continues to investigate the potential benefits of such belief without sacrificing his considerable mental abilities. Rolfe thus unites, in near Ishmaelean fashion, the opposing poles of the book's dialectic by avoiding the dogmatism of overcommitment: "*Evil* do I say? / But speak not evil of the evil: / Evil and good they braided play / Into one cord" (399). He is both head and heart, scholar and man of action, dreamer and "messmate of the elements." Yet perhaps in order to maintain such a balance—like Ishmael shifting from sea to land to sea—Rolfe has come "To Jewry's inexhausted shore / Of barrenness" to search, like the others, for "Some lurking thing" "behind the parrot-lore / Conventional" (96). In other words, despite his doubts, he too hopes to gain some contact with the divine through proximity to the scriptural sites, for though he understands the possible sociological and psychological explanations for religious feeling, he nevertheless senses its value and centrality in human life:

> "Yea, long as children feel affright
> In darkness, men shall fear a God;
> And long as daisies yield delight
> Shall see His footprints in the sod.
> Is't ignorance? This ignorant state
> Science doth but elucidate—
> Deepen, enlarge. But though 'twere made
> Demonstrable that God is not—
> What then? it would not change this lot:
> The ghost would haunt, nor could be laid." (100–101)

Rolfe joins religious desire with aesthetic and sensuous appreciation and so strengthens the former through a connection with human emotion that places belief beyond the reach of scientific logic or "proof." At the same time, the passage clearly implies a self-criticism by suggesting that such "proof" is irrelevant to divine existence and that nature, to the believer, possesses as much power to evoke God as any genuine "footprints in the sod." Thus while Rolfe is capable of entertaining the notion that historical Christianity is either false or a revision of the older myth of Osiris (101), he equally understands that this potential "fact" will have no practical effect on the human need for faith.

Rolfe does occasionally reveal his own difficulties with faith, for he is equally capable of outbursts of spiritual desire in which he yearns for belief in the reality of the divine. In this respect he prays to and praises the "Easter barque," asking, in echo of Pierre and Ahab, for the "touch" of the divine that will bring spirit into flesh: "ah, in bounty launch, / Thou blessed Easter barque, to me / Hither one consecrated branch!" (192). Once again we see the thinker's attempt to seduce the divine into vision and embrace, the desire to touch God, which runs through the poem. Yet such moments are relatively brief for Rolfe because he understands their futility and uselessness except as emotional release; in other words, he fails to believe in such language, even if he occasionally employs it.

In a similar sense, his evocations of a pre-conscious, Polynesian or Hellenic paradise show his ability to accept irrevocable loss. Though he desires the kind of physical and spiritual satisfaction such visions impart, he understands that the world he dreams no longer exists and that Christ's coming, whatever its aims, served only to deepen the split between spirit and body:

"Back rolled the world's effacing tide:
The '*world*'—by Him denounced, defined—
Him first—set off and countersigned,
Once and for all, as opposite
To honest children of the light.
But worse came—creeds, wars, stakes. Oh, men
Made earth inhuman; yes, a den
Worse for Christ's coming, since his love
(Perverted) did but venom prove." (199–200)

The vision of flesh and spirit, God and man unified in a handshake (199), yields to "creeds, wars, stakes" until the purveyors of Christ's message disrupt the union and destroy the vision of earthly paradise with the reality of moral failure and death. Despite Rolfe's sorrow at this loss, however, he remains capable of absorbing such a realization, even to the point of acquiescing to a vision of his own death and rebirth (180–81). Even without the theological underpinning, he is able to envision a playfully symbolic resurrection within the terms of natural cycle: "The years shall run / And green my grave shall be, and play / The part of host to all that stray" (181). His playfulness may be tinged with sadness, but it is the very mixture of hope and acceptance that characterizes his synthetic vision of life.

Vine likewise refuses to champion a singular vision, though his resistance to definition seems more a desire to distance himself from his fellow travelers, to offer a series of masks and evasions, than a struggle to free himself from totalizing ideas. Indeed, Vine possesses a constraining, constantly self-shaping impulse that acknowledges physical reality but shrinks from bodily contact:

> Flesh, but scarce pride,
> Was curbed: desire was mortified;
> But less indeed by moral sway
> Than doubt of happiness thro' clay
> Be reachable. No sackclothed man;
> Howbeit, in sort Carthusian
> Tho' born a Sybarite. And yet
> Not beauty might he all forget,
> The beauty of the world, and charm:
> He prized it tho' it scarce might warm. (91–92)

Vine thus couples the "opulent softness" (91) of body and sensibility with the inner control of the ascetic, creating in the process a personality that equally attracts and repels, offers and withdraws. He doubts both the potential for bodily happiness and the possible certainty of spirit and in his dealings with the other travelers makes no binding relationships.

Instead, he frequently falls behind the group, silently meditating or indulging his taste for ambiguous symbolism: he crushes porous stones and throws them at his shadow or constructs a cairn as an undefined "monument." In fact, it is precisely this sort of teasing irony that finally characterizes Vine, for though he refuses dialectical definition, he does so from an apparent hopelessness that considers any statement or action ultimately useless. Even his own address to the palm at Mar Saba refuses to function as a moment of honest self-revelation. Instead, "to pass the time" Vine consciously attempts "an invocation free" "in a style sublime / Yet sad as sad sincerity" (362), thereby hiding once again—even though he has no audience—behind a self-made mask. Ultimately incapable of self-investigation, Vine is constructed solely of attitudes and strategies that no member of the traveling party can apparently penetrate.[17]

But if Rolfe and Vine create individual formulae for resolving the split between body and mind, Derwent represents a prefabricated resolution of the dialectic—secularized Christianity. He emerges from a long line of negative characters in Melville's work whose commitment to Christianity is coupled with a selective application of Christian doctrine in their worldly lives. Such characters unwittingly embody the paradoxes of Christianity even as they violate the vision they themselves hold sacred. Thus Derwent is described as a "priest" "but in part," for like the Templar he combines "[t]he cavalier and monk in one" (134). The Templar always presents a contradictory image to Melville, whose sense of the "chronometrical" purity of genuine Christianity does not allow for a "Christian warrior." The notion that physical violence can make possible a nonviolent, spiritualist society merely asserts the selective blindness of such "soldiers" as well as the troubling dualism of the world so imagined. As a result, Derwent functions chiefly as apologist for such apparent contradictions, repeatedly offering hopeful explanations that attempt to reconcile physical fact with spiritual truth. He urges commitment to optimistic emotion rather than severe logic and considers the brain a dangerous and misleading mechanism for determining truth:

> "Though much we knew in desert late,
> Beneath no kind auspicious star,
> Of lifted minds in poised debate—
> 'Twas of the brain. Consult the heart!
> Spouse to the brain—can coax or thwart:
> Does *she* renounce the trust divine?" (446)

Though such rhetoric seems to echo Melville's earlier devotion to the heart, it is clear that Derwent conceives the image not as a metaphor for physical and emotional fulfillment but as a figure for the optimistic blindness needed to overcome intellectual doubt. His is, in a sense, an Ishmaelean attitude divorced from the facts of the physical world, a vision of love without hate, life without death, a refusal to acknowledge darkness in the blind adoration of light.

In the end, despite its emphasis on physical location and evidence—and despite the actual journey undertaken in its pages—*Clarel* remains a book of conversations and debates. Regardless of the overwhelming bulk of speech, however, the number of linguistic visions, like the number of philosophical and theological stances, remains relatively low primarily because the poem's dialectic controls the characters' languages. Thus the book as a whole, in part because of the relatively static debate, moves sluggishly to complete its attenuated circle. Just as Clarel seems fated to mire himself in Christian paradox, so does the poem bog down in its own language, losing tone and tension in a variety of repetitious, fruitless debates.[18] Only rarely do such conversations lead to any new understanding or discovery; the speeches and responses simply accumulate into the largely inanimate body of the text itself, a process that forms an ironic counterpart to Clarel's search for divine reality. Ultimately, the body that is discovered in *Clarel* is not the body of Christ but the textual reality—the body of ideas—created by the accumulated language of the characters themselves. All that Clarel or anyone else in the poem finally gains is an experience of language that flows as though from and into the silence of the desert. In attempting to find the Christly body, the characters unknowingly create a linguistic substitute for the missing God. Their questions, doubts, and arguments form a fragmented negative of the body they seek, giving the poem both its ironic continuo and its tenuous, fragmentary structure.

Furthermore, and largely because of the verse, the individual speech patterns of the characters remain more alike than different. There are, for instance, few distinctly separable attitudes toward syntax or rhythm because the restrictions and requirements of meter and rhyme make such stylistic variations difficult. Thus while the ascetic questers speak a brand of Ahabian language, they do so largely in rhetorical rather than syntactical pattern. Perhaps the best example comes from the mouth of the "Wandering Jew," a figure in the masque at Mar Saba who forms a composite of the poem's yearning characters:

> "For, human still, I yearn, I yearn,
> Yea, after a millennium, turn
> Back to my wife, my wife and boy;
> Yet ever I shun the dear abode
> Or site thereof, of homely joy." (335)

If, after the silence of *The Confidence-Man* and the renewal of violent language in *Battle Pieces*, there remains something of Ahab here, it appears chiefly in the sense of distance, separation from the hearth, and the repetitious emphasis on the isolated "I." Yet this speech lacks the self-destructive energy and bitterness that Ahab's language conveys through its painfully direct syntax. The language of the Wandering Jew, by contrast, reflects the uncertain resignation to hopelessness that *Clarel* as a whole speaks; it surrenders to the strictures of verse and rhyme and rests now somewhere between overreaching desire and restrained contentment. Like the Wandering Jew himself, such language yearns without the energy to strike through the mask and without the ability to find comfort within the bonds of human reality.

This same restrained address characterizes the speeches of Celio, Mortmain, and Ungar, while their language, in turn, finds primary opposition in the playfulness of the Dionysian characters, whose songs continue the resurgence of Ishmaelean elements rediscovered in Melville's earlier verse. Such a figure as the Lesbian, for instance, provides most of the very few light moments in the text, though the songs he prods from the pilgrims often seem juvenile and empty. Nevertheless, the lyrics and wine reinforce his commitment to physical comfort even if they finally have more in common with sailor songs than the philosophical comedy of Ishmael. They are, except in their versification, slim evidence that the commitment to emotional and physical fulfillment yields rich linguistic reward, for they sound hollowly against the drear walls of the monastery.

The similarities between the characters' languages in *Clarel* become more pronounced when we consider that the various debates within the text offer no distinct contrasts between the ways different individuals use language. Only in the clash between Margoth and Derwent do we see a notable contrast. The other major characters, regardless of their ideas, speak too often as though from the same mouth and mind and suggest, taken as a whole, that Melville has failed significantly to delineate them as characters. After all, there are few significant variations in the way words are conceived and employed; for many of the characters, language remains the sole yet inadequate tool for questioning the world, and its very inadequacy quickly becomes their common subject. It soon becomes clear that in *Clarel* words tend to function more as evidence of their own weakness than as expression of character. What remains are speeches frequently as static as the movement of the poem itself, voices in which the remnants of Ahab and Ishmael clash but weakly because the world's power to undermine flesh and spirit also disrupts the power of language.

If the poem's language partakes of the futility and stasis of the book as a whole, however, it is also true that there remains a small but counterbalancing desire to provide a more positive meaning to Clarel's search. Whatever anemia we may locate in the texture of the verse, there remains a propelling, if sometimes fatalistic, energy behind the whole that seems bent on making of this material and language, at the very least, an example of potential cathartic renewal.[19] For instance, not only does the poem contain in Nehemiah the most positive religious character since Father Mapple, but also its much disputed epilogue continues to assert a qualified faith in the possibility of renewal:

> Then keep thy heart, though yet but ill-
>   resigned—
> Clarel, thy heart, the issues there but mind;

> That like the crocus budding through the snow—
> That like a swimmer rising from the deep—
> That like a burning secret which doth go
> Even from the bosom that would hoard and keep;
> Emerge thou mayst from the last whelming sea,
> And prove that death but routs life into victory. (499)

Despite the uncertain placement and tone of this ending, as well as its apparent tonal distance from the rest of the poem, it reflects an impulse present at various moments in the work to find in desert and death some manner of redemption.[20] It reveals the modification of Melville's own metaphysical doubt to include the possibility of fulfillment despite the apparent failure of the search. In short, the transcendence of spirit over body appears here for the first time in the Melville ouevre, as though the experience of writing and living *Clarel* has made possible the notion that contentment may be gained in spite of, rather than through, the reality of physical life.

Such a notion prepares the way for the late poetry and especially *Billy Budd,* in all of which the dialectic between physical and spiritual fulfillment receives a new investigation in light of the possibilities discovered in *Clarel.* In this final period of Melville's creative life, the benefits and possible taxes of the Dionysian life stand against the potential liberation offered by such a spiritual release, even as both possibilities are sharpened and shaped by his unrelinquished irony. There is no loss of the tension that animates *Clarel* and the work before it, for in his transformation of the dialectic of mind and body in the pages of *Clarel,* he has discovered the subject matter of his final work.

8

A QUESTION OF DISTANCE
The Late Poetry

THE AMOUNT OF time between the publications of Melville's work, expanding since the shift to poetry, appears to contract somewhat as he approaches his final decade. After *Battle Pieces* in 1866 and *Clarel* ten years later, another twelve years passed before the publication of *John Marr and Other Sailors,* but then only three until *Timoleon* in 1891, the final year of Melville's life. If we include the two major works left in manuscript at his death, *Weeds and Wildings* and *Billy Budd,* it becomes clear that the Melville of the eighties and nineties, now free from his custom house work, increased rather than reduced his productiveness as he approached death. Yet such an apparent vitality in the final years of his life does not presuppose that the questions asked time and again in the earlier work come any closer than before to a solution. In fact, the dialectic between head and heart remains at the vital core of this later work, even if the terms of the struggle have been altered by time and experience.

It is thus no surprise to see that *Clarel*'s failure to find viable connection to either God or humanity reemerges in the late poetry as an attempt to maintain or question the problematic union with community and family, while in *Billy Budd* the same struggle becomes an even more complex attempt to realize and touch a "living" God. What is perhaps most noteworthy about this modified investigation is that language plays the central role in each of these attempts. It is the matter with which John Marr and others seek to bind themselves to their communities and histories, it is the instrument of exploration and celebration of the life of the natural body, and it is the agent that simultaneously produces the combination of tragic irony and divine ascendence in *Billy Budd.* Yet despite its centrality, the vision of language in the later writing presents no single, conclusive statement on the ultimate source or method of human fulfillment. Though altered at times by potential solutions, the now transformed dialectic of head and heart continues to infuse tension and torque into the language and content of Melville's final works.

The Seduction of Memory

At first glance, *John Marr and Other Sailors* appears to resemble the kind of work we might expect from an aging writer and former sailor whose rebellious desires and powers may have soothingly diminished. Its consistently nostalgic tone and sometimes feeble acquiescence to domestic cliché may lull us into a complacent disregard of the volume's otherwise serious and, within the context of Melville's oeuvre, very significant concerns. An adequately contextual vision of the poems will discover that two important interests from Melville's earlier work form the basic material and purpose of *John Marr*. The first continues to question the nature of exile initially considered in the early sea novels by adding the barrier of time to the forces that alienate the individual from society. The quester now experiences physical isolation not only because of his distance from others of similar experience but also because many of those he remembers are now dead. The second, unfolding from the complexities of the first, attempts to understand the ways in which language succeeds or fails to reconnect the isolated body to its distant social counterpart either through an Ahabian attempt to seduce the past into the present or through the difficult realization that language can sometimes form yet another barrier. In this manner the desires of both the metaphysical and physical selves subtilely meld in the half-failed recollections and domestic celebrations of *John Marr*, each forming a part in a variably satisfied but unending need for certainty in the face of spatial and temporal distance.[1]

The world and atmosphere of *John Marr*, despite its retrospective quality, ultimately provide little productive physical or social connection for the individual. The active and retired sailors who populate its pages provide portraits of selves confined to a relatively valueless present and largely isolated from meaningful contact with either nature or humanity. The images of the lone sailor isolated among unreceptive strangers, separated from his bride, or alone on his deathbed consistently haunt the book by placing the unassisted individual against an essentially malicious and compassionless world, permitting him only the mechanisms of language with which to attempt a reunion.

In the title work, for instance, the retired sailor, John Marr, "of a mother unknown" and "disabled at last from further maritime life by a crippling wound" settles in an inland community only to lose "his young wife and infant child" to a fever.[2] In an attempt to "fill that void by cultivating social relations" (160), he then enters the community and household of a narrowly religious and ascetic family who fail to encourage or respond to the sailor's attempts to form significant social ties. Forced into a kind of silence, he realizes that the "desert" plain and its unresponsive people effectively isolate him from any productive human contact; he speaks an alien language and knows and desires a distant, unattainable world far too different from theirs. He thus becomes, by and by, an "absentee from existence" (164), perfectly alone, untouched by the physical world or the human community. As a result, he turns inward, away from the reality that has rejected him and into the potentially accepting folds of memory and language.[3]

"Tom Deadlight," in a similar fashion, provides a more complicated picture of isolation within a community, though the title character's separation comes not from cultural boundaries but from the approach of death "in the *sick-bay* under the tiered gun-decks of the British *Dreadnought*, 98" (182–83). The dying sailor, "wandering in his mind, though with glimpses of sanity" (183), begins to lose his sense of physical presence in the world of the ship. All that remain to tie him to those he is leaving are his final orders for the disposition of his body and "[s]ome names and phrases, with here and there a line, or part of one; these, in his aberration, wrested into incoherency from their original connection and import, he involuntarily derives . . . from a famous old sea-ditty" (183). He forms this amalgam of language into an utterance that alternates between past and present, life and death, as his physical reality alternately fades and reasserts itself and he struggles through words to remain in touch with his world:

> But give me my *tot*, Matt, before I roll over;
>   Jock, let's have your flipper, it's good for to feel;
> And don't sew me up without *baccy* in mouth, boys,
>   And don't blubber like lubbers when I turn up my keel. (184)

The concern for a final physical contact with the receding world relies upon language as the medium for effecting the touch that this farewell attempts. Furthermore, this particular gesture—unlike either the positive "splice" in *Moby-Dick* or the negative touch in "Bartleby" and *Israel Potter*—blends productive and unproductive results because the very body of the speaker exists on the threshold between life and death. The touch, which never occurs in the poem, is thus a physical connection as well as, after death, a physical barrier, for only the language of memory can remain a binding instrument after the spiritless body fails to offer a genuine embrace.

The isolation in *John Marr* deprives its characters not only of the opportunity for social contact but also of the more extensive life of the body connected with their pasts and Melville's mythos of the South Seas. Not only do poems such as "John Marr," "Bridegroom Dick," and "Crossing the Tropics" acknowledge the importance of physical and erotic contact in traditional, domestic terms, but the volume's overall retrospective tone contains a mournful note for the lost Edenic pleasures of the life of a young sailor, the pre-matrimonial days of beachcombing and the experience of paradisiacal, uninhibited sexuality. "To Ned" provides the clearest example of this absence by evoking and idealizing the vagabond past while dwelling on the insurmountable distances that time has created between the two separated sailors and their "Authentic Edens in a Pagan sea" (201):

> But, tell, shall he, the tourist, find
>   Our isles the same in violet-glow
> Enamoring us what years and years—
>   Ah, Ned, what years and years ago! (201)

The answer, of course, need not be given, for it would simply reiterate the absence of the speaker's own youth and link the lost innocence of the individual with the lost innocence of the world. The "violet-glow" of a preconscious eroticism is now distant from all who exist in the poem's present, while the loss both appears and dissolves within the language of the speaker, whose address to the absent Ned simultaneously rejoins and helps to sever the disparate times.

If the human community in *John Marr* offers more barriers than connections to the individual, the natural world is openly hostile to productive contact between individuals and especially to those who seek a redemptive connection to nature. In "John Marr," for instance, the prairie seems to the rebuffed and lonely mariner the unresponsive partner to its phlegmatic inhabitants. The "blank stillness" (162) of the plain shows no evidence of life just as the people themselves offer little sense of geniality. Instead they become associated with machines just as the land begins to seem to the former sailor "the bed of a dried-up sea" (162) or, in other words, a negative version of both vital abundance and sailor geniality.

The more active or seemingly malicious machinations of nature and fate appear in "The Haglets," Melville's retelling of the Timoneer's story in *Clarel*. The tale involves the basic irony of a shipload of conquerors whose booty of swords and other metal alters the ship's compass and so causes the vessel's wreck and the death of its crew. Beyond its primary message of the unpredictability of fate, the poem suggests that nature itself plays a part in the world's treatment of these excessively self-confident "victors." In the first place, the titular trio of seabirds, an image of the fates, forms the primary link between the activities of nature and the fate of the sailors; they follow the doomed ship as untranslatable chorus to its downfall until all nature appears to desire the ship's distress:

> The hungry seas they hound the hull,
> The sharks they dog the haglets' flight;
> With one consent the winds, the waves
> In hunt with fins and wings unite. (192)

But if this apparent conspiracy can be attributed to a superstitious interpretation of the haglets' natural behavior, then their obvious inability to offer any comfort other than harsh screams remains clear and justifiably chilling.[4] They, like the unresponsive prairie in "John Marr," serve to intensify human isolation by failing to act in a way that at least seems friendly or compassionate. Like the silence of the prairie, their cries offer no binding response or communicative balm.[5]

Perhaps the apex of nature's apparent ill will in the volume comes in "The Maldive Shark," a portrait that not only emphasizes the animalistic cruelty and unintelligible voraciousness of the shark itself but also adds an element of sinister irony that restates nature's ability to deceive and threaten. The irony involves the shark's symbiotic relationship with the "sleek little pilot-fish, azure and slim" (200) who "lurk[s] in the port of serrated teeth" (200) and guides the shark to its prey. In other words, nature, like man, apparently possesses two basic parts: the first is pure body, a "saw-pit of mouth" and "charnel of maw," a "dotard lethargic and dull, / Pale ravener of horrible meat" (200). The second becomes "eyes and brains" to the body, an "alert" parasite and seemingly clever tactician. Together they form a horrific, cold-blooded vision of natural function and mutual exploitation that contains absolutely no ability or desire for compassion or connection to human reality. The shark remains a physical and psychological fact that is itself a barrier to human sympathy with nature, while the pilot-fish simply reminds us that nature is neither completely instinctual nor incapable of deception and strategy.

The final depiction of nature's hostility—or in this case, implacability—appears in "The Berg," a dream poem in which "a ship of martial build . . . Directed as by madness mere" (203) steers directly into an iceberg and sinks without having any visible effect upon the ice. Like "Pisa's Leaning Tower" in *Timoleon*, the poem appears to be an extended symbol of a psychological state, and yet whatever sense of frustration and futility it may convey, it clearly dwells upon the failure of nature to respond to so evident an attempt at contact:

> Impingers rue thee and go down,
> Sounding thy precipice below,
> Nor stir the slimy slug that sprawls
> Along thy dead indifference of walls. (204)

The personification of the berg increases the sense of failed contact by again granting the stolid face of nature some sort of potential for motive and reason. After all, it is the very emotional term "indifference" that receives the emphasis both in the last line and throughout the poem and becomes the key to understanding this vision of failed contact and negative natural experience. Whatever its unreadable "motives," nature in *John Marr* offers only resistance in one form or another to those who attempt some connection with it.

What little contact present reality, either human or natural, does offer in *John Marr* appears for the most part in the long poem "Bridegroom Dick." Even so, the comforts offered by the speaker's "old woman" are qualified by the primary contrast between his feeble sweet talk and his forceful descriptions of lost shipmates as well as by the poem's overwhelming emphasis on the superiority of past over present. The speaker is thus forced to resurrect not only his own youth and vitality but the vitality of a world in which the heroism of the individual had yet to succumb to the heartless motions of steel.[6] In fact, it becomes clear that the present is able to offer the comforts of wife and hearth because time has enfeebled the sailor whose heart and mind continue to occupy the distant decks of remembered ships. Thus like John Marr, he invokes the distant world in order to enter it, to leave this year "in decay" (167) that has fallen into the metallic cowardice introduced by the *Merrimac:*

> Under the water-line a *ram's* blow is dealt:
> And foul fall the knuckles that strike below the belt.
> Nor brave the inventions that serve to replace
> The openness of valor while dismantling grace. (181)

The blow "below the belt" replaces the once heroic, honorable struggle between individuals while it once again suggests a negative eroticism that becomes, as in "The Tartarus of Maids," one of the hallmarks of the mechanistic world. The machine era in which Bridegroom Dick now lives provides the poem with little more than the will to yearn for the past; his wife, all that remains to support his now ironic nickname, gives him only the basic social connection he needs to perform his single defining task of reminiscence. His true world, like John Marr's, exists beyond his body, somewhere in the language he employs to recover and attempt to embrace it.

It is ultimately the medium of words that the speakers in *John Marr and Other Sailors* rely upon to find a connection to the distant world. Language thus exists primarily as a tool, a vehicle for evoking, searching, and reconstituting a distant bodiless reality. Somewhat like Ahab's, these sailors' speeches attempt to bring their own histories into the present, though for the most part each exhibits a clearer sense of the impossibility of his desire. In fact, all seem at least partially aware that such language becomes both a connection and a barrier to the past they invoke, just as in their present lives speech may join or separate them from their surrounding communities. In other words, the Ahabian impulse to yearn beyond the limits of reality is here tempered by resignation to the fact of such distances and by a consequent sense of qualified enjoyment or play still derived from such self-fulfilling evocations.

The prose description of "John Marr," for instance, serves to establish the sailor's separation from humanity while providing a context for his poetic monologue. His address intends to elicit the response of his absent friends, to establish "verbal communion" with the fleshless inhabitants of his memory. Yet such a desire for embrace through words leads only to a keener need for the physical touch just as the unreality of the phantoms serves merely to intensify the speaker's yearning:

Ye float around me, form and feature:—
Tattooings, ear-rings, love-locks curled;
Barbarians of man's simpler nature,
Unworldly servers of the world. (166)

The true subject of this passage remains language's ability to create a present-absence, to formulate and decorate the features of immaterial bodies that finally exist exclusively as language, as the creations of a kind of spell that lasts only as long as the words themselves sound and resound from the speaker's lips. The fleeting shades of John Marr's past reside purely in the evanescence of language, and his poem both celebrates and rejects this simultaneous bridge and barrier to the world he dreams.

Painful though its products may be, language persists as an instrument for the repeated and almost ritual reconstruction of the absent body in the volume. For the less isolated Bridegroom Dick, for instance, such attempts to reenter or seduce the past form a ritualistic renewal and return to sources of joy and contentment, a repetitive feeding upon the past in order to revitalize the aging present. The telling and retelling of stories as well as the remembrance of lost friends becomes both a way of maintaining and enlivening the connection between Dick and his wife and a way of ordering and giving meaning to their present existence together.

Even though the wife continually interrupts the old sailor's daydreaming and so reasserts the reality of the present, she provides a stable center that releases Dick from John Marr's more intense desire while offering a listening ear that makes the occasion of his telling less desperate and more integral to a productive life. Indeed, one of the major points of the collection is to see such remembrance as a productively playful, resurrecting activity that allows the speaker to relive and restructure his life from the vantage point of age and acquired wisdom. Though this impulse is frequently countered by a painful isolation and resultant desire, the two finally exist in a neutral balance, each acknowledged and experienced, to different degrees, by the voices that fill the book.

If remembrance has both positive and negative results in the collection, however, the language of the present more frequently prevents contact than facilitates it. John Marr's seafaring tales, for instance, effectively sever whatever ties he has been able to form with the narrow-minded farmers in his community. In a practical sense, words become the sailor's enemy, and he soon learns that silence is preferable to the farmers' "unresponsiveness" (161). Likewise, in "Bridegroom Dick" the positive results of memory clash with the clearly negative description of the rhetoric of the warring South in the Civil War (170–71) as well as the sort of speech that precedes and elicits battle (172–73). Perhaps the most haunting vision of isolation and the related failure of language appears in "The Aeolian Harp," Melville's dark comment on Coleridge's more famous and more optimistically rendered instrument. The poem employs as its representation of "the Real" the image of a dismasted and abandoned ship sailing without course or guidance. Like "The Berg," "The Aeolian Harp" has a visionary quality, as though the aimless ship represents more than the randomness and seeming cruelty of nature and fate. In fact, the symbol echoes the note of isolation and homelessness that much of the volume sounds even as it considers the potentially tragic ironies of fate and the failure of language to prevent or repair the results of such "accidental" collisions:

> O, the sailors—O, the sails!
> O, the lost crews never heard of!
> Well the harp of Ariel wails
> Thoughts that tongue can tell no word of! (196)

As an image of the real, this vision of voiceless destruction and its unspeakable results suggests that reality not only contains a sinister propensity for random violence but also that the reality of language often participates in this dangerous disjunction. As in "The Encantadas," words may drift unmoored and unguided, for if reality is ultimately unreliable, then a language that supposedly reflects it must be equally dangerous, unpredictable, or, at the very least, impotent.

Though "The Aeolian Harp" and "The Berg" offer portraits of an uncaring and potentially malicious world, other poems within the volume provide a contrasting sense of joy and geniality and help balance the book overall. Passages in "Bridegroom Dick," for instance, though tinged with the distance of nostalgia, nevertheless revel in the appetites and antics of remembered sailors, while such a work as "Jack Roy" openly celebrates the balance of levity and heroism in the figure of the "manly king o' the old *Splendid's* crew" (184). The desire to reincarnate the Ishmaelean hero animates the poem, stretching its knowingly comic rhythms to the breaking point in order to imitate the tone of Jack Roy's wit. It is a formal freedom and vitality that appears elsewhere in the volume, whether in Melville's own experiment of combining prose and verse in "John Marr" and "Tom Deadlight" or in the mimetic fragmentation of "Pebbles."

Indeed, the tension between wholeness and disjunction that animates much of Melville's earlier work does not disappear in *John Marr and Other Sailors;* it reveals itself in the textures of the verse and, more significantly, in the content of the volume. The themes of isolation and attempted reconnection that the poems present clearly reflect an abiding concern with form and dissolution, bodily integrity and dismemberment, for the body of the work and the body of the world continue to strain both toward and away from union.

A Failed Synthesis

The poems of *Timoleon* present a world concerned less with the effects of temporal and spatial distance than with the attempt once again to synthesize the dialectic between mind and body. Perhaps because many of these lyrics may have been written earlier than the verse of *John Marr,* the volume as a whole participates more directly than any of the late poetry in the thematic concerns of *Battle Pieces* and *Clarel.*[7] Thus the animating friction in the volume continues *Battle Pieces'* concern with the individual's separation from the familial body as well as *Clarel's* interest in the rival temptations of mental and erotic life. In considering such familiar ground, however, the poems in *Timoleon* also conduct a unique investigation of the potential for art or language to fuse or at least balance Melville's long-abiding dialectic.[8]

The two major poems of the volume, "Timoleon" and "After the Pleasure Party," form together its primary expression of dialectical tension.

Along with "The Margrave's Birthright," "Monody," "Art," "The Marchioness of Brinvilliers," and "The Age of the Antonines," they rely upon internal struggle between opposites to energize their characters and their worlds and further extend Melville's investigation of alternate paths to personal or artistic transcendence. "Timoleon," which has been read as both biography and an important echo of *Pierre,* tells the story of one man's idealistic betrayal of his tyrant brother and his own consequent exile from his family and country. It emphasizes the unsatisfying choice between family and morality and suggests by its unresolved but quiescent ending that only a partial transcendence may be possible for those unwilling to compromise their physical and mental selves.

The poem begins with a general statement (in the form of a question) concerning the speaker's interest in and vision of this intrafamilial, "civil" conflict. He asks, in effect, whether virtue and action are incompatible when the action in question involves the virtuous person in the very evil he hopes to destroy and, if so, whether that act will ultimately be recognized by the world for its righteous end rather than its wicked means. Having posed the question, however, the speaker offers no solution:

> O, crowned with laurel twined with thorn,
> Not rash thy life's cross-tide I stem,
> But reck the problem rolled in pang
> And reach and dare to touch thy garment's hem. (209)

The basic and indivisible duality of both Timoleon's act and his very self here appears as the capstone of the speaker's introduction. The idealistic younger brother wears the double crown of "laurel twined with thorn"— hero and Christ, active and passive—and the speaker's only gesture will be a presentation of this "cross-tide" life that may, by example, heal those who witness it.

Yet the poem's dualistic bent extends beyond Timoleon's inner struggle. After all, he is one of two brothers, sons of an ambitious mother who favors the older, more ruthlessly ambitious Timophanes, in whom she sees herself "In sex translated" (211). Despite the fact that Timoleon saves his rash brother's life in battle, she looks "slackly" on the younger son, in all likelihood because he "knew / For crimes of pride and men-of-prey /" profound hate (212). Unlike the allegorical mother in *Battle Pieces'* "America," she is allied to the less idealistic son in her worldly desire and silently permits the tyrant's immoral maintenance of power. Thus the basic opposition within Timoleon himself reflects and is reflected by the opposition between him and his family, and the test he undergoes will measure the influence of their horological desires on his chronometrical self.

Once he has realized his brother's corruption, Timoleon seeks to preserve his passivity through the language of diplomacy, but the older brother's despotism overwhelms the very basis of the appeal. The failure of language to appease and join leads to "the predetermined word" (213), the signal for assassination that in turn reveals the transformation of language from binding medium to killing weapon at the same time that it signals the irrevocable entrance of the "just heart and humane" (212) of Timoleon into the world of action.[9] He has, on a limited scale, attempted to embody the ideal, to save the state, and his action results not only in his "mother's ban" (213) but also in the country's distrust and his own inner storm. As a result, he considers suicide but decides instead on exile:

> Estranged through one transcendent deed
> From common membership in mart,
> In severance he is like a head
> Pale after battle trunkless found apart. (214)

It is the very transcendence of that deed—its idealistic motivation—that separates him from both the community and, psychologically, from his own body. Having struck a blow for the ideal, Timoleon has, in effect, become his action, and his appeal to the gods for "some little sign" (215), "Low thunder in your tranquil skies" (215), reasserts both his entrapment within the dualism and his futile reliance on a seductive language to evoke the bodiless gods into action. What freedom and absolution Timoleon finally gains come instead from the softening effects of time and his eventual return and victory at Sicily. However, such praise can address only half of his being, for though the people dress his door "with bays," the thorny portion of his crown now seems absent. He has succeeded as a realist and so can maintain his idealism only by returning to exile, a gesture that projects his continued distance from the individual and social body he has continually tried to deny.

Just as Timoleon achieves a partial but unsatisfying balance of thought and action, Urania, the astronomer protagonist of "After the Pleasure Party," similarly attempts to silence the conflicting demands of mind and body, science and sex, through transcendence. Though this poem seems an unusual one for Melville in its presentation of an aging woman's sexual crisis, its fundamental issues nevertheless coincide with the major questions of the earlier work,[10] for Urania has, like Melville's other metaphysical questers, led an ascetic life devoted to the pursuits of the mind. The "reaching ranging tube" of the telescope (217) has taken her attention

away from the flesh and become for her a substitute for physical fulfillment. Yet seemingly secure in her bodiless existence, she suddenly experiences a birth of sensuality and an intense sexual and romantic desire
that violently clash with her hitherto ascetic vision:

> Could I remake me! or set free
> This sexless bound in sex, then plunge
> Deeper than Sappho, in a lunge
> Piercing Pan's paramount mystery!
> For, Nature, in no shallow surge
> Against thee either sex may urge,
> Why hast thou made us but in halves—
> Co-relatives? This makes us slaves.
> If these co-relatives never meet
> Self-hood itself seems incomplete. (219)

The basic perception of the duality of the sexes reflects Urania's recent
discovery of her own double nature, for her intellectual integrity forbids
her either to ignore her new perceptions or to abandon her former vision
of herself. She feels incomplete because her mental union with "Starred
Cassiopea" has fallen to "Love's ambuscade" (217), and yet the ultimate
result is not a commitment to sexual experience but a disillusioned rejection of both potential lives.

Her final appeal before "an antique pagan stone" reasserts her inner
division even as it appears to offer a potential transcendence for the "wanderer":

> But thee, armed Virgin! less benign,
> Thee now I invoke, thou mightier one.
> Helmeted woman—if such term
> Befit thee, far from strife
> Of that which makes the sexual feud
> And clogs the aspirant life—   (221)

The contrasting images of Mary, whose picture Urania has already seen,
and Athena together echo the struggle between passivity and action that
Timoleon faces even as they translate that struggle into the paradoxes of
gender. The poem's narrator quickly undermines what little resolution
Urania's invocation may effect, however, as his final words warn that denial of the body may lead to a despair that neither thought nor "Art inanimate" (221) can dispel.

Some of the shorter poems in *Timoleon* also use the larger lyrics' dualistic interests and yet, as a whole, present a somewhat more optimistic
vision of the attempt to synthesize the various manifestations of flesh and

spirit. "The Margrave's Birthnight," for instance, offers a version of the eucharist disguised as a feudal lord's "mid-winter" "birthnight" (223) celebration for his subjects. Despite the apparently festive nature of the occasion, the initial emphasis of the poem, in echo of *Clarel*, falls on the absence of the margrave-Christ from the feast. Though his place is set "at head of board" (223), he never appears, nor is his name mentioned by his guests. The poetic result is both a criticism of divine distance and an argument for the symbolic presence of the margrave in the food that is the substance of the feast. Christ, in other words, paradoxically offers absence—"Guests as holly-berries plenty, / But no *host* withal" (223, emphasis added)—in his attempt to bring about the miraculous union of flesh and spirit:

> Mindless as to what importeth
> Absence such in hall;
> Tacit as the plough-horse feeding
> In the palfrey's stall.
>
> Ah, enough for toil and travail,
> If but for a night
> Into wine is turned the water,
> Black bread into white. (224)

The "mindless," "tacit" participants do not question the margrave's absence because they have relinquished the mental life for the physical acceptance of the facts of good food and drink and the pleasure received from them. Such acquiescence to the reality of the flesh, the poem finally suggests, may be the key to understanding the transformation of the physical world into spiritual meaning. Yet how genuine a salvation this conversion of wine into water, "Black bread into white," grants the simplistic servants remains uncertain, for while the poem goes further than the previous lyrics in suggesting a Christly reality, the margrave's absence remains just as much a fact in its world as the nourishment received from the food.

A similar sense of distance and loss pervades "Monody," the well-known lyric traditionally interpreted as Melville's description of his friendship with Hawthorne. Whatever the biographical basis for the poem, it is clear that it shares a similar concern for the difficult and frustrating spaces between individuals that death and other absence create. The tension between spiritual identification and physical presence energizes the poem's images and helps to register the overall paradox, almost Christian, of the distant presence and the present distance. The scenes of the friend's former life, like the sites of the passion in *Clarel*, thus become points of worship and tempting but finally frustrating evidence that refuses to lead to the absent friend (229). A winter's shroud falls over the world, transmitting the speaker's lost connection, while the poem ends without hints of either literal spring or symbolic resurrection.

If "Monody" can be said to offer any consolation for the isolated speaker, that solace must come in the form of the poem itself, the act of language suggested in the refrain, "Ease me, a little ease, my song" (228). Similarly, taken as a whole, *Timoleon* does in a few instances entertain the possibility that dualistic conflicts and unbridgeable distances may be reduced through the synthesizing activity of art:

> In placid hours well-pleased we dream
> Of many a brave unbodied scheme.
> But form to lend, pulsed life create,
> What unlike things must meet and mate:
> A flame to melt—a wind to freeze;
> Sad patience—joyous energies;
> Humility—yet pride and scorn;
> Instinct and study; love and hate;
> Audacity—reverence. These must mate,
> And fuse with Jacob's mystic heart,
> To wrestle with the angel—Art. (231)

This short lyric clearly bases its vision on a dualistic division of idea and act, "pulsed life" and "a brave unbodied scheme," for it proposes a theory of art based upon the synthesis of opposing energies. Thus by implication art truly rendered appears capable of reducing the distances between flesh and spirit. Indeed, the overall thrust of the poem moves toward the idea of incarnation, of transforming thought into substance, embodying a brave scheme in order to reunite the fractured world. In its final image of Jacob wrestling with the angel, Melville once again presents us with the desire for the physical touch of spiritual reality. Yet while arguing that such a union is the goal of art, the poem equally asserts the difficulty, if not impossibility, of such a mystical fusion. It establishes a powerfully hopeful vision of art's potential healing powers only to suggest that such an accomplishment may be nothing but a dream.

Perhaps the clearest overall vision of what such a synthesis could mean to the individual and his world appears in the mournful but visionary "The Age of the Antonines." The poem describes the Roman empire in the second century A.D., emphasizing not merely the peace and prosperity of this well-tempered age but, more important, the philosophy enacted by its inhabitants. Evidence of religious tolerance, acknowledgment of death, and the celebration of life (235) help demonstrate the Romans' ability to comprehend and engage both idea and flesh without attempting to exclude either one. These thoroughly balanced inhabitants are neither ascetics dreaming of paradise nor sybarites who indulge the flesh and ignore darker truths. Despite the utopian vision the poem outlines, however, the world it describes no longer exists; indeed, the poem's ending, with its hope that America might come to reincarnate this benign age, finally seems an unlikely dream for the speaker, whose overall purpose is to criticize American failures rather than offer a vision of its future.

Of those shorter poems that eschew a full investigation of the dialectic, some reveal a specific interest in the effects of an exclusively mental life, while others clearly celebrate the life of the body. The first group presents the negative and positive results of asceticism, sometimes mourning the loss of bodily consciousness, other times asserting the validity of the wisdom gained through denial. "The Enthusiast," for instance, portrays the idealistic life in much the same way that it appears in "Timoleon," and yet its speaker's tone is more inspirational and oratorical than balanced by an acknowledgment of the costs of idealism. It asks essentially the same questions as the larger poem but does so only to provide a reason for the poem's final, answering stanza:

> So put the torch to ties though dear,
>   If ties but tempters be.
> Nor cringe if come the night:
>   Walk through the cloud to meet the pall,
>   Though light forsake thee, never fall
> From fealty to light. (231)

By this point the poem comes perilously close to the portrait of madness in "Cock-A-Doodle-Doo." Though the earlier stanzas may call for the maintenance of chronometrical strength, the final lines very nearly push such devotion into the realm of physical denial and suggest that the idealist should, even if opposed by reality itself, nevertheless remain true to his own vision. Such mental constancy thus appears both admirable and dangerous, for the idealist's impulse to "put the torch to ties though dear," to sever himself from social and familial contact, will undoubtedly leave him, like Timoleon, an exile from the life of the flesh. In fact, the result of such devotion may be similar to that depicted in "The Weaver," the portrait of one man's religious commitment to weaving a shawl "For Arva's shrine" at the expense of all but his mental or spiritual life. His "face is pinched" and his "form is bent" (227), and "No pastime knows he nor the wine" (227); he is "abstinent" and lives only to perform his religious duty.

Another such portrait appears in "Lone Founts," a lyric that seems intentionally paired with its obvious opposite, "The Bench of Boors," in order to reflect the dialectical tensions of the collection. Like "The Enthusiast," "Lone Founts" speaks an inspiring rhetoric designed to encourage devotion to "the never-varying lore" (229) and the wisdom that results from its study. However, this poem stays within the bounds of realism, for though it urges the reader to "View not the world with worldling's eyes" (229), it restrains itself from idealistic blindness in a paean to the rewards of the questing life. It reveals the uncomfortable isolation of the devoted thinker without denying the pain of that isolation or suggesting that truth lies only with the devoted individual.

As though to support the validity of such a life, "The Bench of Boors" answers by describing the excessively indulgent but sometimes desirable life of "Tenier's boors" (229), the sleepy, apparently thoughtless inhabitants observed by the "sleepless" speaker. The basic contrast between the observer and the observed echoes the difference between the two juxtaposed poems, for the speaker fails to find the ease and rest that the boors embody because his mind is too active, too searching: "Thought's eager sight / Aches—overbright!" (230). The basic isolation of the speaker thus both quickens his desire for the seemingly carefree life he witnesses and offers an implicit criticism of the apparently valueless lives of the boors.

"The Bench of Boors" also echoes and is echoed by a number of other poems in *Timoleon* that express an interest in or celebrate the thoughtless but potentially regenerative physical life. "Magian Wine," for instance, offers a rather straightforward celebration of the color and associations of the Dionysian element, stressing wine's connection to an early Hellenic paradise of preconscious pastoralism, while "Herba Santa" similarly tallies the physical and emotional benefits of the soothing pipe, playfully offering it as a substitute for the eucharist and as a second, less exalted Christ:

> Again to come, and win us too
>   In likeness of a weed
> That as a god didst vainly woo,
>   As man more vainly bleed? (238)

Comic though its suggestion may be, this passage does offer a serious criticism of Christian salvation; the "higher plain" on which it claims love first appeared produced no results, the poem argues, because it failed to address the effect of bodily reality on the behavior and attitudes of those it hoped to convert to peace and charity. However absurd the poem's proposed substitute may be, it asserts as fact the physical and emotional passivity tobacco produces and suggests that such results, whatever their means, should not be discounted.

A similar attraction to mindless lassitude appears in "Buddha," in which the desire to meld with "nothingness" (232) counters the "Sobs of the worlds, and dole of kinds / That dumb endurers be—" (232). Yet such appeals to induced states of indifference or total physical devotion find a degree of chilling qualification in "Lamia's Song," the sirenic call to "descend" into a pleasure that threatens psychological ruin. Here the object of the seduction is the "Mountaineer" whom the voice urges to come down "From your lonely Alp / With the wintry scalp / To our myrtles in valleys of May" (228). In other words, the song is directed at the isolated ascetic in an attempt to induce him into partaking of the Dionysian life.[11] According to the poem's title, the song's celebration of "the downward way" is merely a trap designed to ensnare the heroic quester into a destructive relationship. The life of the body as associated with sources of feminine power thus becomes both seductive and ultimately threatening to the isolated, masculine quester. Here, as in *Pierre* and *Clarel,* the physical life can be productive only through the absence of the "gorgonian" female.

The similar struggle between such asceticism—with its sense of erotic avoidance, fragmentation, and disease—and the Ishmaelean interest in productivity and linguistic play appears most forcefully in the section of *Timoleon* entitled "Fruit of Travel Long Ago." Here the emergence of "Art" as a principle capable of ordering life into an aesthetic but dangerously fleshless pleasure both reflects and reshapes the tension between mind and body at the same time that it faces the potential threat of eroticism it seeks to supplant.

The lyrics of "Fruit of Travel Long Ago" concentrate on the speaker's encounter with the culture and, most noticeably, the architecture of Europe and the Middle East. Like the highly formalistic classical and Renaissance architecture of Greece and Italy, these poems show an aesthetically playful formality that nevertheless contains an element of asceticism. If the Ishmaelean impulse reappears in this section, it does so stripped of its full associations with primal death-in-life powers; instead, the desire for productivity is now coupled with Ahab's fear of sexuality and his continued pursuit of bodiless truth. Perhaps more significantly, however, Ishmael's playfulness feeds not upon the energies of southern, "pagan" seas but upon the long-trodden sand and stone at the center of western, "Christian" civilization. In this respect a dialectic arises between an increasingly Christianized metaphysical desire and the reemergence of physicality in language. The impulse to formalize the Ahabian fragment has found its power in western architecture, in cathedrals and temples, but in turning away from the pagan sea it has lost its deeper connection to the body itself.

With the continued presence of such a qualified asceticism, it is thus no surprise that signs of disease, sterility, erotic avoidance, and metaphysical questing consistently appear in the poems. For instance, the section's longest lyric, "Pausilippo," concerns the speaker's observance of "Silvio," a poet arrested for political reasons, prematurely "bleached through strange immurement long" (243) and now released to physical debility and poverty. Sitting near the hill whose beautiful prospect, according to tradition, heals all pain, the wasted poet fails in both body and voice, for in truly Ahabian fashion it was "the yearning in a patriot ode" that was "Construed as treason" (243), and that yearning has cost him both sex and speech. As a result, not only is the poet "Unmanned" (244), but the loss of sex translates into a loss of creative power as well: the once "enthusiast" has lost his ability to act either physically or linguistically, and only "the constant maid" (244), the daughter whose filial faithfulness retards and replaces her own sexual development, can supply his voice.

Perhaps of more significance, however, is the attitude and reaction of the lyric speaker whose pain only deepens as a result of seeing the wasted poet. Like a Wordsworthian voice seeking solace in a natural or humanistic encounter, the speaker, in "sorrow's snare" (245), begins by hopefully explaining the tradition surrounding the hill's history and power:

> Its name, in pristine years conferred
> By settling Greeks, imports that none
> Who take the prospect thence can pine,
> For such the charm of beauty shown
> Even sorrow's self they cheerful weened
> Surcease might find and thank good Pan. (242)

The hill's connection to ritual washing and its association with early Greek, Dionysian joy connect it to the anti-ascetic, carnivalesque vision of the "pristine years" of Greek civilization even as the connection reasserts the distance of such a golden age. The present yields only Silvio and the impotence he embodies, the sight of which simply confirms the speaker's conviction that devotion to the body is no longer possible and that senselessness, in fact, is the only cure for his emotional pain.

The contrast between the dream of the Dionysian past and the harsh truth of the present confirms the speaker's hopelessness at the same time that it reinforces the poem's general orientation toward emotional and bodily fulfillment. If happiness comes only in "a dream of years serene"

(244), then such "fulfillment and fruition" (244) cannot exist in any palpable form in the world of the poem. Instead, the reality of the body appears in Silvio's voiceless, crippled bow, the chaste devotion of his daughter's "ministering hand" (243), and the speaker's own language, whose listless diction reasserts the physical debility that such despair can cause. In the absence of the Dionysian past, the Christian present— "bland untroubled heaven" (245)—provides no meaningful substitutes for golden age fulfillment.

Similarly, "In a Bye-Canal" records the presence of disease and, more importantly, erotic distance, danger, and avoidance. It follows a smaller poem, likewise concerned with Venice, and forms with it a significantly contrasting, two-part invention. The first, "Venice," compares the city's architecture to the "marvellous gallery" (238) constructed by the coral worm of the South Seas. The connection between the two seats of "Pantheistic energy" (238) relates significantly to the following poem because it suggests a sacred tie between the pagan, southern seas of Melville's youth and the pre-Christian spirit of Pan that, according to the final stanza, is responsible for Venice's "reefs of palaces" (239). The notion that an encounter with Venetian "reefs" forms a notable counterpart to Melville's earlier experience with anti-ascetic culture suggests that Venice might also reinvigorate the quester by providing another encounter with the "low enjoying power." Furthermore, by connecting the naturalistic "craftsmanship" of the coral "worm" to the "kindred art" (239) of Venetian architecture, the speaker suggests the possibility that "artifice," whether it appears in nature or civilization, retains a consistent validity and power. Organic form, in other words, acts as artifice even as the "artificial" may be fundamentally organic.

The hopeful and inspiring comparison found in "Venice," however, receives a powerfully disruptive shock in the subsequent "In a Bye-Canal." After establishing the possibility that Venice is another Typee of sorts, the speaker sets out to explore the sacred place he has, in part, constructed for himself. Instead of the spirit of Pan rising in palatial facades, the speaker encounters an erotic and psychological threat comparable to those produced by Melville's previous "gorgonian" women. In fact, from the poem's beginning we are immediately aware that this Venice has more in common with the Naples of "Pausilippo" and the Saddle Meadows of *Pierre* than with the Dionysian city imagined in "Venice." The lifeless calm and dreaminess of the scene suggest the hallucinatory, psychological visions of Poe, while the emphasis on languor, sleep, and silence reflects the note of physical debility that "Pausilippo" invokes. The poem also establishes the possibility that, far from a paradisiacal seat of renewing energy, Venice may harbor a similar sort of castrative power for the searcher whose "yearning" is too great:

> A lattice clicks; and lo, I see
> Between the slats, mute summoning me,
> What loveliest eyes of scintillation,
> What basilisk glance of conjuration! (239)

The "response" to the "tinkling" of the oar—an inadvertent, furtively sexual tapping on the wall—erotically threatens the speaker, who, noting that he has faced both physical and metaphysical dangers, cannot accept the sirenic challenge issued by the basilisk eye. Like Ulysses, "Brave, wise, and Venus' son" (240), he avoids the snare of dangerous feminine eroticism, as though aware that genuine love promises not merely an embrace of death but the chance for resurrection and return that Ulysses himself experiences.[12]

After this escape from the physical and psychological threat of the "basilisk glance," the poems of "Fruit of Travel Long Ago" continue to show a marked interest in metaphysical pursuits even as they investigate the aesthetic value of formality. "In a Church of Padua," for instance, demonstrates that Melville's interest in the problems of metaphysical questing has not so much diminished as it has changed its physical and theological focus. The poem describes a Roman Catholic confessional, "An upright sombre box" (241), but relies upon a figure associated with the sea to compare such Christian "soul-searching" to the "deep diving" of Melville's earlier questers:

> Dread diving-bell! In thee inurned
> What hollows the priest must sound,
> Descending into consciences
> Where more is hid than found. (241)

While the rhetoric of the confessional presumably grants liberation from conscience and sin, Melville's powerful metaphor struggles against such a benign vision of the "diving" process by stressing the position of the priest whose quest to locate the hidden transgression is both difficult and forever unassured of result. Thus the "inurned" seeker must "sound" the "hollows" of conscience, that is, not only penetrate and measure the inner spaces of man's soul but also speak the platitudes of forgiveness in an uncertain attempt to liberate the deceptive sinner. Without knowledge of the individual, the priest must rely solely on what the confessor says to guide him in his task, and it is in part the puzzling unreality and potential ambiguity of all such language that the poem asserts.

Though "In a Church of Padua" dwells on the linguistic and theological difficulties of the confessional, such poems as "The Attic Landscape," "The Apparition," and "The Great Pyramid" contrastingly investigate the potential for an aesthetic value that will provide fulfillment akin to Ishmaelean synthesis.[13] "The Attic Landscape" emphasizes the nearly bloodless linearity of the Greek terrain, a "Pure outline pale" echoed in the architecture and art found within it:

> No flushful tint the sense to warm—
> Pure outline pale, a linear charm.
> The clear-cut hills carved temples face,
> Respond, and share their sculptural grace.
>
> 'Tis Art and Nature lodged together,
>   Sister by sister, cheek to cheek;
> Such Art, such Nature, and such weather
>   The All-in-All seems here a Greek. (245–46)

A qualification, both in content and tone, pervades these stanzas, for the value of linear form is severely undercut both by its fleshlessness and by its evocation in the speaker's mind of a false synthesis. In the second stanza, the "Pure outline pale" and "sculptural grace" suggest both positive and negative qualities, an ascetic pallor coupled with an attractive but suspect formality, while the tone of the third stanza shifts from mixed to ironic by picturing Art and Nature as two posing sisters who, along with the "weather" (a jarringly mundane term), serve to parody idealistic notions. Despite the comic ending, however, it is clear that the possibility of such a synthesis interests Melville during this period, even if he remains aware that such "linear charm" seems perilously close to death.

Though less critical overall, "The Apparition" similarly suggests that Greek architecture may provide a spiritual guide, an ascetic formalism that retains the potential to lead the misanthrope toward social synthesis. The poem begins by citing the episode of Constantine's conversion and the "supernatural Cross" (253) of his vision. The cross that "smote" the pagan, converting him to Christian "allegiance" (253), establishes the power of form to change the viewer by its evocation of meaning. That such Christian order is nearly exhausted or greatly qualified to Melville becomes clear with the second stanza's abrupt turn to the Parthenon:

> With other power appealing down,
>   Trophy of Adam's best!
> If cynic minds you scarce convert,
> You try them, shake them, or molest. (253)

The "other power," presumably the Attic grace of Greek architecture, has now taken the place of Christ and cross by becoming the "Trophy of Adam's best!," that is, the best that fallen man has accomplished, including, we must assume, the accomplishments of the "second Adam," Christ himself. Yet the Parthenon only molests "cynic minds," while the cross "turned [the] soul's allegiance" (253), a contrast that suggests that Greek architecture, while powerful, still lacks metamorphic power.[14] Indeed, the best the Parthenon can do, it seems, is convince us that man is after all capable of some good, even if his accomplishments are partial and limited.

The potential terrors rather than benefits of architectural formality finally appear in "The Great Pyramid," in which ascetic, pantheistic beauty yields to the monotheistic pyramid, emblem of silence and the spiritual terror of "this dumb I AM" (255). Here we find little suggestion that aesthetic appreciation can replace bodily fulfillment; instead, the blindness, sterility, and implacability of the ancient formation offer a return to the worlds of "Bartleby" and *Pierre*. We are given, in fact, another version of the Terror Stone and, in echo of Pierre's challenge, another address to the unresponsive Other. Yet instead of attempting to question the unbridgeable distance, the poem simply describes the nature and result of the quest and ends by hinting that certain kinds of form may hold more terror than consolation:

> Slant from your inmost lead the caves
> And labyrinths rumored. These who braves
> And penetrates (old palmers said)
> Comes out afar on deserts dead
>   And, dying, raves. (255)

As we know from Melville's earlier work, the penetration of the stony maze yields madness and sterility, but the transformation of "Stones formless into form" (255)—while potentially productive in a pagan, pantheistic world—produces spiritual horror in the "deserts dead" of Egypt. Thus architectural art, whose potential for saving power Melville continues to question, here appears as an invocation of the "hollow" of metaphysical desire that draws the seeker toward insanity.[15]

Despite the remnants of Ahabian energy that remain in "Fruit of Travel Long Ago," the collection does help reassert an interest in the body as a palpable erotic force. Such a poem as "The Archipelago," for instance, while registering the absence of Edenic life in the apparently blighted Greek islands, resurrects yet another picture of a Polynesian paradise by combining the desire for an absent pleasure with the genuine recognition of the value of that lost Eden.[16] In a like manner, the final section of

"Syra" describes a scene that evokes the Dionysian past, though now without the heavy qualifications of a comparison to south sea innocence. It imagines a golden age of carefree living, "When trade was not, nor toil, nor stress, / But life was leisure, merriment, peace," (252) and emphasizes the failure of commercialism to taint the "immature" "light hearts" of the inhabitants. Likewise, the collection's "L'Envoi," a dramatic monologue of "The Return of the Sire de Nesle," offers evidence of an Ishmaelean voice as the returning quester gives up the "yearning infinite" (256) and declares his devotion to the heart:

> But thou, my stay, thy lasting love
> One lonely good, let this but be!
> Weary to view the wide world's swarm,
>   But blest to fold but thee. (256)

Such a resolution is among the major chord progressions of Melville's later work, for despite occasional and important modifications and criticisms of the pattern, works such as *John Marr and Other Sailors, Weeds and Wildings,* and *Billy Budd* individually echo this movement toward bodily acceptance.

Despite such moments of acquiescence, however, the problems of both physical and temporal distance remain the principal sources of energy and frustration in *Timoleon,* and though language or art may address and even momentarily overcome them, the overall voice of the book speaks from the basic understanding that such attempts usually fail. Nevertheless, artistic failure may be said to form not only one of the book's main subjects but also a part of its principal aesthetic. In poems such as "The Ravaged Villa" and "Fragments of a Lost Gnostic Poem of the 12th Century," for instance, the idea of incompletion appears both as echo of the book's unsatisfied desires and as the broken remains of language that, as in "Monody," Melville shores against his own and the world's ruins. Furthermore, the volume as a whole, perhaps because it was assembled from earlier work, suggests that a rather delicate thematic unity has here been coupled with a randomly fulfilled form; indeed, without the two larger poems at the book's beginning, the whole seems to disintegrate into related but unstructured pieces. Certainly *John Marr,* with its concentration on the sea, sailors, and memory, offers a more resounding and finished vision than *Timoleon,* whose language, content, and construction seem wedded to the earlier, less formally certain Melville of the late 1850s. *Timoleon* thus produces a small dissonance when placed between the aged dreaming of *John Marr* and the joyous pastoralism of *Weeds and Wildings* and reminds us that whatever modest degrees of acceptance these vol-

umes may present, Melville has not found nor does he keep them without
a struggle.

The Triumph of Sense

Of the three later volumes of lyrics, *Weeds and Wildings with a Rose
or Two* offers the most unified and least anxious vision of its world.
Though it contains conflicts similar to those in the earlier volumes, it
nevertheless imagines a dualistic world that provides potential transformation and synthesis through natural sensuality.[17] More than any of
Melville's later works, it relies upon an Ishmaelean sensibility—with its
propensity for regenerative play now transformed into Dionysian and
Christian patterns of salvation—to enable its characters and speakers to
engage the full sensual and mythological form of the bodily world. The
equally fruitful but variously modified figures of Christ and Dionysus
dominate the volume and provide a mythological framework by which the
body attains a spiritual ascendance even as the spirit assumes a sensual
reality. Thus whatever conflicts arise between spirit and flesh, isolation and
embrace, do so within the atmosphere of potential transformation and
joyful acceptance that the book transmits. The playfulness of the world's
body helps reformulate mental and physical distance into the ingredients
of a larger vision that both accepts physical limits and accentuates physical
benefits. In this respect *Weeds and Wildings,* despite or because of its
sometimes saccharine gestures, moves the Christian-Dionysian strain in
Clarel away from the aridities of the larger poem and into a green and
flowering "retirement" in the Berkshires, meanwhile deepening and en-
larging that vision through its naturalistic revision of the mythos.

The poems of the volume offer what is probably Melville's most sensuous and naturalistic bodily world since *Moby-Dick.* Despite the fact that
the volume concerns itself with flowers instead of whales (making it at
times weakly conventional and less powerful), it reveals a commitment to
the senses that clearly echoes Ishmael's delight in substance and contour.
In fact, an almost childlike simplicity of discovery and enjoyment dominates the poems, imparting both lightness of expression and an absence
of complex thought:

> Soft as the morning
>   When South winds blow,
> Sweet as peach-orchards
>   When blossoms are seen,
> Pure as a fresco
>   Of roses and snow,
> Or an opal serene. (266)

That such a moment of descriptive imagism refrains from one of Melville's typical philosophical turns suggests that the poet of *Weeds,* while occasionally grappling with ideas, is often content simply to record the topographies of the mask rather than strike through it. He seeks and attempts to celebrate the fresh, immediate, and "serene" manifestations of life that this notable exterior world presents. Whether such a lack of intellect results from a surrender to simplicity or from a conscious attempt to explore the regenerative powers of the physical world, what remains notable is the reemergence of sensuality as an end in itself.

Part of the character of this book's world is its propensity for simplified play, the apparently innocent, infantile joys of spring and summer. Yet such giddiness, even in its most conventional expressions, seldom lacks the contrasting note that helps locate seasonal joy within the larger patterns of life and death. Though the senses may dominate the world of *Weeds and Wildings,* the absence of extended philosophical questions does not presuppose an absence of mythological or naturalistic wisdom, neither does it suggest a failure to sense the difficulty of transcendence. In other words, the delight in and celebration of life does not fail to record the presence of evil, the limits of self-consciousness, or the power of death in the natural world:

> We'll rove and we'll revel,
>   Concerned but for this,—
> That Man, Eden's bad boy,
>   Partakes not the bliss. (264)

The butterfly's "ditty" begins with the same apparently carefree account of natural beauty and sensual experience that "The Dairyman's Child" provides. Through flatly conventional figures, the butterfly (speaker) transmits at the very least its sense of both physical and mental freedom to "rove" and "revel" in a paradise of pure sensation. Indeed, not until the third stanza's strange twist, in which excessively fallen man seems suddenly thrust from the garden, do we see the poem's complete vision. Rather than simply praising the freedom of nature, it establishes an unconscious world in order to demonstrate man's exclusion from it, his inability to accept the simplicity of natural experience and, most remarkable, nature's apparent attempt to prevent him from such acceptance. The poem, in effect, measures the distance between thoughtful, theological man and thoughtless, zoological nature and so simultaneously reveals a kind of paradise while it refuses self-conscious humanity the freedom to embrace it.

A similar opposition appears in a more abstract form in "Profundity and Levity," in which the distance between man and nature finds broader symbolization in the meditative owl and the "curvetting and caroling" (274) meadowlark. More significant than the familiar struggle between thought and emotion, however, is the infectiousness of the lark's play, for though the owl reveals his engagement with profound questions, the buoyancy and levity of the smaller bird both effect his "expression" and undercut the seriousness of his seemingly ponderous "wisdom." As the prefatory note states, "the weightiness of the [owl's] wisdom ill agrees with its somewhat trilling expression; an incongruity attributable doubt-less to the contagious influence of the reprehended malapert's overruling song" (274). Which attitude, if either, the dualistic poem promotes re-mains unclear, even though it offers little reward to the pursuer of wisdom and apparent joy of spirit to the "fantastic" celebrator of life.

Perhaps the clearest union of these disparate attitudes appears in "Iris," a portrait of "young Miss Rachel Turner, of Savannah," who, as Stanton Garner explains, was "one of the many Southerners who fled the ruin and privation of home for the humming prosperity of New York City."[18] The subject, like the flower that is her symbol, brings to the North sensuous extravagance, hints of "Magnolias in their languor / And sorcery of the South" (276). Yet despite her provocative "raillery," her personality also suggests defeat, destruction, and suffering:

> For under all your merriment
>   There lurked a minor tone;
> And of havoc we had tidings
>   And a roof-tree overthrown.
>
> Ah, nurtured in the trial—
>   And ripened by the storm,
> Was your gaiety your courage,
>   And levity its form?
>
> O'er your future's darkling waters,
>   O'er your past, a frozen tide,
> Like the petrel would you skim it,
>   Like the glancing skater glide? (277)

The extraordinary display of both flower and woman contains equal parts joy and pain, suggesting the efflorescence that suffering can initiate or enlarge; what appears to be joy may actually be courage, while beauty may flow from sorrow as both antidote and transformed power. The result of such experience in this case strikes a new note for Melville and in a sense underlines much of the apparent levity of the volume as a whole. These lines suggest that what the earlier Melville disdainfully termed "skim-ming," the refusal to dive for the deeper truths of life, now may assume a more profound and less negative meaning. In these lines such avoidance results not from timidity but from the icy effects of the struggle to bear individual suffering. In other words, superficiality and the lightness of spirit that sometimes accompanies it may be the result of profound disturbance, the transformation of deeper knowledge into a sorrowful joy that is both celebratory and grimly courageous. Such a vision, with its suggestions of resurrection or transcendence, clearly echoes on a greatly diminished scale the similar process by which Ishmael gains playfulness through encounters with death, thereafter facing life's terrors with a profound levity.

Through such a poem as "Iris," despite its hackneyed and frequently plain imagery, it becomes clear that the world of *Weeds and Wildings* offers more than a resigned, empty vision of aging acceptance. The volume's larger grasp of the resurrective power of natural cycle, with its connections to early Christian and Dionysian mythoi, provides the poems with an increased depth of vision despite their blithe surfaces. By returning to the productive worldly body, Melville has transformed the ascetic strain of Christianity found in *Clarel* into a body-conscious fulfillment of the pattern of death and resurrection. Nature offers, in effect, images of a fleshly Christ whose suffering and death produce not spiritual ascendence but sensual transcendence.[19]

In this respect, nature provides both the power to transfigure and the path to resurrective joy by means of a death that is productive rather than destructive. One of the primary expressions of this notion appears in "The Blue-Bird," in which the death of the bird, yielding to the magic of seasonal change, resurrects the "azure bells" of the larkspur:

> But, look, the clear etherial hue
> In June it makes the Larkspur's dower;
> It is the self-same welkin-blue—
> The Bird's transfigured in the Flower. (265)

The poem's early stanzas describe the bird's physical death and prepare the reader for the final stanza's transformation of the bird's "etherial" color into the earth-bound and earth-fed larkspur. The poem thus employs a basically Christian mythological pattern but transfers it to a naturalistic, sensuous world in an attempt to validate the idea of rebirth by wedding it to reality. That color forms the only connection between bird and flower thus becomes significant rather than disturbing because such a rebirth must occur within the realm of the senses, the sensual experience of nature. It is precisely an element of the bird's body that is reborn in the flower; whatever spiritual resurrection this link suggests must follow and depend upon the immediacy of the senses.

In a larger, more directly social context, "Trophies of Peace" similarly imagines death as part of a peaceful, naturalistic order that helps produce beauty and nourishment. The poem imaginatively transfers "Files on files of Prairie Maize" (266) into "spears" that obviate the need for genuine military "files" of soldiers and spears of steel. Likewise, their deaths replace and prevent the deaths of their human, symbolic counterparts both by means of the food they provide and by their metaphoric displacement of human death. Thus the poem manages to synthesize death and life by allowing natural process to inform the central metaphor with cyclical meaning. The "golden grain" that results thereby becomes the "trophies" of acquiescence to natural order and provides not symbols of egotistical "victory" but palpable matter for the nourishment of the living body.

This opposition between human violence and nature's ability to transform it into productive power continues in "Time's Betrayal," a notation of the effects of tapping a premature maple. The poem's prefatory note informs us that such early "bleeding" does not kill the "sylvan younker" (273) but "can hardly contribute to the tree's amplest development or insure patriarchal long life to it" (273), for "the annual tapping would seem to make precocious the autumnal ripening or change of the leaf" (273). Thus the young maple becomes a symbol for the stunting but often extraordinary effects of early suffering, the kind of virginal shock that propels Pierre into idealism and sexual disfunction. It is the "tapping" of the premature tree that undoubtedly functions as a symbolic sexual act. Such diction as "conscience," "makes bleed," "poignards," and "shapely young maple" clearly establishes the scene as a kind of virgin's rape (273). Yet while the act itself is decried, the poem attempts to convert this violence into beauty by noting that "the leafage will tell" (274) and "all beauty excell / For a time, for a time!" (274) like the brief, productive lives of poets "who die early" but yield "a splendor!" (274). In other words, tragedy produces intensity of life just as death accelerates and intensifies both pain and beauty.

Though the volume as a whole relies upon echoes of Christian mythos, however, it refuses to push that reliance beyond a generally secular naturalism. Despite the Christ-like reappearance of spring flowers, the formal Christianity that comes under attack in *Clarel* still provides no valuable source of comfort for the poem's speakers. Even in the largely joyous and celebratory Christmas poems that conclude "The Year," for instance, there remain mildly sardonic barbs and cynical thrusts at Christian theology and tradition:

O the delight to believe in a wight
More than mortal, with something of man,
Whisking about, an invisible spright,
Almoner blest of Oberon's clan.

Stay, Truth, O stay in a long delay!
Why should these little ones find you out?
Let them forever with fable play,
Evermore hang the Stocking out! (270)

Though the subject of "Stockings in the Farm-House Chimney" is undoubtedly Santa Claus, the description of him as "More than mortal, with something of man" equally applies to his non-secular counterpart, whose "fable" requires, in the speaker's mind, a similar faith. Indeed, the tone of the last stanza, with its wish for eternal innocence, expands beyond simple Christmas folklore in its desire for childlike acceptance and the act that is based purely on faith. Similarly, in the second Christmas poem, "A Dutch Christmas Up the Hudson in the Time of Patroons," a careful and loving catalogue of Christmas delights ends with a strangely deflating stab at the inconsistency and practicality of worldly Christians: "Happy harvest of the conscience on many Christmas Days" (272).

A similar though somewhat more qualified look at official Christianity occurs in "Rose Window," the description of a churchgoer's dream of natural potency and sensual validity. This lyric offers a clear picture of the contrast between Melville's naturalization of Christian rebirth and his criticism of organized religiosity by pitting the minister's exposition on "The Resurrection and the Life" (299) against the bored listener's dream of floral splendor:

And I saw the Rose
Shed dappled down upon the dead;
The shrouds and mort-cloths all were lit
To plaids and chequered tartans red. (299)

The "lullaby" of the "minister gray" (299) clearly offers no viable power; only through its metamorphosis into natural force does it begin to operate effectively. In other words, conventional, nineteenth-century Christianity, with its ascetic commitments and benign impotence, is remade into the religion of the rose, whose power colors the pale shrouds of the dead and sensually quickens them. Even the final stanza's explanation of the sources of the dream fails to weaken the poem's substitution of sensual power for homily. Though the change here recorded may be illusory and transitory, it nevertheless asserts the validity and superiority of bodily experience as the only rebirth both available and reliable.

Yet man's ability to experience some sort of rebirth requires more than simple recognition of its presence. In this respect, though *Weeds and Wildings* records sensual experience, it becomes clear that the body's chances for natural rebirth are significantly qualified; nature may contain the power to transfigure, but the machinations of intellect may also interfere with human reception of that power. In this respect, though such poems as "A Dutch Christmas" and "Madcaps" present some human involvement in sensual delight, most of the human activity in the volume contains more complicated responses to natural and bodily experience. There remains, for instance, as in "Stockings in the Farm-House Chimney," the frequent suggestion that humanity has been irrevocably severed from such experience by knowledge and self-consciousness. Likewise, in such a pastoral revision as "When Forth the Shepherd Leads the Flock," the golden age serenity of the first three stanzas confronts the lapsarian obsession with "profit" and utility; infantile playfulness, in other words, must struggle against mature humanity's tendency to destroy useless pleasure in favor of productivity. The tacit result of such an ongoing battle is the understanding that those motivated solely by profit cannot participate in Edenic joy. Their capacity for self-supporting play—the simultaneous beginning and end of rebirth—has succumbed to the dictates of utility.

This same argument, as well as its dualistic embodiment, appears in the prose preface to "Rip Van Winkle's Lilac," in which the Bohemian painter confronts a severely utilitarian and ascetic religionist. The "meditative vagabondo" "in his summer wanderings after the Picturesque" (287) has come upon "the pink Lilac relieved against the greenly ruinous home" of the long absent Rip and, charmed by it, opens "his box of colors, brushes, and so forth" and begins to "make a study of it" (287). But soon "a gaunt hatchet-faced stony-eyed individual, with a gray sort of salted complexion like that of a dried cod-fish" approaches and criticizes the painter's choice of subject: " 'Why,' said he, 'if you *must* idle it this way—can find nothing more useful to do, paint something respectable, or, better, something godly; paint our new tabernacle—there is it,' pointing right ahead to a rectangular edifice stark on a bare hill-side, with an aspiring wooden steeple" (287). The ascetic's vision of art allows for the depiction of only that which turns away from nature toward the spirit; that which is useful becomes equal to that which denies the body and exalts the trapped and "aspiring" soul. To the palpably sensitive painter the desiccated flesh of the stranger, his lank horse, and the pallid white church suggest little more than a death that demands the destruction of the body and the loss of the fecund sensations of nature. He therefore counters with his own vision of art, which includes the presence of "ruin" and a "decay" that "is often a gardener" (288). Such images both support and elaborate the poem's general examination of resurrection in the Rip Van Winkle legend, but they also expand the volume's argument that natural process provides rebirth only for those who acquiesce to its patterns and sensations. The individual who turns away from the life of the body becomes blind to the symbolic value of the natural world, becomes, as in the vision of the painter, a figure of death whose "ignorance is extreme" when it comes to the inherent values present in the full life of the body.

A variation of this same theme dominates the longer poem "The Rose Farmer," in which the speaker attempts to determine whether it is better to keep and enjoy the "heaps of posies" or to distill from those blossoms "some crystal drops of Attar" that he can sell and that will outlast the flowers. The opposition arises between direct immersion in bodily experience and the deferral of pleasure in favor of attempts to capture a "transcendental essence" (309). The rose farmer—who has, like Melville, "after rugged scrambles / Through fate's blessed thorns and brambles / Come unto [his] roses late" (303)—was granted his farm by the will of "A corpulent grandee of the East" (304) for whom he once "Prepared a *chowder* for his feast" "against his Ramadan" (304). The clear reference to Queequeg, or his historical source, strongly connects the rose farm— "laved by streams that sacred are, / Pharpar and twin-born Abana" (304)—not only to Eden but also to the pagan sources of sensuous experience. As a result, when the farmer asks the older, wiser florist which method and which philosophy he should adopt, the more experienced man describes his neighbor, "The Parsee," "Lean as a rake with his distilling" (307), whom "No neighbor loves" (307) and who neither enjoys nor profits from his roses. By contrast, the healthy, "flourishing" "veteran" only occasionally picks his roses and accepts and celebrates the "evanescence" of their beauty, enjoying the rewards of sensuality without attempting to alter nature's patterns. It is no surprise that his answer—"I am for roses—*sink* the Attar!" (309)—directly echoes the language of the earlier Melville who had recently completed *Moby-Dick:* "I stand for the heart. To the dogs with the head!"[20] The wise man expresses his preference for the senses, the life of the body and emotions over an exclusively mental existence:

> Discreet, in second thought's immersion
> I wended from this prosperous Persian
> Who, verily, seemed in life rewarded
> For sapient prudence not amiss,
> Nor transcendental essence hoarded
> In hope of quintessential bliss:
> No, never with painstaking throes
> Essays to crystallize the rose. (309)

"To crystallize the rose" is, in effect, to alter nature in order to make it equal or justify an idea, the "hope of quintessential bliss" that attempts to defer bodily pleasure in favor of a bodiless reward. "The Rose Farmer" clearly argues against such desire, promoting instead the very Ishmaelean attitude of the "prosperous Persian."

Despite the argument in "The Rose Farmer," however, an exclusive devotion to the senses remains an alternately positive and negative lifestyle in *Weeds and Wildings,* and perhaps no other poem makes this uncertainty more prominent than "Rip Van Winkle's Lilac." The "good-hearted good-for-nothing" Rip stands as a figure of both sensuality and dangerous mental vacuity. Like the inhabitants of Typee, though happy, he is equally capable of sleeping through most of his life and, in consequence, neglects his house and family in a life of aimless loafing. At the same time, however, he is clearly a figure of rebirth (even though his resurrection fails to bring him renewed youth), and his devotion to sensuous pleasure eventually transforms the landscape into a veritable "Paradise embowered" (293):

> Go ride there down one charmful lane,
> O reader mine, when June's at best,
> A dream of Rip shall slack the rein,
> For there his heart flowers out confessed.
> And there you'll say,—O, hard ones, truce!
> See, where man finds in man no use,
> Boon Nature finds one—Heaven be blest!" (293)

While the final lines suggest that nature retains the power to transform, they also clearly recognize Rip as an ironic life-model, imbalanced to the point of near uselessness, and consequently offer their blessing more as a token of acceptance than a genuine celebration of such emptiness. Rip, after all, lacks the experience and wisdom of the elder rose farmer; despite his age, he retains the immature self he bore into the woods, and *Weeds and Wildings* clearly asserts that whatever values a devotion to heart or rose may produce, such a vision must be tempered by suffering and time if it is to sustain and enrich the individual.

Though Melville's late poetry varies little in formal terms (with the exception of *Clarel*, each is equally idiosyncratic), *Weeds and Wildings* most directly links the natural sensuousness of verse with a vision that highlights bodily play as a productive end in itself. If the turn to poetry reveals a desire to return to Ishmaelean language, then *Battle Pieces, John Marr,* and *Timoleon* can be said to investigate the potential benefits and shortcomings of such a verse as part of the process of revitalizing the dialectic between head and heart. The experimental forms and sometimes rugged versification undoubtedly helped lead Melville away from the deceptive, often unmoored language of *The Confidence-Man,* back toward a dualism that partially echoes and partially transforms the conflict found in *Moby-Dick.* In this respect, these volumes, along with *Clarel,* help make room for the cautious, resurrective syntheses of *Weeds and Wildings* by effectively clearing the ground upon which such a remarkably sensuous, bodily vision might grow. As a result, the poetic language of this late collection encounters much less resistance to its exuberance and playfulness. The tension between desire and acceptance that appears even in the language of *John Marr* and *Timoleon* barely surfaces because the poems of *Weeds and Wildings* offer a less tortured, more resigned vision of both word and deed. What had been rugged in the verse becomes, in effect, the results of playfulness and does so largely because the Ahabian impulse to stretch or fragment form barely exists in these poems.

Such a verse as "Madcaps" provides a clear example of the gentle, unstrained roughness that *Weeds and Wildings* consistently, if somewhat monotonously, offers:

> Through the orchard I follow
> Two children in glee.
> From an apple-tree's hollow
> They startle the bee.
> The White Clover throws
> Perfume in their way
> To the hedge of Red Rose. (263)

Trivial though the subject matter certainly is, such verse clearly echoes, with its simple meter and irregular rhyme, the kind of sailor poetry that Melville first attempted in *Mardi*. It is, once again, the poetry of geniality and high spirits that neither forces nor struggles with the irregularities of the verse. A simple, accentual rhythm drives the song onward, and the awkward extra syllable of "To the hedge of Red Rose" has little effect beyond the comic failure of the verse to follow the established pattern. The air of improvisation and spontaneity certainly does not produce great poetry, but on the other hand it does account for the poem's lack of polish while attempting to make of that slight ungainliness a cause for joy.

What is finally more significant in the development of Melville's own voice late in his career is the notable presence in the later poetry and especially in *Weeds and Wildings* of both small and extended prose introductions. This predilection for mixed genres is nothing new to Melville, who in *Moby-Dick* made such generic variety a veritable modus operandi. Yet in *John Marr and Other Sailors* and especially *Weeds and Wildings*, we begin to see greater and greater quantities of a prose more vital and exuberant than any Melville has produced since the late 1850s. The long contours of *Clarel*, which itself approaches a remarkably prosy verse at times, seem to have pushed Melville more toward extended character investigation and farther away from compressed lyric revelation. Similarly, the verbal solidity and playfulness of the lyrics have revitalized his prose and given it a measure of its former brio. Not only does the vocabulary frequently show high spirit and fecundity, but the very length of some of the introductions in *Weeds and Wildings* causes them to outshine the poems they supposedly introduce. Thus the prefatory "note" to "Rip Van Winkle's Lilac" becomes, in effect, a short story to which is appended a brief poem, while in *Billy Budd* the prose finally overwhelms the verse it pretends to introduce.[21] In other words, the impulse that moves Melville after *Clarel* toward more frequent prose pieces finally makes possible the novella-length "note" that caps his career and continues to overshadow "Billy in the Darbies."

IV

An Open Ending

9

BILLY BUDD AND THE TOUCH OF A GOD

IF *Weeds and Wildings* offers a partially successful deification of the body, an elevation of the senses to the level of spirituality, then *Billy Budd* can be termed its similar opposite, a work in which spirituality takes on flesh, in which the underlying desire of Ahabian questers from *Moby-Dick* through *Clarel* apparently and finally confronts the miraculous answer. Having addressed the question of divine absence in *Clarel,* Melville moves in *Billy Budd* beyond previous limits to ask what would happen to the quester were his desire for physical proof of the metaphysical fulfilled. What effect would such a discovery have upon the society in which it occurred, and what flaws and failures would it reveal in that world's vision of language and its ability to determine truth? *Billy Budd* asks these questions by presenting in "the handsome sailor" a figure who appears to possess a mystical, paradoxical body, a fusion of spiritual and corporeal vigor. It measures and records Billy's responses to the worlds he enters as well as the responses of others to the unprecedented appearance and behavior of the foretopman.[1] The result relies upon and enacts the ironies of distance, for Claggart—the metaphysical quester who has denied his own body—remains frustratingly separate from the now incarnate spirit even as Vere, the leader and protector of a bellicose social body, must sever his only contact with passivity and innocence. The only "touch" that does occur between these fundamentally disparate individuals comes in the form of the equally paradoxical blessing-blow of body and word that simultaneously destroys and creates, fuses and tears apart.

Though we should certainly acknowledge *Billy Budd*'s tonal connection to the poetry of *John Marr and Other Sailors,* it differs from that collection and *Weeds and Wildings* both in the complexity of its subject and in its engagement with difficult philosophical and theological problems.[2] It offers neither the retired examination of temporal distance that *John Marr* exhibits nor the sensuous celebrations of *Weeds and Wildings,* but instead turns back to the tortured sexual and social questions of *Timoleon* and the theological snares of *Clarel.* It is especially the paradoxical

dilemma and failure of Clarel's search for physical evidence of an absent
God that the character of Billy appears to address. Whatever identification
we grant to the "welkin-eyed" sailor, it is clear that he exists in the narration and, most importantly, in the eyes of Claggart as an individual who
approaches if not embodies the contradiction of a fully developed, even
extraordinarily beautiful body without a consciousness of either sexuality
or evil.[3] He is, in other words, both sexed and sexless, body and nonbody.
Though his "aspect" resembles the prototypical "handsome sailor," he
combines the contradictory attributes of delicacy and strength, youth and
physical maturity: "He was young; and despite his all but fully developed
frame, in aspect looked even younger than he really was, owing to a lin-
gering adolescent expression in the as yet smooth face all but feminine in
purity of natural complexion but where, thanks to his seagoing, the lily
was quite suppressed and the rose had some ado visibly to flush through
the tan."[4] The conjunction of lily and rose, given Melville's flower symbolism in *Weeds and Wildings,* suggests a melding of spirit and body even
as it focuses on the exterior reality of Billy. Just as his "frame" reflects
both bodily maturity and youthful innocence, so does his overall appearance combine "a mold peculiar to the finest physical examples of those
Englishmen in whom the Saxon strain would seem not at all to partake
of any Norman or other admixture" with "something suggestive of a
mother eminently favored by Love and the Graces" (51). He thus seems
both in and out of place, lower and upper class, for his physical form
suggests nobility while he possesses "about as much" "self-consciousness
. . . as we may reasonably impute to a dog of Saint Bernard's breed" (52).
Illiterate Billy reflects little of civilization's deferral of physical life in favor
of intellectual development; he is a body, "found" rather than born, who,
though somatically complete, is "much such perhaps as Adam presumably
might have been ere the urbane Serpent wriggled himself into his company" (52), namely, unconscious of his own physical dimension and his
own and others' propensity for evil.

   This ignorance of all but the surfaces of self and other reveals itself
not only in Billy's repeated failure to comprehend Claggart but also in
his reaction to shipboard justice and the mechanisms of the "civilized"
world: "When Billy saw the culprit's naked back under the scourge, grid-
ironed with red welts and worse, when he marked the dire expression
in the liberated man's face as with his woolen shirt flung over him by
the executioner he rushed forward from the spot to bury himself in the
crowd, Billy was horrified" (68). The nature of Billy's horror at this scene
is more complicated than it may at first appear. Because it is his first experience of such a punishment, he not only fears for his own physical and

emotional safety but also comprehends for the first time the reality of the body and its potential connection to shame and degradation. Until this episode, Billy has behaved purely by instinct, decking Red Whiskers, for instance, as though by reflex to his insulting "dig under the ribs" (47). But with his perception of "the culprit's naked back under the scourge," Billy begins to perceive not only individual and social evil but also his involvement in the limits of physical existence, his own susceptibility to bodily punishment and bodily shame. His avoidance of the scene and his ultimate failure to achieve just such a consciousness thus become partially responsible for his fatal "reflex" later in the narrative.

By contrast, a clear indication that consciousness of bodily reality accompanies an understanding of deceptive human behavior—that knowledge of surface yields a knowledge of depth—comes in the form of the Dansker, to whom Billy turns for advice after the flogging. As Melville's figure of sibylline wisdom, the old "*Agamemnon* man" carries "a long pale scar like a streak of dawn's light falling athwart the dark visage" (69), and "his wizened face, time-tinted and weather-stained to the complexion of an antique parchment, was here and there peppered blue by the chance explosion of a gun cartridge in action" (69). The Dansker has gained his sagacity, in other words, not simply from time and experience but, in part at least, at the expense of physical pain and a forced acknowledgment of bodily limits. Like Melville's other aged and knowing protagonists— Israel Potter, Daniel Orme, the Timoneer in *Clarel*—he bears the marks of his knowledge, scars or signs that, like Queequeg's tattoos, encode the understanding of suffering and the memory of physical pain. To Billy, despite his physical prowess or stature, the reception of the wound is impossible; his body cannot be marred because he cannot fathom or accept the knowledge that accompanies the experience. It is partially for this reason that he remains handsome and unmarked even in death.

Billy's status as innocence incarnate also attains various degrees of significance depending upon the different interpretations of those he encounters. For instance, Claggart, the most important of these readers, clearly sees in Billy more than a virginal, handsome sailor, for though it is in fact Billy's "significant personal beauty" (77) that first moves the master-at-arms against him, it is more particularly Claggart's devotion to metaphysical desire that determines his vision of Billy. Claggart is the last and most degenerate figure in Melville's long line of questers. Like Billy, he is physically handsome, but his "pallid" complexion, his "somewhat spare and tall" figure (64), and his large brow "of the sort phrenologically associated with more than average intellect" (64) suggest that, like Ahab's ideal man, he is all brain and no heart, all mind and little body. The accompanying attributes of such an intense devotion to intellect include not merely a consciousness of evil but an understanding so deep that it stains the seeker with an indelible darkness: "Not many are the examples of this depravity which the gallows and jail supply. At any rate, for notable instances, since these have no vulgar alloy of the brute in them, but invariably are dominated by intellectuality, one must go elsewhere. Civilization, especially if of the austerer sort, is auspicious to it" (76). This depravity is both civilized and strangely ascetic, for it lacks the "alloy of the brute" and "partakes nothing of the sordid or sensual" (76). Yet its deeper origin cannot be attributed to education or experience; it is "the mania of an evil nature, not engendered by vicious training or corrupting books or licentious living, but born with him and innate" (76). In other words, the propensity for evil, in such a case, emerges in tandem with the propensity for complex thought so that the figure is separated from both bodily experience and the capacity for innocence.

If Claggart stands as a figure of physical and moral isolation, however, then Billy's appearance must frustrate and tantalize him with those qualities he lacks. Claggart is, in effect, the last embodiment of metaphysical desire now reduced—very much like the figure of the confidence-man— to a perverse hatred for that which earlier manifestations of his spirit once yearned. He has, in fact, discovered a physical reality that seems to him evidence of spiritual truth, an incarnation for which he may once have hoped but from which he now remains separate because of his denial of the body: "If askance he eyed the good looks, the cheery health, and frank enjoyment of young life in Billy Budd, it was because these went along with a nature that, as Claggart magnetically felt, had in its simplicity never willed malice or experienced the reactionary bite of that serpent" (78). The physical facts of Billy accompany and are part of his innocent nature. He thus becomes in Claggart's eyes another Adam, a form capable of a robust, joyous physical existence that flows from his innocence and lack of self-consciousness. "Baby Budd" (44) possesses the innocent eroticism of childhood, yet he has gained it not through Ishmael's resurrective experience but miraculously, extraordinarily in Claggart's eyes, and it is precisely this infantile and innocent pleasure that the master-at-arms cannot attain and therefore must destroy: "And the insight but intensified his passion, which . . . at times assumed that of cynic disdain, disdain of innocence—to be nothing more than innocent! Yet in an aesthetic way he saw the charm of it, the courageous free-and-easy temper of it, and fain would have shared it, but he despaired of it" (78). This "aesthetic" appreciation is nothing less than Claggart's sense of the physical and erotic benefits of innocence. His desire is for both the moral purity *and* the joyous erotic and emotional existence that Billy possesses and exemplifies.

Claggart's behavior towards Billy thus begins a kind of negative court-ship, a string of gestures designed to initiate a consummative embrace that will both join and destroy the figurative "lovers." The first of these "touches" occurs in chapter 10 when Claggart notices "the streaming soup" that Billy has spilled: "Pausing, he was about to ejaculate something hasty at the sailor, but checked himself, and pointing down to the stream-ing soup, playfully tapped him from behind with his rattan, saying in a low musical voice peculiar to him at times, 'Handsomely done, my lad! And handsome is as handsome did it too!' " (72). The sexual diction and symbolism of this passage have been frequently noted and explained, but what remains significant is the initiatory contact between Claggart and Billy. The "playful" tap with the rattan is more than a symbolic gesture: it both foreshadows Billy's later blow and echoes the previous flogging scene even while, more significantly, it physically links the two protago-nists through the agency of the master-at-arms' rattan, the instrument of official justice. It furthermore suggests that Claggart's legal power func-tions as his only viable body, for having severed himself from participation in the bodily world, he requires an agent that will bridge the distance between him and the society of the ship. His "courtship" of Billy will thus necessarily take place via the law, for only through its mechanisms can he produce a palpable effect on the handsome sailor.

This negative "romance" between the previously frustrated quester and the object of his partially abandoned desire climaxes in Billy's re-sponding "touch" in Captain Vere's cabin. Claggart converts his playful tap into its more powerful, linguistic correlative and in his final attempt to join and destroy his vision of incarnate innocence strikes out with words. Here, however, for the first time in Melville's oeuvre, the divine sphere responds to the embittered intellectual, as Billy—whose voice at this crucial moment is as silent as that of Pierre's God—in effect brings the terror stone down upon him: "The next instant, quick as the flame from a discharged cannon at night, his right arm shot out, and Claggart dropped to the deck. Whether intentionally or but owing to the young athlete's superior height, the blow had taken effect full upon the forehead, so shapely and intellectual-looking a feature in the master-at-arms; so that the body fell over lengthwise, like a heavy plank tilted from erectness" (99). The blow on the forehead, both an inverted blessing and a criticism of the intellectualism that sought it, effectively consummates the relation-ship. The seduction of the "divine" has succeeded, and its reward, as the seducer hopes, appears to be a mutual destruction, a death-union that will fulfill the promise of the negative embrace.[5]

Billy's death, like his "birth," serves more to reaffirm and increase his bodily mystery than to reduce him, as it does to Claggart, to simple substance. If Claggart begins by seeing a frustrating combination of physical prowess and spiritual innocence, then the ship's crew transforms his vision of the handsome sailor into a mystical and miraculous one of its own. In this respect Billy's dramatic "ascension" into "the full rose of the dawn" (124), the strange motionlessness of his "pinioned figure" (124), and the actions of the Haglet-like seafowl operate together on the social body of the *Bellipotent* to produce in the minds of the sailors a mystical figure whose death becomes the birth of faith, no matter how superstitious and ignorant its basis may be.[6] More important, their simplistic fervor leads them to perform the function of the faithful, for they, like the seekers in *Clarel,* attempt to reconstruct the mystical body, to recover its physical reality and thereby unite flesh and spirit by transforming the palpable "evidence" of Billy's existence into religious relics: "The spar from which the foretopman was suspended was for some few years kept trace of by the bluejackets. Their knowledge followed it from ship to dockyard and again from dockyard to ship, still pursuing it even when at last reduced to a mere dockyard boom. To them a chip of it was as a piece of the Cross" (131). This description becomes simultaneously an ironic criticism of religious weakness and an assertion of Billy's continued power both despite and because of Claggart's vision,[7] for the master-at-arms, by partially transforming the simple sailor into a divine challenge, has ultimately created the figure he sought to embrace and destroy. Like Judas, he has defined and confirmed the mystical body by assuring both its destruction and its figural resurrection.

The basic relationship between Claggart and Billy, however, remains only part of the problem of *Billy Budd,* for at every moment aboard the *Bellipotent,* regardless of his actual presence, Captain Vere both defines and partially creates the action of the book's world. Even at the climactic moment between Billy and Claggart, Vere is present, acting as both "matchmaker" and official voyeur. It is his vision of Billy, as much as Claggart's, that ultimately transforms the foretopman into a human mystery, for Vere, clearly the "one person excepted" who can appreciate "the moral phenomenon presented by Billy Budd" (78), extends Claggart's vision of Billy as innocence incarnate in order to reveal the implications for the ship's society he strives to protect. If Claggart has partially replaced his own body with the language and instruments of law, Vere has gone even further, taking his own bodily reality from the world of the ship itself:

"But a true military officer is in one particular like a true monk. Not with more self-abnegation will the latter keep his vows of monastic obedience than the former his vows of allegiance to martial duty" (104). The equation of monastic bodily denial and martial duty clearly emphasizes Vere's assumption of the ruling responsibility of his ship onto his own denied and replaced self. He is, after all, "Starry Vere" (61), given to "a certain dreaminess of mood" (61); he loves books "treating of actual men and events" (62) and solidly possesses "settled convictions" (62) that oppose innovations in social theory because such ideas "seemed to him insusceptible of embodiment in lasting institutions, . . . at war with the peace of the world and the true welfare of mankind" (63). He also possesses "a mind resolute to surmount difficulties even if against primitive instincts strong as the wind and the sea" (109). In short, he has devoted himself to the task of preserving the form of the social body, its "lasting institutions," and of preventing the infection of new ideas and potential fevers that may accompany them:

> To some extent the Nore Mutiny may be regarded as analogous to the distempering irruption of contagious fever in a frame constitutionally sound, and which anon throws it off. (55)
>
> . . . .
>
> But do these buttons that we wear attest that our allegiance is to Nature? No, to the King. Though the ocean, which is inviolate Nature primeval, though this be the element where we move and have our being as sailors, yet as the King's officers lies our duty in a sphere correspondingly natural? So little is that true, that in receiving our commissions we in the most important regards ceased to be natural free agents. (110)

The first passage not only establishes a background for the story but also introduces a significant metaphor that clearly represents the official vision of social crisis. It obviously prepares us, in other words, both for Vere's apparent echo of the concept and for his own figural position as the representative "frame," the social "agent," which must linguistically and legally exorcise its own disease.[8]

The initial form of that virus is clearly Billy himself, for his blessing-blow strikes both at the social body's legal sinews—the law itself and Claggart, its agent—but also, by extension, at the assumed form of Vere, in terms of both his authority and his own ideas of order.[9] After the fatal moment of contact, Billy suddenly enters Vere and becomes the threat of his own conscience, a "disease" that speaks with Vere's own voice and against which the *Bellipotent*'s captain must fight in order to maintain his own form. After all, there is a sense in which the whole scene of consummation between Claggart and Billy is both orchestrated and simultaneously takes place in the person of Captain Vere, unfolding as though at his unconscious bidding and at the cue of his unknowing touch: "Going up close to the young sailor, and laying a soothing hand on his shoulder, he said, 'There is no hurry, my boy. Take your time, take your time.' Contrary to the effect intended, these words so fatherly in tone, doubtless touching Billy's heart to the quick, prompted yet more violent efforts at utterance—efforts soon ending for the time in confirming the paralysis, and bringing to his face an expression which was as a crucifixion to behold" (99). The touch and response pattern of Billy and Claggart thus receives a third actor, and it becomes uncertain whether Billy's blow is purely a response to Claggart's physical and verbal approach or, at least in part, a further answer of sorts to the captain's "soothing hand" and "fatherly" tone.[10] Billy, in other words, must respond to two Claggarts in the end, each, for related reasons, committed to the seduction and destruction of innocence. If Claggart wishes to destroy what he cannot possess, Vere wishes to cure himself and his bellicose world of the infections and potential anarchies of conscience.

To Vere as well as Claggart, Billy manages a final response, a wounding benediction that solidifies Vere's denial of his own reality and his transformation into an agent of the warring society he leads and represents. "At the pronounced words" ("God bless Captain Vere!") first uttered by Billy and then echoed by the "ship's populace" (123), "either through stoic self-control or a sort of momentary paralysis induced by emotional shock, [Vere] stood erectly rigid as a musket in the ship-armorer's rack" (123–24). He becomes, in other words, not merely the bodily substitute of institutional man but the very agent or weapon of the man-of-war himself.

Further support for the effect of Vere's vision on Billy's position on the *Bellipotent* comes from the anecdotal history of Billy's previous role aboard the *Rights of Man*. To Captain Graveling, who has not denied his own identity in favor of social form ("he was fifty or thereabouts, a little inclined to corpulence" [45]), Billy has functioned not as a legal and moral challenge to a denied conscience but as a peacemaker. The world of the *Rights of Man*, at least titularly devoted to individuality rather than social hegemony, receives and in a sense transforms the handsome sailor into the organizing lodestone of a sphere of "love," for the threat to the integrity of the *Bellipotent*'s social body had been the savior of form aboard the *Rights of Man*. The transformation hinges upon a positive version of the later "embrace," as Billy confronts the troublesome Red Whiskers: "So, in the second dogwatch one day, the Red Whiskers in presence of the others, under pretense of showing Billy just whence a sirloin steak was cut—for the fellow had once been a butcher—insultingly gave him a dig under the ribs. Quick as lightning Billy let fly his arm. . . . And will you believe it, Lieutenant, Red Whiskers now really loves Billy—loves him, or is the biggest hypocrite that ever I heard of." (47) This consummation, freed from the disturbing influence of Vere's bellicose world, produces a fruitful union, a coupling that acknowledges the reality of the body and employs it as an avenue to social stability.[11] The blow thus produces love in a world where individual form and function are recognized and death where the body is subsumed by unyielding devotion to the ideal.

The Living Word

Given the importance of all such physical contacts in *Billy Budd*, it remains to be seen just how significant a role language plays within these courtships and consummations. As Barbara Johnson has suggested, each character does indeed represent and enact a unique vision of language, and it is, in part, the collision of these exclusive linguistic attitudes that binds and energizes the text's consummative moments.[12] For Billy, the significant linguistic factor remains his stutter; it is both his "flaw" and his response to the deception he encounters aboard the *Bellipotent*. After all, "To deal in double meanings and insinuations of any sort was quite foreign to his nature" (49), and therefore language remains clean and simple to the foretopman: it transmits meaning in a direct, vehicular manner and is as pure and unambiguous as the blow. Thus when he enters the world of the *Bellipotent*, with its nearly urban sense of sophistication and decadence, he encounters in the actions of Claggart and his men as well as in the gnomic evasiveness of the Dansker a language he can neither understand nor speak.[13] The stutter, the image of the failure of language itself, becomes his only response. In fact, it is possible to trace the decay of Billy's speech from his confused questioning of the Dansker to his half-stuttered response to the afterguardsman (82) to his silence in Captain Vere's cabin. In other words, not only is Billy unable to respond in kind to the doubleness of the language spoken to and about him, but his brief existence aboard the *Bellipotent* also appears to tell the story of his growing distrust of language and the eventual systemic failure of a speech that insists on one-to-one correspondences between signifier and signified. His "language" thus steps backward into the purity of physical response: "Could I have used my tongue I would not have struck him. But he foully lied to my face and in presence of my captain, and I had to say something, and I could only say it with a blow, God help me!" (106). The blow fulfills

Billy's vision of what language should accomplish: it transmits a message without equivocation, frankly, and in his eyes is incapable of misconstruction.

What Billy still fails to understand is that the meaning of the "linguistic" act, whether physical or verbal, refuses to fix itself firmly to its apparent vehicle. Though the physical effects of his contact with Claggart seem clear, the meaning of the blow shifts according to the vision and language of the viewer. In Billy's eyes, it is clearly a purification of the uncertainties associated with statement, a way around the murkiness of words. In truth, however, this action seems no clearer or more definite than Billy's final utterance, this time delivered in words instead of flesh but equally capable of mirroring the listener's own ratio of love and hate. Again, what Billy clearly conceives as a pure gesture becomes both a benediction and a curse, for if in striking Claggart he partially blesses the master-at-arms by fulfilling his desire for divine contact, then by frankly blessing Vere, he similarly strikes the captain with what may be his death blow as well. Furthermore, the fact that Billy fails to stutter through his final words suggests that the purely physical agency of the blow, so swift and immediate, has somehow been transferred to his speech. Having struck the purifying blow against duplicity, he seems liberated from both physical limitation and linguistic failure. He does, in a real sense, become the word just as earlier the word became him.

It is, in part, this purity of linguistic and physical act that attracts Claggart to Billy, and it becomes Claggart's linguistic task to seduce and fatally absorb a purity that is, at least to him, both evidence of divine incarnation and the destructive antidote to civilization's duplicity. Claggart is not only the late manifestation of the confidence-man but also a detective with "a peculiar ferreting genius" (67) for uncovering the hidden underside of his world. He himself embodies the ship's doubleness: "Though the man's even temper and discreet bearing would seem to intimate a mind peculiarly subject to the law of reason, not the less in heart he would seem to riot in complete exemption from that law, having little to do with reason further than to employ it as an ambidexter implement for effecting the irrational" (76). The rational surface does not correspond to the irrational depth, a disjunction that makes Claggart more than "sinister": he is the double-dealing "ambidexter," a sleight-of-hand artist whose predisposition is both unusual and inherently deceptive.[14] He possesses the "sinister dexterity" that Billy lacks (49), and yet, for all his seemingly genetic doubleness, he moves throughout the action of the story toward the overwhelmingly homogenous presence of Billy. Despite his inextricable involvement with deception and linguistic casuistry, his maneuvers push him further toward the encounter with the frankness of Billy's touch. His shifting, insinuating syntax creates an image of himself, for the "mantrap" he imagines clearly lurks in him and there lies prepared for the "fair cheek" of Billy (94). In linguistic terms, moreover, it is the syntax itself that seems to weave the snare in order to catch another kind of syntax, in order to absorb and, paradoxically, be destroyed by a sentence structure translated into bodily action.

In Claggart's mind and language actor and action grow clouded—subject and verb qualified and bled of all but indirect power—and his seduction of Billy similarly becomes an attempt to regain vigorous language, to recapture the ability to see, think, and act without indirection. Billy's presence is thus divine to Claggart both because of his paradoxicality and because of his language. Billy speaks and acts directly, vigorously; in fact, speech and action are so closely related in his character that they seem to shift and blend together. As a result, Claggart's accusation amounts to a demand for a purity of which he himself remains incapable: "Those lights of human intelligence, losing human expression, were gelidly protruding like the alien eyes of certain uncatalogued creatures of the deep. The first mesmeric glance was one of serpent fascination; the last was as the paralyzing lurch of the torpedo fish" (98). Claggart, like the confidence-man, turns finally from language to the "mesmeric glance," the attempt to surpass the body's limits, to act beyond the boundaries of physical form. It is ultimately the nearest thing to a physical threat he can muster, for having denied his body he retains only words and the wordless stare, the eye almost disembodied. Billy's responding blow thus momentarily returns Claggart's body even as it destroys it. The touch brings Claggart into contact with a language and action free from duplicity, and he becomes, for the first time in the text, an object, made so by an action and actor unconcealed and responsible for his "word."

Again, the mediator and pander in this relationship is Vere, who is devoted to preserving the language of society along with the social body itself. It is his task to provide the shipboard conglomeration of cultures and languages with a single, overarching linguistic theory that will, often at the expense of the ideal, continue to construct and maintain them as a single unit. In service of this goal, he apparently attempts to avoid all unnecessary utterance, keeps his sea and shore languages neatly separate (60), and shuns humor and geniality. His fellow officers sense that "there is a queer streak of the pedantic running through him" (63) precisely because he restricts his conversation to practical matters and tailors his language to fit the captain's uniform. Though his avoidance of the "jocosely familiar" (63) is meant to solidify his official position and streamline his command, his pedantry works against these goals by revealing his tendency to misread his audience and so at times to fail to communicate. The captain thus speaks in a kind of monologue and though aiming at "directness" (63) inevitably ends by following his own course, unaware of those around him. He remains caught in the paradoxes of his character; after all, he is a sedentary, bookish man in command of a man-of-war, and he speaks a language that will follow only the contours of the forms within his mind. It is Vere's constant goal to align these interior patterns with exterior reality, and yet his attempts to do so end by stretching his words to transparency.

Such self-involvement, however, does not preclude Vere from recognizing and practicing deception, but the deception he identifies is inevitably not his own, and the deceptions he practices apparently remain the unconscious maneuvers of his attempt to retain the shape of social reality. In this respect, though he clearly recognizes and intends to unmask Claggart's false accusations (95–96), he himself turns surreptitious stage manager in his attempt to arrange the face-to-face meeting (97). Similarly, after the violence has occurred, he continues his machinations in the arrangement of the drumhead court and even to the point of Billy's hanging believes it is his duty to deceive the crew in order to save the ship's stability.

What becomes even more significant than his physical duplicity is the combination of official force and officialized language that he employs in the trial. Here his ability to engage in deception transforms itself into a language that attempts to deny that portion of reality that fails to fit his predetermined vision of social form. By refusing to allow consideration of any aspect of the incident except the physical, Vere produces a language that refuses to acknowledge ambiguity even as it uses it for its own ends: " 'That is thoughtfully put,' said Captain Vere; 'I see your drift. Ay, there is a mystery; but, to use a scriptural phrase, it is a "mystery of iniquity," a matter for psychological theologians to discuss. But what has a military court to do with it? Not to add that for us any possible investigation of it is cut off by the lasting tongue-tie of—him—in yonder,' again designating the mortuary stateroom. 'The prisoner's deed—with that alone we have to do' " (108). Vere acknowledges the "mystery" in order to dismiss it, and yet his division of the world into "military" and theological carries its own inherent mysteriousness. To separate the physical from the metaphysical, to deny any connection or tangent between the two, is to split the world severely and artificially, creating an unbridgeable distance between thought and action. It is, in effect, to create a mystery, for Vere's denial of explicability in the case not only results in Billy's condemnation but also assures that Billy's emerging mythos will flourish. The "super-stitious" explanations of "the people" consequently pour in to fill the space created by Vere's division of the *Bellipotent*'s world. As such, Vere's language and vision foster both injustice and martyrdom; he is, indeed, as the text suggests, the "father" of Billy, for out of his paradoxically destructive and retentive language, the post-mortem Billy of legend is born.

Though *Billy Budd* finally provides the dramatic locus for the collision of a variety of linguistic visions, the language and form of the text itself reflect the essential incompatibility of its materials in its tenuous lack of integrity and uncertain status as prefatory "note" to "Billy in the Dar-bies." As recent critics have continued to remind us, *Billy Budd* remains an unpolished and very possibly unfinished text, a manuscript with a checkered editorial and textual history that demands caution of the reader.[15] What Newton Arvin originally termed the text's "stiff-jointed prose" and "torpidity of movement" has combined with later critics' res-ervations about the formal ineffectiveness of the later chapters and is ca-pable of producing in any reader an uneasy doubt about the work's status as a complete, self-supporting structure.[16] Yet both Billy's archetypal "passion" and Vere's insistence on social form provide the tale with pow-erful lines against which Claggart's destructive desire and the tale's own admission of the "raggedness" of truth energetically rebel: "The symme-try of form attainable in pure fiction cannot so readily be achieved in a narration essentially having less to do with fable than with fact. Truth uncompromisingly told will always have its ragged edges; hence the con-clusion of such a narration is apt to be less finished than an architectural finial" (128). The sentiment of this passage echoes not only Ishmael's fa-mous prayer against completion but also *The Confidence-Man*'s arguments against consistency. It includes Claggart's descended Ahabianism and Ish-mael's perception of the inexhaustible wealth of reality. Even more, it alerts us to its own consciously established tension between form and frag-ment and its deliberate conflation of fulfillment and frustration. *Billy Budd*, like the poetry from which it emerges, relies upon the energizing effects of desire and distance, form and dissolution, to fuel its rhetorical engines. Claggart's encounter with Billy thus becomes the central, para-doxical moment that not only drives the narrative but shapes the text's self-conflicting body. Therein form is both born and destroyed; desire moves equally for and against the limits of existence, and the tale that grows around it makes evident both Billy's Christology and Claggart's yearning against physical limit, both Vere's legalism and Billy's "chro-nometrical" force as mystical body. Even Billy himself stands equally as archetypal savior and benign idiot, peacemaker and murderer, perfect body and imperfect language. In other words, there remains in the form of *Billy Budd* the conflicting nature of its substance, and its shape therefore becomes both successful in its failure and a failure in its success. It is, as it has suitably been considered, the fitting conclusion to Melville's life and career, not because it relents and not because it condemns, but because it continues the dualistic struggle with life and world and receives from that timeless clench of recalcitrant doubles an unending power.

EPILOGUE

He lies buried among other sailors, for whom also strangers performed
one last rite in a lonely plot overgrown with wild eglantine uncared for
by man.   —"Daniel Orme"

WITH THE POETRY of *John Marr* and the prose of *Billy Budd*, the
sea returns as a productive force in Melville's work for the first time
since *Moby-Dick*. Despite the presence of water in "Benito Cereno," "The
Encantadas," and *The Confidence-Man*, not since the sinking of the *Pequod*
do we find traces of Ishmael's "live sea" that "swallows up ships and
crews," that miraculous realm of death and rebirth, the seat of the "low
enjoying power." Of course, the world of *Moby-Dick* is not that of *Billy
Budd*, and the vital energy of the larger novel returns only after its transformation by both Christian mythos and bitter experience into a simultaneously sincere and ironic spirit that offers transcendence even as it
questions human value. Nevertheless, as Billy's sewn and shotted body
plunges into the water and the screaming haglets dive and rise above it,
there are discernible echoes of that previous water birth when "the black
bubble upward burst" from the heart of the creamy vortex, the ascending
motion of the first finally descending in the dive of the second, bodies
rising from and falling into their world's essential element. Despite his arguments against symmetry, Melville's work offers this rhyming. The re-
sponding gestures gather and hold together forty years of life and writing.

The tremendous personal toll of such a search, the palpable physical
and emotional costs, are still being revealed to us. Whatever the biographical motives and results, however, it remains clear that Melville's life
was consistently devoted to the attempt to find form and expression for
the dialectical fires that fueled him. The troubling struggle of head and
heart, Ahab and Ishmael, weaves and shifts through that forty years of
work, binding disparate genres and voices into a concentrated investigation of human knowledge and fulfillment. From *Pierre*'s ascetic idealism
through *The Confidence-Man*'s bodiless fragmentation to the political and
theological revisions of *Battle Pieces* and *Clarel*, Melville pushes always in

search of the double voices that offer the potential for reunion, the way toward rebirth and transcendence that Ishmael's experience and the whale's "live sea" provide. Thus from the resurrection of the body at the close of *Moby-Dick,* we move to the resurrection of spirit that *Billy Budd* tentatively provides. It is the end of a long and self-destructive argument, the answer to which is finally both satisfying and disturbing, the synthesis of paradox in the unity of long-strained voices.

The same sort of doubleness informs one of Melville's other late prose pieces, "Daniel Orme." The "old man-of-war's man" wears "a crucifix in indigo and vermillion tattooed on the chest and on the side of the heart," while "[s]lanting across the crucifix and paling the pigment there ran a whitish scar, long and thin."[1] This image, with its complex connection of Christian mythos to Ishmael's symbolic "heart," scarred now and distorted by the violence of human struggle, not only recalls *Moby-Dick*'s celebration of the "low enjoying power" but connects it to the dualistic violence of *Battle Pieces* and to *Clarel*'s search for Christ. It is "the cross of the Passion" (120), the figure of desire inscribed on the aged body as a sign of passage, that same desire that leaves Orme leaning dead against the rusty cannons overlooking the sea, "his clay pipe broken in twain, the vacant bowl and no spillings from it, attesting that his pipe had been smoked out to the last of its contents" (121–22). As one of Melville's final images, this description speaks neither of acceptance nor of triumph but of a self emptied, its thoughts uncertain, unattainable, with only the scars of the body, the signs of a passion, to guide us.

NOTES

Chapter 1. *Moby-Dick* and the Divided Body

1. Of the recent commentators on the Melville-Rabelais connection, Bainard Cowan states that "the connection . . . is not without justification, for it is Rabelais above all who 'bolts down all events, all creeds, and beliefs' . . . and who thus lights the way for Ishmael's imagination in perceiving the 'general joke' of earthly existence." *Exiled Waters: Moby-Dick and the Crisis of Allegory* (Baton Rouge: Louisiana State University Press, 1982), 115. For the most thorough treatments of comic influence, see Jane Mushabac, *Melville's Humor: A Critical Study* (Hamden: Archon Books, 1981); Edward H. Rosenberry, *Melville and the Comic Spirit* (Cambridge: Harvard University Press, 1955); and Robert Schulman, "The Serious Function of Melville's Phallic Jokes," *American Literature* 33, no. 2 (1961): 179–94.

2. Mikhail Bakhtin, *Rabelais and His World,* trans. Helene Iswolsky (Cambridge: MIT Press, 1968), 21. All subsequent references will appear in the text.

3. Though Cowan acknowledges Bakhtin's importance in an understanding of the Melville-Rabelais relationship, he primarily stresses the role of the Bakhtin's "carnivalesque."

4. *Moby-Dick or The Whale,* vol. 6 of *The Writings of Herman Melville,* ed. Harrison Hayford, Hershel Parker, and G. Thomas Tanselle (Evanston and Chicago: Northwestern University Press and Newberry Library, 1988), 164, 167. Subsequent references will appear in the text.

5. The serpentine imagery also recurs in the sperm-squeezing scene in chapter 94.

6. For a systematic reading of this double whale, see Robert Zoellner, *The Salt-Sea Mastodon: A Reading of Moby-Dick* (Berkeley: University of California Press, 1973), 146.

7. Indeed, one can say that a shortcoming of most of the classificatory brand of *Moby-Dick* criticism results from a failure to deal with the narrative whale in preference to the second-hand whale of rumor and speculation. Only by examining the whale itself (as Ishmael does) can we begin to understand the characters' interpretations and their languages of reading, as well as, finally, the characters themselves.

8. Zoellner makes a related point about perception when he says that Ahab "forgot, or never understood, that the image he saw in the world was in part an image of himself" (266). Likewise, David Simpson states that "the paradoxical identity of Moby-Dick consists in the doubling of motives whereby he is both the object on whom revenge must be taken and at the same time the image of the lost member which must be conquered and regained." *Fetishism and Imagination: Dickens, Melville, and Conrad* (Baltimore: Johns Hopkins University Press, 1982), 79–80.

9. In support of a related point, Sharon Cameron writes that "Melville deprives us of metaphoric consolation and makes us see the self's relation to its own body as *literal." The Corporeal Self: Allegories of the Body in Melville and Hawthorne* (Baltimore: Johns Hopkins University Press, 1981), 17.

10. The best description of the history of Ahabian psychology comes from Norman O. Brown: "For two thousand years or more man has been subjected to a systematic

effort to transform him into an ascetic animal. He remains a pleasure-seeking animal. Parental discipline, religious denunciation of bodily pleasure, and philosophic exaltation of the life of reason have all left man overtly docile, but secretly in his unconscious unconvinced, and therefore neurotic." *Life Against Death: The Psychoanalytic Meaning of History* (Middletown: Wesleyan University Press, 1959), 31.

11. Franklin, *The Wake of the Gods: Melville's Mythology* (Stanford: Stanford University Press, 1963), 74.

12. This division was clearly in Melville's mind when he wrote to Hawthorne that "[i]t is a frightful poetical creed that the cultivation of the brain eats out the heart. But it's my *prose* opinion that in most cases, in those men who have fine brains and work them well, the heart extends down to hams. And though you smoke them with the fire of tribulation, yet, like veritable hams, the head only gives the richer and the better flavor. I stand for the heart. To the dogs with the head!" *Correspondence,* vol. 14 of *The Writings of Herman Melville,* ed. Lynn Horth (Evanston and Chicago: Northwestern University Press and Newberry Library, 1993), 192.

13. Martin Leonard Pops notes that "it may even be argued, as D. H. Lawrence first argued on behalf of another American hero, Natty Bumppo, that Ishmael not only does not grow older (i.e., overripe with fulfillment) as the quest continues but that he grows younger and younger." See *The Melville Archetype* (Kent, Ohio: Kent State University Press, 1970), 87.

14. For an analysis of the possibly deceptive tone in the book's opening chapters, see Edgar A. Dryden, *Melville's Thematics of Form: The Great Art of Telling the Truth* (Baltimore: Johns Hopkins University Press, 1968), 86.

15. See Leslie Fiedler, *Love and Death in the American Novel,* rev. ed. (New York: Stein and Day, 1966), 381, for an explanation of Yojo.

16. Brown, 308.

17. E. H. Rosenberry, *Melville and the Comic Spirit,* 94.

18. See especially Zoellner on Ishmael's changing attitude towards Moby-Dick (185).

19. F. O. Matthiessen, *American Renaissance: Art and Experience in the Age of Emerson and Whitman* (New York: Oxford University Press, 1941), 426; and Charles Olson, *Call Me Ishmael* (New York: Reynal & Hitchcock, 1947), 68.

20. Gayle L. Smith states, for instance, that "Ahab's linguistic choices reflect a rigid, correspondential notion of language, a faith that meaning and reality somehow inhere in language itself" (260–61). "The Word and the Thing: *Moby-Dick* and the Limits of Language," *ESQ: A Journal of the American Renaissance* 31, no. 4 (1985): 260–71.

21. He has a further adjunct or counterpart in Elijah, who likewise hints and tempts, though in a less notably malicious manner.

22. For instance, Elaine Barry notes a similarity between Pip's language and the nonsense talk of Azzageddi in *Mardi.* "The Changing Face of Comedy," *American Studies International* 16, no. 4 (1978): 19–33. The point is worth stressing primarily because the extreme philosophical searching of Babbalanja's demonic voice performs a function similar to Pip's experience at sea. Both have gone deeply into the self and, because of what they saw or did not see there, are driven into the realm of non-reason.

23. *Correspondence,* 122.

24. Olson, 42.

25. As Robert K. Martin states, "Ahab's language is another reflection of his intrusive sexuality and aggressive politics. If Ishmael, taught by Queequeg, is to bring about any change, it must include a questioning of that linguistic order that privileges meaning over the words in themselves, with their erotic surfaces fully alert." *Hero, Captain, and Stranger: Male Friendship, Social Critique, and Literary Form in the Sea Novels of Herman Melville* (Chapel Hill: University of North Carolina Press, 1986), 11.

26. It is this aspect of Ishmael's playfully double language that so often misleads commentators into either suggesting that he doesn't mean what he says or ignoring the comedic delivery altogether. See, for instance, James Guetti, *The Limits of Metaphor: A Study of Melville, Conrad, and Faulkner* (Ithaca: Cornell University Press, 1967), 118.

27. E. H. Rosenberry, *Melville and the Comic Spirit*, 119.

28. It is important to note that during this episode Stubb becomes identified with the sharks and with the lower stratum as a whole. Only he and Ishmael, for instance, ever actually attempt to ingest the whale itself.

29. *Correspondence*, 193.

30. *Correspondence*, 162.

31. *Correspondence*, 193.

Chapter 2. Language and the Ascetic Body in *Pierre* and "Bartleby"

1. *Correspondence*, 191.

2. Among these, Edward H. Rosenberry states that "Pierre is an Ahab, . . . but there is no Ishmael in the picture." *Melville and The Comic Spirit*, 142. Likewise, William Ellery Sedgewick, in *Herman Melville: The Tragedy of Mind* (New York: Russel & Russel, 1944) sees Pierre as a young Ahab (147), and, most cogently, Richard H. Brodhead states that "[i]n *Pierre* the process of discovery presented in Ahab's case in the foreshortened form of flashback is stretched out so that we can observe all its stages." *Hawthorne, Melville, and the Novel* (Chicago: University of Chicago Press, 1976), 169. On the other hand, Wai-chee Dimock has recently suggested that Pierre is a version of Ishmael. See *Empire for Liberty: Melville and the Poetics of Individualism* (Princeton: Princeton University Press, 1989), 144.

3. *Pierre; or, The Ambiguities*, vol. 7 of *The Writings of Herman Melville*, ed. Harrison Hayford, Hershel Parker, and G. Thomas Tanselle (Evanston and Chicago: Northwestern University Press and Newberry Library, 1971), 3. All subsequent references will appear in the text.

4. This change of foundation is also evident in the shift in *Pierre* from the mixture of Rabelaisian and Elizabethan influences found in *Moby-Dick* to the, at least psychologically, ascetic combination of Spenser, Dante, and *Hamlet*.

5. *Moby-Dick*, 3.

6. *Moby-Dick*, 274.

7. *Moby-Dick*, 273.

8. As Richard Gray states, "Pierre's life is fictive, not just because Melville has invented it, but to the extent that . . . there is a certain fictitiousness in all Pierre's relationships." " 'All's o'er, and ye know him not': A Reading of *Pierre*," in *Herman Melville: Reassessments*, ed. A. Robert Lee (London: Vision Press, 1984), 116–34.

9. Nicholas Canaday likewise suggests that Pierre's masculinity has been "crushed in the egg and left abandoned in the domestic circle" in which he has been raised (397). "Pierre in the Domestic Circle," *Studies in the Novel* 18, no. 4 (1986): 395–402. For the further suggestion of homosexuality, see Paula Miner-Quinn, "A Psychoanalytic Interpretation of Herman Melville's *Pierre*," *University of Hartford Studies in Literature: A Journal of Interdisciplinary Criticism* 13, no. 2 (1981): 111–21.

10. Lucy's mother, Mrs. Tarton, also contributes to the artificial and repressive background of their relationship. The "match-maker to the nation" (28) and "lady thimble-rigger" (27), as Brodhead notes, "constructs a scene that arouses and plays upon sexual desire without, however, letting it be frankly acknowledged or fully expressed" (172).

11. Several critics have noted the paradoxically destructive nature of Pierre's idealism. H. Bruce Franklin states that "this role [as Christ] leads [Pierre] to a granite hell

and self-destruction. It also destroys all those whom he believed divine." *The Wake of the Gods*, 113. Likewise, Brian Higgins and Herschel Parker note that "in *Pierre* Melville sets out to demonstrate . . . that chronometrical altruism leads inevitably to catastrophe." "The Flawed Grandeur of Melville's *Pierre*," in *New Perspectives on Melville*, ed. Faith Pullin (Edinburgh: Edinburgh University Press, and Kent, Ohio: Kent University Press, 1978), 264.

12. For a further examination of Pierre's idealism, see Michael S. Kearns, "Phantoms of the Mind: Melville's Criticism of Idealistic Psychology," *ESQ: A Journal of the American Renaissance* 35, no. 2 (1989): 147–60; and James C. Wilson, "The Sentimental Education of Pierre Glendinning: An Exploration of the Causes and Implications of Violence in Melville's *Pierre*," *American Transcendental Quarterly* 1, no. 13 (1987): 167–77.

13. As Leslie Fiedler notes, Pierre's speech is a weaker version of the Ahabian voice, a "pseudo-Shakespearean rant, the rhetoric of the deepest gothic melodrama, a theatrical debasement of the pure Faustian cry of terror" (421).

14. See Pops, 95, upon whose discussion I am here relying, for the primary perception of the stone's cetological resemblances.

15. As early as E. L. Grant Watson's foundational essay that cites the "deliberate artificiality" of the early chapters, the majority of critics have acknowledged some degree of intention in Melville's stylistic excesses. "Melville's *Pierre*," *New England Quarterly* 3 (April 1930): 195–234. More recently Brodhead, Alan Holder in "Style and Tone in Melville's *Pierre*," *ESQ: A Journal of the American Renaissance* 60 (1982): 76–86, and Higgins and Parker have agreed, the latter noting that "Melville is in fact mocking Pierre's adolescent heroics, his unearned sense of security, and his unwillingness to force those dark truths that are to be the burden of the novel" (245).

16. Newton Arvin, *Herman Melville* (William Sloan Associates, 1950), 225. Likewise, John Seelye states that in the latter episodes of the book "the style takes on a dry, acerb quality, reminiscent of the complex sarcasm of the eighteenth century." *Melville: The Ironic Diagram* (Evanston: Northwestern University Press, 1970), 78.

17. *Correspondence*, 195.

18. "Bartleby, the Scrivener: A Story of Wall Street," *The Piazza Tales and Other Prose Pieces 1839–1860*, vol. 9 of *The Writings of Herman Melville*, ed. Harrison Hayford, Hershel Parker, and G. Thomas Tanselle (Evanston: Northwestern University Press and Newberry Library, 1987), 15. All subsequent references will appear in the text.

19. We should note not only the portion of the letter quoted above but also Melville's frequent conflation of eating, reading, and writing—from saying that Hawthorne (as a writer) "needs roast-beef, done rare" to offering to send him "a fin of the *Whale* by way of a specimen mouthful" (*Correspondence*, 181, 196).

20. William B. Dillingham, *Melville's Short Fiction* (Athens: University of Georgia Press, 1977), 27–28, stresses the connection between food and money in the lawyer's mind but, instead of noting a basic bodily orientation, sees in them a symbolic representation of the lawyer's "hunger" to purchase self-approval.

21. Lewis H. Miller, Jr., calls "Bartleby's persistent, automatic reiteration" of a single phrase "a triggered response, an empty counter much akin to the mimicry performed by certain trained birds" (3). " 'Bartleby' and the Dead Letter," *Studies in American Fiction* 8 (1980): 1–12.

Chapter 3. *Israel Potter* and the Search for the Hearth

1. *Journal of a Visit to London and the Continent by Herman Melville, 1849–1850*, ed. Eleanor Melville Metcalf (Cambridge: Harvard University Press, 1948), 75.

2. Charles N. Watson, Jr., "Melville's *Israel Potter:* Fathers and Sons," *Studies in the Novel* 7 (1975): 563–68; Robert Zaller, "Melville and the Myth of Revolution," *Studies in Romanticism* 15 (Fall 1976): 607–22. For an example of the novel's generic rebellion, see Brian Rosenberry, "Israel Potter: Melville's Anti-History," *Studies in American Fiction* 15, no. 2 (Autumn 1987): 175–86.

3. Joyce Sparer Adler, *War in Melville's Imagination* (New York: New York University Press, 1981), 79–87; and Daniel Reagan, "Melville's *Israel Potter* and the Nature of Biography," *American Transcendental Quarterly* 2, no. 1 (March 1988): 41–55.

4. Sedgewick, *Herman Melville.*

5. Seelye, 117; Joseph Flibbert, *Melville and the Art of the Burlesque* (Rodolphi N. V. Amsterdam, 1974), 146; and William B. Dillingham, *Melville's Later Novels* (Athens: University of Georgia Press, 1986), 248.

6. For a discussion of Melville's modifications of his source, see Walter E. Bezanson, "Historical Note," in *Israel Potter: His Fifty Years of Exile,* vol. 8 of *The Writings of Herman Melville* (Chicago: Northwestern University Press and Newberry Library, 1982), 173–235; and Hennig Cohen, "*Israel Potter:* Common Man," *A Companion to Melville Studies,* ed. John Bryant (New York: Greenwood Press, 1986), 279–314.

7. For discussions of this aspect of the novel, see Charles N. Watson, Jr. (563), and Zaller (608).

8. *Israel Potter: His Fifty Years of Exile,* vol. 8 of *The Writings of Herman Melville,* eds. Harrison Hayford, Hershel Parker, and G. Thomas Tanselle (Evanston and Chicago: Northwestern University Press and Newberry Library, 1982), 7. All subsequent references will appear in the text.

9. Both Seelye (116) and Alan Lebowitz have suggested a connection between Melville's Franklin and the figure of the confidence-man. See *Progress into Silence: A Study of Melville's Heroes* (Bloomington: Indiana University Press, 1970), 174.

10. See Lebowitz on Jones's "prudence" (178).

11. See also Zaller for a different reading of the blanket scene (612).

12. See especially the "pickled powder" incident in chapter 18.

13. For instance, Cohen states that "the variety of literary forms in *Moby-Dick* has been remarked often, and on a much more modest scale *Israel Potter* includes a like variety" (301).

Chapter 4. Toward Deception: The Short Fiction and the Failing Body

1. Melville's letter proposing the manuscript is suggestive but unclear about his compositional method overall. The guarantee of "at least ten printed pages in ample time for each issue" does hint, however, at a fragmentary vision of the story. *Correspondence,* 265. For a possible chronology of the short fiction, see Merton M. Sealts, Jr., "Historical Note," in *The Piazza Tales and Other Prose Pieces, 1839–1860,* vol. 9 of *The Writings of Herman Melville,* ed. Harrison Hayford, Hershel Parker, and G. Thomas Tanselle (Evanston and Chicago: Northwestern University Press and Newberry Library, 1987), 457–533.

2. Of the theories concerning Melville's shift to shorter forms, Newton Arvin's notion of "flagging inventiveness" has long been the basic assumption of many readers (244). Yet Charles G. Hoffman argues that the turn to new genres is the conscious move of a writer interested in shorter forms. "The Shorter Fiction of Herman Melville," *South Atlantic Quarterly* 52 (1953): 414–30. A. W. Plumstead also sees Melville moving to forms over which he could maintain greater control. "Bartleby: Melville's Venture into a New Genre," *Melville Annual 1965 A Symposium: Bartleby the Scrivener* (Kent: Kent State University Press, 1966), 82–93; while Beryl Rowland suggests that

the short fiction is an "underground" writing that "seems to have provided experimental answers to the problem" of saying what he wanted to say in works still commercially viable. "Melville's Bachelors and Maids: Interpretation Through Symbol and Metaphor," *American Literature* 41, no. 3 (1969): 389–405. Marvin Fisher, on the other hand, claims that Melville's subject, "the social and political ideas of American life . . . rather than Melville's talent or intellect—were going under." *Going Under: Melville's Short Fiction and the American 1850's* (Baton Rouge: Louisiana State University Press, 1977), xi. Likewise, William Wasserstrom says the irregularity of the tales reflects "the irregularity in the very fabric of national culture." "Melville the Mannerist: Form in the Short Fiction" in *Herman Melville: Reassessments,* ed. A. Robert Lee (London: Vision Press, 1984), 135–56.

3. "Cock-A-Doodle-Doo!," *The Piazza Tales,* 268.

4. For the standard interpretation of the cock as a figure for transcendentalism, see Egbert S. Oliver, " 'Cock-A-Doodle-Doo!' and Transcendental Hocus-Pocus," *New England Quarterly* 21 (June 1948): 204–16; Hershel Parker, "Melville's Satire of Emerson and Thoreau," *American Transcendental Quarterly* 7 (Summer 1970): 61–67; and William Bysshe Stein, "Melville Roasts Thoreau's Cock," *Modern Language Notes* 74 (1959): 218–19. For a contrasting claim that the tale is "the happiest in the Melville canon," see Sidney P. Moss, " 'Cock-A-Doodle-Doo!' and Some Legends in Melville Scholarship," *American Literature* 40, no. 2 (May 1968): 192–210.

5. *Moby-Dick,* 434.

6. For a related discussion of language in these stories, see Dillingham, *Melville's Short Fiction,* 120.

7. As Dillingham notes, "[Melville's] references to cannibalism suggest that the frenzied poor in the Guildhall have atavistically regressed so far that they are more animal than human" (134).

8. Fisher (78) is one of the few to suggest such a connection and to note the importance in this context of the "seed" metaphor in Melville's letters to Hawthorne.

9. *Correspondence,* 213.

10. Richard Harter Fogle notes, for instance, that " 'The Encantadas' moves steadily from general to particular. The sketches are strongly visual; indeed, Melville consistently makes use of seeing as a physical symbol for knowing." *Melville's Shorter Tales* (Norman: University of Oklahoma Press, 1960), 93.

11. There is a rhythmic similarity between Melville's first two phrases and the ballad's first two lines, each ringing the accentual tetrameter of the ballad stanza. William H. Shurr notes that in the early paragraphs of "The Paradise of Bachelors and the Tartarus of Maids," "dactyls tumble over anapests" and "assonance and consonance seem to draw the reader's attention to some highly metaphoric images." "Melville's Poems: The Late Agenda," in *A Companion to Melville Studies,* ed. John Bryant (New York: Greenwood Press, 1986), 355.

12. Henry F. Pommer, *Milton and Melville* (Pittsburgh: University of Pittsburgh Press, 1950), 106. Several critics have followed and elaborated upon Jay Leyda's original description of the tales. See Jay Leyda, ed., *The Complete Stories of Herman Melville* (New York: Random House, 1949), xx; also R. Bruce Bickley, Jr., in *The Method of Melville's Short Fiction* (Durham: Duke University Press, 1975), 76; and Dillingham, who calls them "bipartite stories." *Melville's Short Fiction,* 8.

13. Fogle, *Melville's Shorter Tales,* (58) and Bickley (124).

Chapter 5. Inverted Worlds: "Benito Cereno" and *The Confidence-Man*

1. "Benito Cereno," *The Piazza Tales,* 48, 49. All subsequent references will appear in the text.

2. For a reading of the "inseparability of master and slave" that does not emphasize sexuality, see Adler, 96–97. In a similar vein, Michael Paul Rogin claims that "[the
servant's] subversion is an entrapment, and he is still yoked to his former lord." *Subversive Genealogy: The Politics and Art of Herman Melville* (New York: Alfred A. Knopf,
1983), 215, 217; and William B. Dillingham sees the master/slave relationship as "role
playing," stating that "There is no fundamental difference between the two positions."
Melville's Short Fiction, 233.

3. The notion, suggested by textual evidence, that Aranda's body may have been
cannibalized before being attached to the prow both supports the unification of master
and slave (via ingestion) and increases the darkness of the sexuality to which Delano
remains blind. See Dillingham, *Melville's Short Fiction*, 241–42; John Harmon McElroy,
"Cannibalism in Melville's 'Benito Cereno,'" *Essays in Literature* 1, no. 2 (Fall 1974):
206–18; and Barbara J. Baines, "Ritualized Cannibalism in 'Benito Cereno': Melville's 'Black-letter' Texts," *ESQ: A Journal of the American Renaissance* 30, no. 3 (1984):
163–69.

4. For a wider reading of Melville's bachelors, see Richard Harter Fogle, *Melville's
Shorter Tales* (Norman: University of Oklahoma Press, 1960), 132–34; and Guy Cardwell, "Amasa Delano's Plain Good Sense," in *A Benito Cereno Handbook,* ed. Seymour
L. Gross (Belmont, Calif.: Wadsworth Publishing Co., 1965), 100. We should note that
there exist other, more balanced "bachelor" figures in Melville's work who, while not
specifically labeled bachelors, are clearly unmarried. Thus it appears that in order to be
a quester it helps to be free of familial obligations, and yet such a lack of ties does not
necessarily denote a devotion to the cloistral "bachelor" existence that Melville appears
to view critically.

5. Pops, 154.

6. For an examination of the language of Southern slavery, see Carolyn L.
Karcher, *Shadow over the Promised Land: Slavery, Race, and Violence in Melville's America* (Baton Rouge: Louisiana State University Press, 1980), 132. Other readings focus
upon slavery as an institution and the cultural assumptions that support it; see Rogin,
Adler, Jean Fagin Yellin, "Black Masks: Melville's 'Benito Cereno,'" *American Quar-
terly* 22, no. 3 (Fall 1970): 678–89; and Sandra A. Zagarell, "Reenvisioning America:
Melville's 'Benito Cereno,'" *ESQ: A Journal of the American Renaissance* 30, no. 4
(1984): 245–59. For a more general political orientation of the tale, see Allan Moore
Emery, "'Benito Cereno' and Manifest Destiny," *Nineteenth Century Fiction* 39, no. 1
(June 1984): 48–68.

7. Criticism of *The Confidence-Man* has come to mirror its subject's almost vertiginous complexity. However, it may be said, in general, that there are two basic approaches to the book and its central figure. The first attempts to identify the confidence-man in order to fix a full or partial allegorical pattern that will then help
unlock the stubborn text. Among these, suggested identities include the devil, Christ,
Christ-and-devil, the critic, a figure of self-knowledge, and a manipulator of fictions.
Elizabeth S. Foster, Introduction to *The Confidence-Man: His Masquerade* (New York:
Hendricks House, 1954); Daniel G. Hoffman, *Form and Fable in American Fiction*
(New York: Oxford University Press, 1961), 279–313; Franklin, *The Wake of the Gods,*
177; Edward H. Rosenberry, *Melville and the Comic Spirit,* 153; Seelye, 121; Mushabac,
138; Dillingham, *Melville's Later Novels,* 306; and Roelof Overmeer, "'Something Further': *The Confidence-Man* and Writing as a Disinterested Act," *Études De Lettres* (1987):
43–53.

On the other hand, more recent readings have focused on the resistance of the
text to any reading and have suggested that the confidence-man is a concealing author-
figure, a type of the inconsistency of all character, a ventriloquist or deconstructor, or
a combination of an allegorical and anti-allegorical figure. Dryden; Paul Brodtkorb,

Jr., "*The Confidence-Man:* The Con-Man as Hero," *Studies in the Novel* 1, no. 4 (Winter 1969): 421–35; Henry Sussman, "The Deconstructor as Politician: Melville's *The Confidence-Man,*" *Glyph* 4 (1978): 32–56; A. Robert Lee, "Voices Off, On and Without: Ventriloquy in *The Confidence-Man,*" in *Herman Melville: Reassessments,* ed. A. Robert Lee (London: Vision Press, 1984), 157–75; and John Bryant, "Allegory and Breakdown in *The Confidence-Man:* Melville's Comedy of Doubt," *Philological Quarterly* 65, no. 1 (1986): 113–30.

8. *The Confidence-Man: His Masquerade,* vol. 10 of *The Writings of Herman Melville,* ed. Harrison Hayford, Hershel Parker, and G. Thomas Tanselle (Evanston and Chicago: Northwestern University Press and Newberry Library, 1984), 3. All subsequent references will appear in the text.

9. As Martin Leonard Pops notes, it is significant that the small, highly descriptive portion of the text known as "The River" was probably taken out by Melville in order to contribute to the effect of impalpability (168). Newton Arvin was perhaps the first to note that "sensuously, pictorially, kinaesthetically, one has little or no sense of being on such a boat or such a river" (249). On the other hand, Foster is one of the few to claim that "it is the River, and it flows with unmistakable reality past bluffs and shot towers and vine-covered banks" (xciii).

10. For a general notation of disease and decay, see Adler, 113. Edward H. Rosenberry's suggestion that the *Fidèle* is also a classic "ship of fools" contributes to the sense of both mental and physical debility aboard the riverboat. See "Melville's Ship of Fools," *PMLA* 75, no. 5 (December 1960): 604–8.

11. Readings of Colonel Moredock and the Indians he hates have varied widely over the years. John W. Shroeder's early reading claimed that "the Indian-hater is the world's only remedy against the confidence-man; a severe disease calls for a strong purge." "Sources and Symbols for Melville's *Confidence-Man,*" *PMLA* 66 (June 1951) 363–80. More recently Wai-chee Dimock has contended that he represents "the imperial self: a self so encompassing that it encompasses even opposites" (182). Other opinions include Roy Harvey Pearce's claim that the Indian-hater "loses sight of his human self" through blind hatred; Hershel Parker's argument that the tale "is a tragic study of the impracticability of Christianity, and, more obviously, a satiric allegory in which the Indians are devils and the Indian-haters are dedicated Christians"; William M. Ramsey's perception that the story is "a *reductio ad absurdum* of logic" and too completely fictional to decipher; and Adler's claim that Melville conflates "Indian" evil with "European" treachery, thereby undermining any allegorical equivalences. "Melville's Indian-Hater: A Note on a Meaning of *The Confidence-Man,*" *PMLA* 67 (December 1952): 942–48; "The Metaphysics of Indian-hating," *Nineteenth Century Fiction* 8, no. 2 (September 1963): 165–73; "The Moot Points of Melville's Indian-Hating," *New England Quarterly* 52, no. 2 (May 1980): 224–35; and Adler, 120.

12. *Moby-Dick,* 302.

13. Adler's point (120)—that the descriptions of Indian treachery are made up of European examples—supports the generality of the "Indian" idea.

14. The cosmopolitan's admission that he never uses the chamber-pot or life-preserver (251) reinforces the perception of the confidence-man's essential bodilessness.

15. Of those to argue for or against the book's completion, Bruce L. Grenberg calls it "a collocation of broken threads and loose ends" in *Some Other World to Find: Quest and Negation in the Works of Herman Melville* (Urbana: University of Illinois Press, 1989), 180; and Daniel Hoffman, "a book of brilliant fragments." *Form and Fable in American Fiction,* 310. On the other hand, Edward H. Rosenberry considers it "an ironic fugue—a *perpetuum mobile,* in fact" (*Melville and the Comic Spirit,* 148); John G. Cawelti notes that it "is structured around incomplete reversals at every level," in

"Some Notes on the Structure of *The Confidence-Man*," *American Literature* 29, no. 3 (November 1957): 278–88. Seelye claims that "the structure is such that it could be expanded forever by continued accretion" (118), and Bryant describes "a mixture of didactic and mimetic modes" (128) in an allegory that fails to fulfill itself.

16. For an excellent description of the book's style, see R. W. B. Lewis, *The Trials of the Word* (New Haven: Yale University Press, 1965), 65. There remains a small difference of opinion on the nature and effectiveness of the book's language. For instance, Daniel Hoffman sees the "new rhythm" dramatizing "the serpentine twistings of reason proposed by the confidence-man" (281), and Brodtkorb notes "the extraordinary frequency of double-negative litotes" (430). On the other hand, Franklin argues that the book is "Melville's most nearly perfect work" and notes a controlled language throughout. *The Wake of the Gods*, 153.

17. See Dryden (165, 174) for a broader discussion of the book's confidence-game. Lee also argues that " 'The Author' plays one more co-partner in the overall Masquerade" (174).

18. It has become customary among some critics to pretend that Melville wrote nothing between *The Confidence-Man* and *Billy Budd*. Dryden states, for instance, that " 'Truth is voiceless,' and for thirty-four years after *The Confidence-Man*, so was Herman Melville" (195). See also Daniel Hoffman (312).

Chapter 6. The Fissure in the Hearth: *Battle Pieces*

1. Thomas McFarland, *Romanticism and the Forms of Ruin: Wordsworth, Coleridge, and Modalities of Fragmentation* (Princeton: Princeton University Press, 1981), 13.

2. In this context, it is important to remember Ishmael's prayer: "God keep me from ever completing anything. This whole book is but a draught—nay, but the draught of a draught." *Moby-Dick*, 145.

3. Critics have devoted only minimal energy to understanding why Melville changed genres after *The Confidence-Man*. In fact, the long-held theory of failing health and sanity often prompts readers to see the change to shorter forms simply as evidence of lost energy. More recently, however, commentators such as Warren Rosenberg have attributed it to "a need to reject an organic creative mode which blurred the distinction between writer and work in favor of a mode . . . which emphasized aesthetic distance and therefore increased [Melville's] control over his materials." " 'Deeper Than Sappho': Melville, Poetry, and the Erotic," *Modern Language Studies* 14, no. 1 (Winter 1984): 70–78. On the other hand, Andrew Hook has suggested that "Melville turned to poetry because he could regard it as a more private act." "Melville's Poetry," in *Herman Melville: Reassessments*, ed. A. Robert Lee (London: Vision Press, 1984), 186.

4. *Herman Melville* (New York: William Sloan Associates, 1950), 262; and Shurr, *The Mystery of Iniquity: Melville as Poet, 1857–1891* (Lexington: University of Kentucky Press, 1972), 20.

5. Along similar lines, Robert Penn Warren suggests that the Civil War provided Melville with a larger struggle in which his own "personal failure" could both shrink "to a manageable scale" and find "an appropriate image" for his own "deep divisions." See Introduction to *Selected Poems of Herman Melville* (New York: Random House, 1970), 9. Similarly, Arvin suggests that "the war had roused Melville . . . from the mood of disbelief and apathy into which he had fallen in the 'fifties" (269).

6. Other critics have noted the lack of resolution in these poems. Lee, for instance, notes that "Melville's poems in *Battle Pieces* rarely seek to resolve their typical inversions and oppositions" (132).

7. Herman Melville, *Battle Pieces and Aspects of the War,* ed. Sidney Kaplan (Amherst: University of Massachusetts Press, 1972), 11. All subsequent references will appear in the text.

8. Melville's horror of modern warfare reemphasizes the individual's tenuous position in the crushing, machine-like movements of battle. See Arvin (267) and Catherine Georgoudaki, *"Battle Pieces and Aspects of the War:* Melville's Poetic Quest for Meaning and Form in a Fallen World," *American Transcendental Quarterly* (March 1987): 21–32. Shurr's description of the book as "a philosophical meditation on human impotence in the face of the power of destructiveness and evil" also owes something to this inherent tension. "Melville's Poems," 356.

9. William Bysshe Stein argues, for instance, that Melville "settled upon ugly discordance and incongruity—in meter, rime, image, symbol, and language"—because "he became convinced that the measured euphony of verse belied experiential reality." *The Poetry of Melville's Late Years: Time, History, Myth, and Religion* (Albany: State University of New York Press, 1970), 4. Similarly, Richard Harter Fogle calls Melville's variations in meter "a more radical departure, a reaction, almost a revolt from a mechanically regular scheme preestablished by himself." "Melville's Poetry," *Tulane Studies in English* 12 (1962): 81–86. Warren also suggests that Melville's style reflects the Civil War's conflict (17–18).

10. See Shurr for a discussion of Melville's traditional metrics. *The Mystery of Iniquity,* 20.

11. See Adler for a description of how the pieces fall into "the three-part causal sequence that is characteristic of tragedy: origin and building up of the fate; agony; enlightenment" 133.

12. *Moby-Dick,* 226.

Chapter 7. *Clarel* and the Search for the Divine Body

1. Critics have long recognized the fundamental choice facing Clarel. For instance, Walter Bezanson sees the final decision as between "the ascetic ideal of a Celibate . . . and the apostasy of a Prodigal." "Introduction" to *Clarel: A Poem and Pilgrimage in the Holy Land* (New York: Hendricks House, 1960), lxi. See also Arvin, 277. Nina Baym suggests that the poem examines the connection between philosophical questing and antierotic misogyny. "The Erotic Motif in Melville's *Clarel,*" *Texas Studies in Literature and Language* 16, no. 2 (Summer 1974): 315–28. Shirley M. Detlaff follows Melville's interest in the Arnoldian distinction between Hebraic and Hellenic visions of life. "Ionian Form and Esau's Waste: Melville's View of Art in *Clarel,*" *American Literature* 54, no. 2 (May 1982): 212–28.

2. There is no consensus on the tone of the poem's ending. While Richard Harter Fogle claims that the "final appeal is to the heart, with its intimation of immortality," William B. Dillingham contends that Melville's "was neither the Yea nor the Nay voice, but the clear, strong sound of a man who sensitively perceived the endless ambiguities of existence." "Melville's *Clarel:* Doubt and Belief," *Tulane Studies in English,* vol. 10 (New Orleans: Tulane University Press, 1960), 114; and " 'Neither Believer Nor Infidel': Themes of Melville's Poetry," *The Personalist* 46, no. 4 (October 1965): 501–16. On the other hand, Joseph G. Knapp claims that Melville "found this dynamic synthesis which once and for all integrated his famous polarities." "Melville's *Clarel:* Dynamic Synthesis," *American Transcendental Quarterly* 7 (Summer 1970): 67–76. Joseph Flibbert suggests that Clarel "isn't surrendering to despair; he is facing the darkness in himself." "The Dream and Religious Faith in Herman Melville's *Clarel,*" *American Transcendental Quarterly* 50 (Spring 1981): 129–37. Basem L. Ra'ad states that "Melville

leads Clarel through a sequence of deaths to arrive not at despair . . . but rather at a constructive kind of bereavement." "The Death Plot in Melville's *Clarel*," *ESQ: A Journal of the American Renaissance* 27, no. 1 (1981): 14–27.

3. As William H. Shurr notes, "geography here has become highly symbolic, and the landscape psychologic." He also states that Jerusalem "is dead; it has no eye for [Clarel's] problems, no voice to speak to him. . . . The implication is that the city, like the Jew, offered churlish taunts as response to Jesus; both then are abandoned, damned." *The Mystery of Iniquity*, 60, 50, 55.

4. Herman Melville, *Clarel: A Poem and Pilgrimage in the Holy Land*, vol. 12 of *The Writings of Herman Melville*, ed. Harrison Hayford, Alma A. MacDougall, Hershel Parker, and G. Thomas Tanselle (Evanston and Chicago: Northwestern University Press and Newberry Library, 1991), 162, 266–67. All subsequent references will appear in the text.

5. As Bezanson notes, "In Part I, Clarel makes two responses to his desolate plight. One is to find some person who can solve his spiritual crisis. So begins a major pattern of the poem: the lost hero in search of a guide." Introduction, liv.

6. *Moby-Dick*, 416.

7. As Ra'ad suggests "Clarel, in desiring Ruth, is clearly attempting to combine the 'now' and the 'hereafter'—a paradise that is removed not simply from religious doubt but from doubt which permeates the roots of man's origin" (19). On the other hand, Robert Penn Warren claims that "when [Clarel] falls in love with Ruth, he falls in love with an idea, a symbol, and not with a young female of flesh and blood" (39).

8. See Clarel's discussion with the Celibate (373–78) and his dream during his night with the Lyonese (476).

9. Baym similarly states that "Love for women is identified with the physical, and gratification of the physical side of the self is taken to be incompatible with a spiritual development of the personality and, consequently, with a pure love for God" (317), and further suggests that "a horror of women . . . produces the quest for God" (318).

10. As Martin Leonard Pops notes, "the quest for sex is inextricably associated with the quest for sacrament, and as Clarel fails in one, he fails in both" (211). On the other hand, Shurr suggests that it is less Clarel's failure than the failure of romantic love: "Romantic love has not proved to be the real locus for the edenic" (*Mystery of Iniquity*, 104).

11. As James Baird contends, "the monks of Mar Saba become the sign not only of the desolation of Judea but also of the total apostolic history of a distorted Christianity, terminating finally in man's disavowal of his nature as a human being." *Ishmael* (Baltimore: Johns Hopkins Press, 1956), 416.

12. We should also note that Nathan, another American enthusiast of New England stock, forms a kind of similar opposite to Nehemiah, for while each commits himself to an otherworldly vision, Nehemiah's remains the passive shadow of Nathan's violent life-and-death attempt to recreate yet another "promised land."

13. From Hawthorne's journal, reprinted in volume two of Jay Leyda's *The Melville Log: A Documentary Life of Herman Melville, 1819–1891* (New York: Harcourt, Brace & Co., 1951), 529.

14. For an overview of Celio, Mortmain, and Ungar as negative lessons for Clarel, see Vincent S. Kenny, "Clarel's Rejection of the Titans," *American Transcendental Quarterly* 7 (Summer 1970): 76–81.

15. As Flibbert states, "[The Banker's] response is almost exclusively of the senses, the corpulence of his frame and the weight of his elaborate French clothes making him especially vulnerable to the heat of the desert." "The Dream and Religious Faith," 131.

16. Bezanson, 539.

17. It should be noted that the long-held theory that Vine is a portrait of Hawthorne probably owes as much to Vine's ironic attitudes as it does to his emotional resistance to Clarel and others. For a reading of Vine as an unfavorable portrait of Hawthorne, see Hershel Parker, "The Character of Vine in Melville's *Clarel*," *Essays in Arts and Science* 15 (June 1986): 91–113. On the other hand, for a description of Vine as a balanced "union of opposites," see Merlin Bowen, *The Long Encounter: Self and Experience in the Writings of Herman Melville* (Chicago: University of Chicago Press, 1960), 256.

18. Both Ronald Mason and Fogle suggest that Clarel "fails structurally of attaining unity and development" (Fogle, "Melville's *Clarel*," 103); Mason, *The Spirit Above the Dust: A Study of Herman Melville* (London: John Lehman, 1951), 227. On the other hand, Bryan C. Short argues in behalf of the poem's organic form. "Form as Vision in Herman Melville's *Clarel, American Literature* 50, no. 4 (1970): 553–69.

19. As Short suggests, "Although [Melville's] themes reflect the depression which adorns his family correspondence, his incessant technical experiments bespeak an undying vitality" (553).

20. For a reading of the epilogue as "forced, if sincere," see Seelye (138).

Chapter 8. A Question of Distance: The Late Poetry

1. In contrast, William Bysshe Stein sees the volume as "almost devoid of anxiety, melancholia, or spiritual unrest." *The Poetry of Melville's Late Years: Time, History, Myth, and Religion* (Albany: State University of New York Press, 1970), 19. Other critics have argued for the thematic unity of the volume in different ways. Shurr, for instance, states that "the real subject of the volume is Melville's exploration of the vast sea-as-universe metaphor." *Mystery of Iniquity*, 127. Douglas Robillard suggests a number of unifying devices, including "a kind of plot for the reader to follow through the successive poems, as [Melville's] protagonist passes from the condition of depression and illness to recovery and health." "Theme and Structure in Melville's *John Marr and Other Sailors*," *English Language Notes* 6 (March 1969): 187–92.

2. *Collected Poems of Herman Melville*, ed. Howard P. Vincent (Chicago: Hendricks House, 1947), 159. All subsequent references to *John Marr, Timoleon*, and *Weeds and Wildings* are to this volume and will appear in the text.

3. A more conventional bodily isolation confronts the speaker of "Crossing the Tropics," who finds himself separated from his bride and so yearns against the direction of his sailing to return to her. "The Figure-head" likewise offers a vision of erotic failure in the image of the decayed wooden couple who comprise the *Charles and Emma*'s figurehead which, after years of deterioration, eventually falls apart.

4. On the other hand, the sea as it appears in "Pebbles" is unmistakably hostile, though as Robillard reminds us, "the inhumanity of the sea [in this poem] is inseparable from its healing powers" (190).

5. In Stein's reading, on the other hand, "these shadows of death . . . exemplify the paradox of the Great Mother as destroyer and creator." *Poetry of Melville's Late Years*, 46.

6. As Aaron Kramer states, "A second major theme of 'Bridegroom Dick' . . . is the superiority of heart over head, instinct over strategy, naturalness over formalism, spontaneity over prudence." *Melville's Poetry: Toward the Enlarged Heart* (Rutherford: Fairleigh Dickinson University Press, 1972), 15.

7. The dates of individual poems in the volume is uncertain at best. For varying conjectures see Vincent's introduction to *Collected Poems* and Shurr, *Mystery of Iniquity, 4*.

8. In Darrel Abel's slightly more biographical approach, the book "is unified by its varied reiteration of the theme that . . . bold and original thinking alienates artists and intellectuals from their fellow-man." " 'Laurel Twined with Thorn': The Theme of Melville's *Timoleon*," *The Personalist* 41 (Summer 1960): 330–40.

9. Vernon Shetley likewise notes that "the assassination is represented as an act of verbal aggression." "Melville's 'Timoleon,' " *ESQ: A Journal of the American Renaissance* 33 (1987): 83–93.

10. Stein, for instance, sees it as the "symbolic disclosure of a compulsive desire to write and the inability to do so." *Poetry of Melville's Late Years*, 98.

11. As Stein notes, "Lamia's task is to overcome conventional inhibitions, to discourage studied poses of icy aloofness" (97).

12. Rosenberg, 72.

13. For descriptions of Melville's interest in classical form, see Jane Donahue, "Melville's Classicism: Law and Order in His Poetry," *Papers on Language and Literature* 5, no. 1 (Winter 1969): 63–72; and Dettlaff, 212–28. As Rosenberg suggests, "Only in his poetry, protected by a defined and cryptic form, could Melville successfully integrate the erotic theme *and* overcome the guilt and confusion which marred his best prose works" (72).

14. We should note, however, that given his depiction of worldly Christianity in *Pierre* and *The Confidence-Man*, Melville would hardly have seen the conversion of Constantine as a positive step for a fundamentally "chronometrical" religion.

15. Herman Melville, *Journals*, vol. 15 of *The Writings of Herman Melville*, eds. Harrison Hayford, Hershel Parker, and G. Thomas Tanselle (Evanston and Chicago: Northwestern University Press and Newberry Library, 1989), 78. "They must needs have been terrible inventors, those Egyptian wise men. And one seems to see that as out of the crude forms of the natural earth they could evoke by art the transcendent mass & symmetry & unity of the pyramid so out of the rude elements of the insignificant thoughts that are in all men, they could rear the transcendent conception of a God. But for no holy purpose was the pyramid founded." (78)

16. "Contrast between the Greek isles & those of the Polynesian archipelago. The former have lost their virginity. . . . The former look worn, and are meagre, like life after enthusiasm is gone. The aspect of all of them is sterile & dry." *Journals*, 72.

17. Lucy M. Freibert, for instance, sees the speaker of the poems as "a mature persona who has grasped the eternal youthfulness of nature . . . [and] who speaks with a levity that recognizes the profundity of life but refuses to be paralyzed by it." "*Weeds and Wildings*: Herman Melville's Use of the Pastoral Voice," *Essays in Arts and Sciences* 12, no. 1 (March 1983): 61–85.

18. Stanton Garner, *The Civil War World of Herman Melville* (Lawrence: University of Kansas Press, 1993), 403.

19. Stein offers a slightly different vision of Melville's attitude toward Christianity, noting that he "seems mainly concerned with undermining the ascetic principles of Christianity—with subordinating the comforting gift of the passion to the fulfilling moment of sexual passion." *Poetry of Melville's Late Years*, 200.

20. *Correspondence*, 192.

21. Merton M. Sealts, Jr. "Innocence and Infamy: *Billy Budd, Sailor*," in *A Companion to Melville Studies*, ed. John Bryant (New York: Greenwood Press, 1986), 412.

Chapter 9. *Billy Budd* and the Touch of a God

1. The readings of Billy include John W. Rathburn's claim that he is an extraordinary individual whom society misunderstands, "*Billy Budd* and the Limits of Per-

ception," *Nineteenth Century Fiction* 20, no. 1 (June 1965): 19–34; Edward H. Rosenberry's contention that the "American Adam . . . [is] fit to be forgiven anything after he has struck his sacrificial blow at oppressive authority," "The Problem of *Billy Budd*," *PMLA* 80, no. 5 (December 1965): 489–98; Walter Sutton's connection of Billy to Buddhism, "Melville and the Great God Budd," in *The Merrill Studies in Billy Budd*, ed. Haskell S. Springer (Columbus, Ohio: Charles E. Merrill, 1970); Lyon Evans, Jr.'s ironic reading of Billy as a fraudulent Christ allied to the christology of nineteenth-century biblical criticism, " 'Too Good to Be True': Subverting Christian Hope in *Billy Budd*," *New England Quarterly* 55, no. 3 (September 1982): 323–53; and R. Evan Davis's equation of Billy with America, "An Allegory of America in Melville's *Billy Budd*," *Journal of Narrative Technique* 14, no. 3 (Fall 1984): 172–81.

2. E. H. Rosenberry, "The Problem of *Billy Budd*," 491.

3. Of course, some have suggested that the narrator is unreliable, uncertain, or simply ironic and that all descriptions of Billy contribute to his presentation as an ironic figure caught in a variety of interpretations by those around him. See Lawrence Thompson, *Melville's Quarrel with God* (Princeton: Princeton University Press, 1952); Paul Brodtkorb, Jr., "The Definitive *Billy Budd*: 'But Aren't it All Sham?' " *PMLA* 82, no. 7 (December 1967): 602–12; Grenberg; and James Duban and William J. Scheick, "The Dramatis Personae of Robert Browning and Herman Melville," *Criticism* 32, no. 2 (Spring 1990): 221–40.

4. *Billy Budd, Sailor*, ed. Harrison Hayford and Merton M. Sealts, Jr. (Chicago: University of Chicago Press, 1962), 50. All subsequent references will appear in the text.

5. Merlin Bowen first noted the target of the blow (220).

6. See William B. Dillingham's discussion of Melville's revision of "*shekinah*" to "rose." *Melville's Later Novels*, 381. Richard Harter Fogle also suggests "a second crucifixion." "*Billy Budd*—Acceptance or Irony," *Tulane Studies in English* 8 (1958): 107–13. For the connection of the seafowl to "The Haglets," see William H. Shurr, 249.

7. The question of Melville's attitude toward Billy has produced extensive critical disagreement. Those who see only irony and thus criticism of social injustice and religious ignorance include Joseph Schiffman, "Melville's Final Stage, Irony: A Re-examination of *Billy Budd* Criticism," *American Literature* 22 (1950): 128–36; Thompson; and Evans. The line of so-called "acceptance" readings, on the other hand, moves from E. L. Grant Watson's early essay, "Melville's Testament of Acceptance," *New England Quarterly* 6 (1933): 319–27; Newton Arvin; and Rosenberry's 1965 essay, "The Problem of *Billy Budd*." In contrast, Stanton Garner offers a more complicated picture of the narrator as confidence-man aware of his own deceptions. See "Fraud as Fact in Herman Melville's *Billy Budd*," *San Jose Studies* 4 (May 1978): 82–105. A less combative view that the novel contains both attitudes is put forth by Fogle in "*Billy Budd*—Acceptance or Irony," and by Robert Milder, who sagely states that "the humbling reality . . . is that Melville seems to contain both emotions not simply at once but *as one*." Introduction to *Critical Essays on Melville's Billy Budd, Sailor*, ed. Robert Milder (Boston: G. K. Hall & Co., 1989), 7.

8. Those who see some sort of struggle in Vere include Bowen (216), Dillingham (*Melville's Later Novels*, 377), and Charles A. Reich, "The Tragedy of Justice in *Billy Budd*," *Critical Essays on Melville's Billy Budd, Sailor*, ed. Robert Milder (Boston: G. K. Hall, 1989), 143. Other readers variously denounce Vere for the choices he makes. H. Bruce Franklin calls the narrative "unambiguous" in its condemnation of Vere's rhetoric of order and compromise of principles, while Christopher S. Durer brands the captain "a mouthpiece for the mores of [an] inadequate high social group." See "From Empire to Empire: *Billy Budd, Sailor*, in *Herman Melville: Reassessments*, ed. A. Robert

Lee (London: Vision Press, 1984), and "Captain Vere and Upper-Class Mores in *Billy Budd,*" *Studies in Short Fiction* 19 (Winter 1982): 9–18. For modifications of similar views, see Barbara Johnson, "Melville's Fist: The Execution of *Billy Budd,*" *Studies in Romanticism* 18, no. 4 (Winter 1979): 567–99; James F. Farnham, "Captain Vere's Existential Failure," *Arizona Quarterly* 37, no. 4 (Winter 1981): 362–70; Karl E. Zink, "Herman Melville and the Forms—Irony and Social Criticism in *Billy Budd,*" *Accent* 12 (Summer 1952): 131–39; and Grenberg, 201. Wendell Glick, by contrast, claims that Melville and the narrative approve of Vere's attempt to preserve the stability of society. "Expediency and Absolute Morality in *Billy Budd,*" in *The Merrill Studies in Billy Budd,* ed. Haskell S. Springer (Columbus: Charles E. Merrill, 1970), 55.

9. As Charles Mitchell states, "Vere responds to Billy's act as though Billy had attacked the very system of legally constituted authority in which Vere's own being is grounded." "Melville and the Spurious Truth of Legalism," *The Centennial Review* 12, no. 1 (Winter 1968): 110–26.

10. Vere's denial of the natural body in favor of the social is also strengthened by the suggestion that in condemning Billy he is sacrificing his own son. See 115. Merton M. Sealts, Jr., also notes Vere's precipitation of Billy's blow. "Innocence and Infamy," 416. For a biographical reading of the father-son relationship, see Peter L. Hays and Richard Dilworth Rust, " 'Something Healing: Fathers and Sons in *Billy Budd,*" *Nineteenth Century Fiction* 34, no. 3 (December 1979): 326–36.

11. For a reading of the sexual symbolism of the act, see Pops, 239.

12. Johnson, 573.

13. For more comment on Billy's impressment see Thomas J. Scorza, *In the Time Before Steamships: Billy Budd, The Limits of Politics, and Modernity* (DeKalb: Northern Illinois University Press, 1979), 32; and Pops, 238.

14. Johnson, 573.

15. See Hershel Parker, *Reading Billy Budd* (Evanston: Northwestern University Press, 1990), for extensive discussions of the textual background. Parker sees the late Melville as intentionally suspicious "of the literary work which is elaborated down to the last ornament." (28). Others, from Brodtkorb to Johnson to Duban and Scheick also consider the text formally imbalanced. See Dryden, 216. Notably, Garner in "Fraud as Fact" argues for the purposeful inclusion of factual errors and other anomalies.

16. Arvin, 294.

Epilogue

1. "Daniel Orme," in Melville, *Billy Budd and Other Prose Pieces,* ed. Raymond W. Weaver (New York: Russel & Russel, 1963) 120. All subsequent references will appear in the text.

BIBLIOGRAPHY

Abel, Darrel. " 'Laurel Twined with Thorn': The Theme of Melville's *Timoleon*." *The Personalist* 41 (Summer 1960): 330–40.

Adler, Joyce Sparer. *War in Melville's Imagination*. New York: New York University Press, 1981.

Arvin, Newton. *Herman Melville*. William Sloan Associates, 1950.

Baines, Barbara J. "Ritualized Cannibalism in 'Benito Cereno': Melville's 'Black-letter' Texts." *ESQ: A Journal of the American Renaissance* 30, no. 3 (1984): 163–69.

Baird, James. *Ishmael*. Baltimore: Johns Hopkins Press, 1956.

Bakhtin, Mikhail. *Rabelais and His World*. Trans. Helene Iswolsky. Cambridge: MIT Press, 1968.

Barry, Elaine. "The Changing Face of Comedy." *American Studies International* 16, no. 4 (1978): 19–33.

Baym, Nina. "The Erotic Motif in Melville's *Clarel*." *Texas Studies in Literature and Language* 16, no. 2 (Summer 1974): 315–28.

Bezanson, Walter E., "Explanatory Notes" to *Clarel: A Poem and Pilgrimage in the Holy Land*. New York: Hendricks House, 1960.

———. "Historical Note." In *Israel Potter: His Fifty Years of Exile*, Vol. 8 of *The Writings of Herman Melville*, edited by Harrison Hayford, Hershel Parker, and G. Thomas Tanselle, 173–235. Chicago: Northwestern University Press and Newberry Library, 1982.

———. Introduction to *Clarel: A Poem and Pilgrimage in the Holy Land*. New York: Hendricks House, 1960.

Bickley, R. Bruce, Jr. *The Method of Melville's Short Fiction*. Durham: Duke University Press, 1975.

Bowen, Merlin. *The Long Encounter: Self and Experience in the Writings of Herman Melville*. Chicago: University of Chicago Press, 1960.

Brodhead, Richard H. *Hawthorne, Melville, and the Novel*. Chicago: University of Chicago Press, 1976.

Brodtkorb, Paul, Jr. "*The Confidence-Man:* The Con-Man as Hero." *Studies in the Novel* 1, no. 4 (Winter 1969): 421–35.

———. "The Definitive *Billy Budd:* 'But Aren't it All Sham?' " *PMLA* 82, no. 7 (December 1967): 602–12.

Brown, Norman O. *Life Against Death: The Psychoanalytic Meaning of History*. Middletown: Wesleyan University Press, 1959.

Bryant, John. "Allegory and Breakdown in *The Confidence-Man:* Melville's Comedy of Doubt." *Philological Quarterly* 65, no. 1 (1986): 113–30.

Cameron, Sharon. *The Corporeal Self: Allegories of the Body in Melville and Hawthorne*. Baltimore: Johns Hopkins University Press, 1981.

Canaday, Nicholas. "Pierre in the Domestic Circle." *Studies in the Novel* 18, no. 4 (1986): 395–402.

Cardwell, Guy. "Amasa Delano's Plain Good Sense." In *A Benito Cereno Handbook,* edited by Seymour L. Gross, 99–103. Belmont, Calif.: Wadsworth Publishing Co., 1965.

Cawelti, John G. "Some Notes on the Structure of *The Confidence-Man.*" *American Literature* 29, no. 3 (November 1957): 278–88.

Cohen, Hennig. "*Israel Potter:* Common Man." In *A Companion to Melville Studies,* edited by John Bryant, 279–314. New York: Greenwood Press, 1986.

Cowan, Bainard. *Exiled Waters: Moby-Dick and the Crisis of Allegory.* Baton Rouge: Louisiana State University Press, 1982.

Davis, R. Evan. "An Allegory of America in Melville's *Billy Budd.*" *The Journal of Narrative Technique* 14, no. 3 (Fall 1984): 172–81.

Detlaff, Shirley M. "Ionian Form and Esau's Waste: Melville's View of Art in *Clarel.*" *American Literature* 54, no. 2 (May 1982): 212–28.

Dillingham, William B. *Melville's Later Novels.* Athens: University of Georgia Press, 1986.

———. *Melville's Short Fiction.* Athens: University of Georgia Press, 1977.

———. " 'Neither Believer Nor Infidel': Themes of Melville's Poetry." *The Personalist* 46, no. 4 (October 1965): 501–16.

Dimock, Wai-chee. *Empire for Liberty: Melville and the Poetics of Individualism.* Princeton: Princeton University Press, 1989.

Donahue, Jane. "Melville's Classicism: Law and Order in His Poetry." *Papers on Language and Literature* 5, no. 1 (Winter 1969): 63–72.

Dryden, Edgar A. *Melville's Thematics of Form: The Great Art of Telling the Truth.* Baltimore: Johns Hopkins University Press, 1968.

Duban, James, and William J. Scheick. "The Dramatis Personae of Robert Browning and Herman Melville." *Criticism* 32, no. 2 (Spring 1990): 221–40.

Durer, Christopher S. "Captain Vere and Upper-Class Mores in *Billy Budd.*" *Studies in Short Fiction* 19 (Winter 1982): 9–18.

Emery, Allan Moore. " 'Benito Cereno' and Manifest Destiny." *Nineteenth Century Fiction* 39, no. 1 (June 1984): 48–68.

Evans, Lyon, Jr. " 'Too Good to Be True': Subverting Christian Hope in *Billy Budd.*" *New England Quarterly* 55, no. 3 (September 1982): 323–53.

Farnham, James F. "Captain Vere's Existential Failure." *Arizona Quarterly* 37, no. 4 (Winter 1981): 362–70.

Fiedler, Leslie. *Love and Death in the American Novel,* rev. ed. New York: Stein and Day, 1966.

Fisher, Marvin. *Going Under: Melville's Short Fiction and the American 1850's.* Baton Rouge: Louisiana State University Press, 1977.

Flibbert, Joseph. "The Dream and Religious Faith in Herman Melville's *Clarel.*" *American Transcendental Quarterly* 50 (Spring 1981): 129–37.

———. *Melville and the Art of the Burlesque.* Rodolphi N. V. Amsterdam, 1974.

Fogle, Richard Harter. "*Billy Budd*—Acceptance or Irony." *Tulane Studies in English* 8 (1958): 107–13.

———. "Melville's *Clarel:* Doubt and Belief." *Tulane Studies in English* 10 (1960): 101–16.

———. "Melville's Poetry," *Tulane Studies in English* 12 (1962): 81–86.

———. *Melville's Shorter Tales.* Norman: University of Oklahoma Press, 1960.

Foster, Elizabeth S. Introduction to *The Confidence-Man: His Masquerade.* New York: Hendricks House, 1954.

Franklin, H. Bruce. "From Empire to Empire: *Billy Budd, Sailor.*" In *Herman Melville: Reassessments,* edited by A. Robert Lee, 199–216. London: Vision Press, 1984.

———. *The Wake of the Gods: Melville's Mythology.* Stanford: Stanford University Press, 1963.

Freibert, Lucy M. "*Weeds and Wildings:* Herman Melville's Use of the Pastoral Voice." *Essays in Arts and Sciences* 12, no. 1 (March 1983): 61–85.

Garner, Stanton. *The Civil War World of Herman Melville.* Lawrence: University of Kansas Press, 1993.

———. "Fraud as Fact in Herman Melville's *Billy Budd.*" *San Jose Studies* 4 (May 1978): 82–105.

Georgoudaki, Catherine. "*Battle Pieces and Aspects of the War:* Melville's Poetic Quest for Meaning and Form in a Fallen World." *American Transcendental Quarterly* (March 1987): 21–32.

Glick, Wendell. "Expediency and Absolute Morality in *Billy Budd.*" In *The Merrill Studies in Billy Budd,* edited by Haskell S. Springer, 53–61. Columbus: Charles E. Merrill, 1970.

Gray, Richard. " 'All's o'er, and ye know him not': A Reading of *Pierre.*" In *Herman Melville: Reassessments,* edited by A. Robert Lee, 116–34. London: Vision Press, 1984.

Grenberg, Bruce L. *Some Other World to Find: Quest and Negation in the Works of Herman Melville.* Urbana: University of Illinois Press, 1989.

Guetti, James. *The Limits of Metaphor: A Study of Melville, Conrad, and Faulkner.* Ithaca: Cornell University Press, 1967.

Hays, Peter L., and Richard Dilworth Rust. "Something Healing: Fathers and Sons in *Billy Budd.*" *Nineteenth Century Fiction* 34, no. 3 (December 1979): 326–36.

Higgins, Brian, and Herschel Parker, "The Flawed Grandeur of Melville's *Pierre.*" In *New Perspectives on Melville,* edited by Faith Pullin, 162–96. Edinburgh: Edinburgh University Press, and Kent, Ohio: Kent University Press, 1978.

Hoffman, Charles G. "The Shorter Fiction of Herman Melville." *South Atlantic Quarterly* 52 (1953): 414–30.

Hoffman, Daniel G. *Form and Fable in American Fiction.* New York: Oxford University Press, 1961.

Holder, Alan. "Style and Tone in Melville's *Pierre.*" *ESQ: A Journal of the American Renaissance* 60 (1982): 76–86.

Hook, Andrew. "Melville's Poetry." In *Herman Melville: Reassessments*, edited by A. Robert Lee, 176–88. London: Vision Press, 1984.

Johnson, Barbara. "Melville's Fist: The Execution of *Billy Budd*." *Studies in Romanticism* 18, no. 4 (Winter 1979): 567–99.

Karcher, Carolyn L. *Shadow over the Promised Land: Slavery, Race, and Violence in Melville's America*. Baton Rouge: Louisiana State University Press, 1980.

Kearns, Michael S. "Phantoms of the Mind: Melville's Criticism of Idealistic Psychology." *ESQ: A Journal of the American Renaissance* 35:2 (1989): 147–60.

Kenny, Vincent S. "Clarel's Rejection of the Titans." *American Transcendental Quarterly* 7 (Summer 1970): 76–81.

Knapp, Joseph G. "Melville's *Clarel*: Dynamic Synthesis." *American Transcendental Quarterly* 7 (Summer 1970): 67–76.

Kramer, Aaron. *Melville's Poetry: Toward the Enlarged Heart*. Rutherford: Fairleigh Dickinson University Press, 1972.

Lebowitz, Alan. *Progress into Silence: A Study of Melville's Heroes*. Bloomington: Indiana University Press, 1970.

Lee, A. Robert. "Voices Off, On and Without: Ventriloquy in *The Confidence-Man*." In *Herman Melville: Reassessments*, edited by A. Robert Lee, 157–75. London: Vision Press, 1984.

Lewis, R. W. B. *The Trials of the Word*. New Haven: Yale University Press, 1965.

Leyda, Jay, ed. *The Complete Stories of Herman Melville*. New York: Random House, 1949.

———. *The Melville Log: A Documentary Life of Herman Melville, 1819–1891*. 2 vols. New York: Harcourt, Brace & Co., 1951.

McElroy, John Harmon. "Cannibalism in Melville's 'Benito Cereno.' " *Essays in Literature* 1, no. 2 (Fall 1974): 206–18.

McFarland, Thomas. *Romanticism and the Forms of Ruin: Wordsworth, Coleridge, and Modalities of Fragmentation*. Princeton: Princeton University Press, 1981.

Martin, Robert K. *Hero, Captain, and Stranger: Male Friendship, Social Critique, and Literary Form in the Sea Novels of Herman Melville*. Chapel Hill: University of North Carolina Press, 1986.

Mason, Ronald. *The Spirit Above the Dust: A Study of Herman Melville*. London: John Lehman, 1951.

Matthiessen, F. O. *American Renaissance: Art and Experience in the Age of Emerson and Whitman*. New York: Oxford University Press, 1941.

Melville, Herman. *Battle Pieces and Aspects of the War*, edited by Sidney Kaplan. Amherst: The University of Massachusetts Press, 1972.

———. *Billy Budd and Other Prose Pieces*, edited by Raymond W. Weaver. New York: Russel & Russel, 1963.

———. *Billy Budd, Sailor*, edited by Harrison Hayford and Merton M. Sealts, Jr. Chicago: University of Chicago Press, 1962.

———. *Clarel: A Poem and Pilgrimage in the Holy Land*, vol. 12 of *The Writings of Herman Melville*, edited by Harrison Hayford, Alma A. MacDougall, Hershel Parker, and G. Thomas Tanselle. Evanston and Chicago: Northwestern University Press and Newberry Library, 1991.

——. *Collected Poems of Herman Melville,* edited by Howard P. Vincent. With corrigenda. Chicago: Hendricks House, 1947.

——. *The Confidence-Man: His Masquerade,* vol. 10 of *The Writings of Herman Melville,* edited by Harrison Hayford, Hershel Parker, and G. Thomas Tanselle. Evanston and Chicago: Northwestern University Press and Newberry Library, 1984.

——. *Correspondence,* vol. 14 of *The Writings of Herman Melville,* edited by Lynn Horth. Evanston and Chicago: Northwestern University Press and Newberry Library, 1993.

——. *Israel Potter: His Fifty Years of Exile,* vol. 8 of *The Writings of Herman Melville,* edited by Harrison Hayford, Hershel Parker, and G. Thomas Tanselle. Chicago: Northwestern University Press and Newberry Library, 1982.

——. *Journal of a Visit to London and the Continent by Herman Melville, 1849–1850,* edited by Eleanor Melville Metcalf. Cambridge: Harvard University Press, 1948.

——. *Journals,* vol. 15 of *The Complete Writings of Herman Melville,* edited by Harrison Hayford, Hershel Parker, and G. Thomas Tanselle. Evanston and Chicago: Northwestern University Press and Newberry Library, 1989.

——. *Moby-Dick or The Whale,* vol. 6 of *The Writings of Herman Melville,* edited by Harrison Hayford, Hershel Parker, and G. Thomas Tanselle. Evanston and Chicago: Northwestern University Press and Newberry Library, 1988.

——. *The Piazza Tales and Other Prose Pieces 1839–1860,* vol. 9 of *The Writings of Herman Melville,* edited by Harrison Hayford, Hershel Parker, and G. Thomas Tanselle. Evanston: Northwestern University Press and Newberry Library, 1987.

——. *Pierre; or, The Ambiguities,* vol. 7 of *The Writings of Herman Melville,* edited by Harrison Hayford, Hershel Parker, and G. Thomas Tanselle. Evanston and Chicago: Northwestern University Press and Newberry Library, 1971.

Milder, Robert. Introduction to *Critical Essays on Melville's Billy Budd, Sailor,* edited by Robert Milder. Boston: G. K. Hall & Co., 1989.

Miller, Lewis H., Jr. " 'Bartleby' and the Dead Letter." *Studies in American Fiction* 8 (1980): 1–12.

Miner-Quinn, Paula. "A Psychoanalytic Interpretation of Herman Melville's *Pierre.*" *University of Hartford Studies in Literature: A Journal of Interdisciplinary Criticism* 13, no. 2 (1981): 111–21.

Mitchell, Charles. "Melville and the Spurious Truth of Legalism." *The Centennial Review* 12, no. 1 (Winter 1968): 110–26.

Moss, Sidney P. " 'Cock-A-Doodle-Doo!' and Some Legends in Melville Scholarship." *American Literature* 40, no. 2 (May 1968): 192–210.

Mushabac, Jane. *Melville's Humor: A Critical Study.* Hamden: Archon Books, 1981.

Oliver, Egbert S. " 'Cock-A-Doodle-Doo!' and Transcendental Hocus-Pocus." *New England Quarterly* 21 (June 1948): 204–16.

Olson, Charles. *Call Me Ishmael*. New York: Reynal & Hitchcock, 1947.

Overmeer, Roelof. " 'Something Further': *The Confidence-Man* and Writing as a Disinterested Act." *Études De Lettres* (1987): 43–53.

Parker, Hershel. "The Character of Vine in Melville's *Clarel*." *Essays in Arts and Sciences*, vol. 15 (June 1986): 91–113.

———. "Melville's Satire of Emerson and Thoreau." *American Transcendental Quarterly* 7 (Summer 1970): 61–67.

———. "The Metaphysics of Indian-hating." *Nineteenth Century Fiction* 8, no. 2 (September 1963): 165–73.

———. *Reading Billy Budd*. Evanston: Northwestern University Press, 1990.

Pearce, Roy Harvey. "Melville's Indian-Hater: A Note on a Meaning of *The Confidence-Man*." *PMLA* 67 (December 1952): 942–48.

Plumstead, A. W. "Bartleby: Melville's Venture into a New Genre." *Melville Annual 1965 A Symposium: Bartleby the Scrivener*. Kent, Ohio: Kent State University Press, 1966.

Pommer, Henry F. *Milton and Melville*. Pittsburgh: University of Pittsburgh Press, 1950.

Pops, Martin Leonard. *The Melville Archetype*. Kent, Ohio: Kent State University Press, 1970.

Ra'ad, Basem L. "The Death Plot in Melville's *Clarel*." *ESQ: A Journal of the American Renaissance* 27, no. 1 (1981): 14–27.

Ramsey, William M. "The Moot Points of Melville's Indian-Hating." *New England Quarterly* 52, no. 2 (May 1980): 224–35.

Rathbun, John W. "*Billy Budd* and the Limits of Perception." *Nineteenth Century Fiction* 20, no. 1 (June 1965): 19–34.

Reagan, Daniel. "Melville's *Israel Potter* and the Nature of Biography." *American Transcendental Quarterly* 2, no. 1 (March 1988): 41–55.

Reich, Charles A. "The Tragedy of Justice in *Billy Budd*." *Critical Essays on Melville's Billy Budd, Sailor*, edited by Robert Milder, 127–43. Boston: G. K. Hall, 1989.

Robillard, Douglas. "Theme and Structure in Melville's *John Marr and Other Sailors*." *English Language Notes* 6 (March 1969): 187–92.

Rogin, Michael Paul. *Subversive Genealogy: The Politics and Art of Herman Melville*. New York: Alfred A. Knopf, 1983.

Rosenberg, Warren. " 'Deeper Than Sappho': Melville, Poetry, and the Erotic." *Modern Language Studies* 14, no. 1 (Winter 1984): 70–78.

Rosenberry, Brian. "Israel Potter: Melville's Anti-History." *Studies in American Fiction* 15, no. 2 (Autumn 1987): 175–86.

Rosenberry, Edward H. *Melville and the Comic Spirit*. Cambridge: Harvard University Press, 1955.

———. "Melville's Ship of Fools." *PMLA* 75, no. 5 (December 1960): 604–8.

———. "The Problem of *Billy Budd*," *PMLA* 80, no. 5 (December 1965): 489–98.

Rowland, Beryl. "Melville's Bachelors and Maids: Interpretation Through Symbol and Metaphor." *American Literature* 41, no. 3 (1969): 389–405.

Schiffman, Joseph. "Melville's Final Stage, Irony: A Re-examination of *Billy Budd* Criticism." *American Literature* 22 (1950): 128–36.

Schulman, Robert. "The Serious Function of Melville's Phallic Jokes." *American Literature* 33, no. 2 (1961): 179–94.

Scorza, Thomas J. *In the Time Before Steamships: Billy Budd, The Limits of Politics, and Modernity.* DeKalb: Northern Illinois University Press, 1979.

Sealts, Merton M., Jr. "Historical Note." In *The Piazza Tales and Other Prose Pieces, 1839–1860,* vol. 9 of *The Writings of Herman Melville,* edited by Harrison Hayford, Hershel Parker, and G. Thomas Tanselle, 457–533. Evanston: Northwestern University Press and Newberry Library, 1987.

———. "Innocence and Infamy: *Billy Budd, Sailor.*" In *A Companion to Melville Studies,* edited by John Bryant, 407–30. New York: Greenwood Press, 1986.

Sedgewick, William Ellery. *Herman Melville: The Tragedy of Mind.* New York: Russel & Russel, 1944.

Seelye, John. *Melville: The Ironic Diagram.* Evanston: Northwestern University Press, 1970.

Shetley, Vernon. "Melville's 'Timoleon.' " *ESQ: A Journal of the American Renaissance* 33 (1987): 83–93.

Short, Bryan C. "Form as Vision in Herman Melville's *Clarel.*" *American Literature* 50, no. 4 (1970): 553–69.

Shroeder, John W. "Sources and Symbols for Melville's *Confidence-Man.*" *PMLA* 66 (June 1951): 363–80.

Shurr, William H. "Melville's Poems: The Late Agenda." In *A Companion to Melville Studies,* edited by John Bryant, 351–74. New York: Greenwood Press, 1986.

———. *The Mystery of Iniquity: Melville as Poet, 1857–1891.* Lexington: University of Kentucky Press, 1972.

Simpson, David. *Fetishism and Imagination: Dickens, Melville, and Conrad.* Baltimore: Johns Hopkins University Press, 1982.

Smith, Gayle L. "The Word and the Thing: *Moby-Dick* and the Limits of Language." *ESQ: A Journal of the American Renaissance,* 31, no. 4 (1985): 260–71.

Stein, William Bysshe. "Melville Roasts Thoreau's Cock." *Modern Language Notes* 74 (1959): 218–19.

———. *The Poetry of Melville's Late Years: Time, History, Myth, and Religion.* Albany: State University of New York Press, 1970.

Sussman, Henry. "The Deconstructor as Politician: Melville's *The Confidence-Man.*" *Glyph* 4 (1978): 32–56.

Sutton, Walter. "Melville and the Great God Budd." In *The Merrill Studies in Billy Budd,* edited by Haskell S. Springer, 83–89. Columbus, Ohio: Charles E. Merrill, 1970.

Thompson, Lawrence. *Melville's Quarrel with God.* Princeton: Princeton University Press, 1952.

Vincent, Howard P. Introduction to *Collected Poems of Herman Melville,* edited by Howard P. Vincent. Chicago: Hendricks House, 1947.

Warren, Robert Penn. Introduction to *Selected Poems of Herman Melville*. New York: Random House, 1970.

Wasserstrom, William. "Melville the Mannerist: Form in the Short Fiction." In *Herman Melville: Reassessments*, edited by A. Robert Lee, 135–56. London: Vision Press, 1984.

Watson, Charles N., Jr. "Melville's *Israel Potter:* Fathers and Sons." *Studies in the Novel* 7 (1975): 563–68.

E. L. Grant Watson. "Melville's *Pierre.*" *New England Quarterly* 3 (April 1930): 195–234.

——. "Melville's Testament of Acceptance." *New England Quarterly* 6 (1933): 319–27.

Wilson, James C. "The Sentimental Education of Pierre Glendinning: An Exploration of the Causes and Implications of Violence in Melville's *Pierre.*" *American Transcendental Quarterly* 1, no. 13 (1987): 167–77.

Yellin, Jean Fagin. "Black Masks: Melville's 'Benito Cereno.'" *American Quarterly* 22, no. 3 (Fall 1970): 678–89.

Zagarell, Sandra A. "Reenvisioning America: Melville's 'Benito Cereno.'" *ESQ: A Journal of the American Renaissance* 30, no. 4 (1984): 245–59.

Zaller, Robert. "Melville and the Myth of Revolution." *Studies in Romanticism* 15 (Fall 1976): 607–22.

Zink, Karl E. "Herman Melville and the Forms—Irony and Social Criticism in *Billy Budd.*" *Accent* 12 (Summer 1952): 131–39.

Zoellner, Robert. *The Salt-Sea Mastodon: A Reading of Moby-Dick*. Berkeley: University of California Press, 1973.

INDEX

Rabelais, François, 3–4, 22
Rosenberry, Edward H., 11, 20

Sea, 24, 25, 37, 38, 201. See also *Moby-Dick*
Shakespeare, William, 3, 11, 16
Shark, 95. See also *Moby-Dick; John Marr and Other Sailors*
Spenser, Edmund, 81, 205 (n. 4)
Sterne, Laurence, 3

"Tartarus of Maids," 72–74
Timoleon, x, 151, 155, 159–74, 183, 187; architecture in, 167, 168, 169, 171, 172; and asceticism, 161–62, 165, 167, 168, 169, 171, 172; disease in, 167–69; and Dionysian elements, 166–69, 173, 174; and isolation, 166; madness in, 165, 172; and mind-body dialectic, 159, 165, 167; playful language in, 167; rebirth in, 164, 170; INDIVIDUAL POEMS: "Aeolian Harp, The," 158–59; "After the Pleasure Party," 159, 161; "Age of the Antonines, The," 160, 164–65; "Apparition, The," 171–72; "Archipelago, The," 172; "Art," 160, 164; "Attic Landscape, The," 171; "Bench of Boors, The," 166–67; "Dutch Christmas Up the Hudson in the Time of Patroons, A," 179, 180; "Enthusiast, The," 165, 166; "Fragments of a Lost Gnostic Poem of the 12th Century," 173; "Fruit of Travel Long Ago," 167–73; "Great Pyramid, The," 171, 172; "Herba Santa," 166;

"In a Bye-Canal," 169–70; "In a Church of Padua," 170–71; "Lamia's Song," 167; "L'Envoi," 173; "Lone Founts," 166, 167; "Magian Wine," 166; "Marchioness of Brinvilliers, The," 160; "Margrave's Birthnight, The," 163; "Monody," 160, 163, 173; "Pausilippo," 168; "Ravaged Villa, The," 173; "Syra," 173; "Timoleon," 159–61, 165; "Venice," 169; "Weaver, The," 165
"Traveling," 81
Tristram Shandy, 66
"Two Temples, The," x, 80
Typee, 69

Weeds and Wildings with a Rose or Two, x, 151, 173–84, 187, 188; and asceticism, 177, 179, 180; Christian-Dionysian dialectic in, 174, 177, 178; and mind-body dialectic, 183; and nature, 175–78, 180–82; play in, 174–76, 180, 183; and rebirth, 177–82; sexuality in, 167; INDIVIDUAL POEMS: "Blue-bird, The," 177; "Dairyman's Child, The," 174–75; "Iris," 176, 177; "Madcaps," 180, 183–84; "Profundity and Levity," 175; "Rip Van Winkle's Lilac," 180, 182, 184; "Rose Farmer, The," 181–82; "Rose Window," 179; "Stockings in the Farm-House Chimney," 178–80; "Time's Betrayal," 178; "Trophies of Peace," 178; "When Forth the Shepherd Leads the Flock," 180; "Year, The," 178

ABOUT THE AUTHOR

CLARK DAVIS, winner of the 1993 Elizabeth Agee Prize in American Literature for his manuscript "After the Whale: Melville in the Wake of *Moby-Dick*," is Assistant Professor of English at Northeast Louisiana University. He received his bachelor's degree from Rice University and his doctorate from the State University of New York at Buffalo. His articles have appeared in several journals, including *American Transcendental Quarterly, Studies in American Fiction,* and *ESQ: A Journal of the American Renaissance.*